HERD

How to Change Mass
Behaviour by Harnessing
Our True Nature

HERD

How to Change Mass Behaviour by Harnessing Our True Nature

MARK EARLS

1807
WILEY
2007

John Wiley & Sons, Ltd

Other Wiley Editorial Offices

John Wiley & Sons Inc., 111 River Street, Hoboken, NJ 07030, USA

Jossey-Bass, 989 Market Street, San Francisco, CA 94103-1741, USA

Wiley-VCH Verlag GmbH, Boschstr. 12, D-69469 Weinheim, Germany

John Wiley & Sons Australia Ltd, 42 McDougall Street, Milton, Queensland 4064, Australia

John Wiley & Sons (Asia) Pte Ltd, 2 Clementi Loop #02-01, Jin Xing Distripark, Singapore 129809

John Wiley & Sons Canada Ltd, 6045 Freemont Blvd, Mississauga, ONT, L5R 4J3

Wiley also publishes its books in a variety of electronic formats. Some content that appears in print
may not be available in electronic books.

Anniversary Logo Design: Richard J. Pacifico

Library of Congress Cataloging-in-Publication Data

Earls, Mark.
    Herd? – how to change mass behaviour by harnessing our true nature / by Mark Earls.
       p.   cm.
    Includes bibliographical references and index.
    ISBN-13: 978-0-470-06036-0 (cloth : alk. paper)
    ISBN-10: 0-470-06036-0 (cloth : alk. paper)
    1. Communication in marketing.   2. Consumer behavior.   3. Social interaction.   4. Social
influence.   I. Title.   II. Title: How to change mass behaviour by harnessing our true nature.
    HF5415.123.E37 2007
    658.8′343 – dc22

                                                                                2006027031

A catalogue record for this book is available from the British Library

ISBN 13: 978-0-470-06036-0

Typeset by SNP Best-set Typesetter Ltd, Hong Kong
Printed and bound in Great Britain by TJ International Ltd, Padstow, Cornwall
This book is printed on acid-free paper responsibly manufactured from sustainable forestry in which
at least two trees are planted for each one used for paper production.

Dedication

To the memory of Tony Orchard (1941–2005) and
Andrew Mattey (1957–2005)

Contents

Dedication v
Foreword by Russell Davies xv
Acknowledgements xix

Introduction 1
At the 'cellotaph' 1
So how are we to explain this kind of thing? 2
Bigger boys made me do it 5
A book about mass behaviour 5
Mass behaviour is hard to change 6
Bad theory, bad plan. Better theory? Better plan? 7
Old news? 8
I and the other 9
Market research and me 10
We're all individuals   I'm not 11
Understanding the *how*, not just the what 12
What the book will cover 12
How to use this book 15

Part One: A 'We-Species' with an illusion of 'I'

1: The Super-Social Ape 19
Tea and kindness 21
Advertising works 22
Even more advertising works 23
We want to be together 23
Say what you see 25
A we-species 26
Are we stardust? 27
The successful ape 28
Homo or Pan? 29
When I grow up 30
Primates are social 31
Why the *naked* ape? 32
Sexuality 33
The infant ape 33
So why *naked* then? 34
The brain of a social ape par excellence 36
How others shape us 37

How we make each other unhappy 38
The social brain 39
The sound of the crowd 40
The empathetic ape 41
Language and stroking 42
The loneliness of autism 42
Collaboration: the keys to the kingdom 45
Self-interest and collaboration 46
Game on 46
Game over and over 47
Collaboration across the nation? 48
Learning from each other 49
How collaboration built the world 50
Shirts – the work of many hands 50
Summary of this chapter 51
Questions to ponder 52
Questions and issues for marketers 52

2: The Illusion of 'I'   **53**
Pepper's ghost 56
What does Pepper's ghost tell us? 57
I woke up this morning . . . 58
What it is – oh, I forgot 59
Eternal sunshine and spotless minds 59
False memories 60
Monkey see 61
Lazy minds 62
Don't think too hard 64
Retelling the story 64
The big when 66
The illusion of consciousness 67
Depression and the distorted self 70
Treatments 71
Summary of this chapter 73
Issues arising 74
Questions and implications for marketers 74

3: 'I' vs. 'Us'   **75**
A blast of hot air 77
Travelling for real 78
Beware Greeks 80
Ubuntu 81
Peace and reconciliation 82
Wo die Zitronen blühn 83
Studying consumer tribal behaviour 85
Beyond marketing 86
Far from the madding crowds 87
The politics of 'I' 88
The collective mind 88
No such thing as society 90
Is the rest of the world so wrong? 90

'I' ideology 91
How social psychology got individualized 91
'I' research 92
Expert opinion 93
Heroes and villains, and other individuals 95
Unhappy feet? 96
The curious tale of curious George 97
What this chapter has demonstrated 97
Some questions 98
Issues for marketers arising from this chapter 98

Part Two: The Seven Principles of Herd Marketing

4: Key Principle No. 1: Interaction 101
At the market 103
At the urinal 104
In the lecture theatre 107
Complexity vs. complicated 108
Complexity as a way of seeing the world 108
Interactive animals 110
Interactive humans 110
Back to the football 111
Learning from the Mexican wave 112
At the office 113
Meanwhile, somewhere in Aberdeen 114
Summary so far 115
Every day, every day, in every way . . . 115
Crime and punishment 117
New York, New York 117
The physics of crime 119
More crime, less physics 120
Crims, saints and floaters 121
Fighting on the beaches (and in the suburbs) 122
The facts 123
Analysis 125
What to do about such riots 126
Markets and interaction 127
Behavioural markets 128
The challenge for market research 129
Issues arising 129
Implications and questions for marketing and business 130

5: Key Principle No. 2: Influence 133
Saturday night's all right 135
Faces in the crowd 136
1-2-3-4 . . . 137
Brainwashing 137
Brainwashing and conformity 138
Parallel lines 139
Fear and needles 140

Hands together, please 141
The placebo effect 142
What do you do to me? 142
Stupid boy 143
Marky Mark and his influence 144
Why one-to-one is wrong 145
Charidee, my friends 146
Relation-canoes 146
Relationships 147
Channel tunnel vision 148
From me to you 148
Getting beyond egotism 150
More influence 151
More conformity 151
The Milgram experiment 151
Let the tapes roll 152
How good people do bad things 153
Targeting rethought 155
Born unequal? 155
At the soap bar 157
Naturally influential? 157
Social influencers 158
Connectedness 159
Meet Lois 160
Targeting rethought (2) 161
Alison's new Mercedes 162
Learning from Decision Watch 164
What this chapter has shown 165
Some questions for marketing 165

6: Key Principle No. 3: Us-Talk 167

Don't believe the hype 169
Children of the revolution 170
So why is the record industry so scared? 171
Scary Mary 172
What can we learn from the Arctic Monkeys' success? 173
Boom time for WoM 174
What do we (really) know about WoM? 175
WoM Fact 1. Word of mouth is more important than other influences on individual purchases 176
WoM Fact 2. Word of mouth is getting more and more important over time 177
WoM Fact 3. Word of mouth operates in both B2B and B2C 178
WoM Fact 4. Word of mouth is a global – and not just a North American – phenomenon 179
New opportunity, traditional thinking? 181
How did everything get viral? 181
A wolf in sheep's clothing 182
The wrong end of the stick? 184
The whole cake (not just the icing) 184
How bad science changed the mind of a nation 184
Real impacts 187
What can we learn from the MMR case? 188
Grooming gossip and feeling good 189

Talk and grooming 190
More grooming talk 190
The conversation has already started 191
It's not all (or even mostly) about you! 192
Paying for it 193
Talk in the real world 193
One number to rule them all 195
Talk talk 196
Talking about telly 197
That one number again 198
One number in reality 200
What this chapter has shown 200
What's next? 201
Questions for marketing 201

7: Key Principle No. 4: Just Believe 203
Disappointed of Desmoines (or Dunstable)? 205
Meaning in a world of oversupply 206
Three principles explained 206
Goodnight Vienna 208
I believe 209
Cardigan Bay's third biggest clothing company 209
Outdoor threads 210
Nice to have? 211
Think differently 212
The journey (home) 213
Jamie's dinners 214
Being Naked 216
The empty office 218
Enron and everything after 219
A challenge – *does belief pay*? 220
So what does the study show? 221
You are not alone 221
Let everyone shine 222
A is for . . . 224
Before we go 225
1. Be who you are 226
2. What do you believe in? Find it and live it! 226
3. Act like you mean it (and don't act like you don't) 228
Summary: taking a stand 228
Some questions arising for marketing 229

8: Key Principle No. 5: (Re-)Light the Fire 231
Keep the home fires burning 233
The fire inside 234
Easier to extinguish than light 236
The misfits 237
Relighting my fire 238
The power of dreams 239
Dream a little dream 240
Vile bodies 241
A familiar situation 242

Girl talk   243
The danger of missions   243
You too can look like this   244
More belief   246
'T ain't what you say   247
The fire inside – summary so far   249
Where next?   250
How to work out what to do?   251
More behaviour thinking   251
Show, don't tell   252
Interlude: Beyond Petroleum   254
Belief in a cynical age   256
Cynics and dogs   257
Spotting cheaters   258
Conclusions   259
Questions for marketers   259

9: Key Principle No. 6: Co-Creativity   261
Unlikely popstars vol. 103   263
Charidee, my friends   264
Number one and everything after   265
So what does the 'Amarillo' syndrome teach us?   267
Originality and creativity   268
Value (chain) of fools?   269
Is this new news?   271
Hi-tech co-creativity   271
Welcome to SIM City   272
Rewriting history (together?)   273
Galileo, Newton and Einstein   274
Another 'pencil squeezer'?   275
Co-creativity – summary so far   276
Meetings, bloody meetings   276
Kick-off   278
At the theatre   279
Co-creative marketing attempts to change mass behaviour   280
I saw this and I thought of you   281
Using co-creativity to change internal audience mass behaviour   282
The Hawthorne effect and after   283
Co-creative innovation   284
Two types of co-creative networks   285
The *Ocean's 11* dream team   286
Co-creativity and market research (1)   287
Co-creativity and market research (2)   288
Some ideas that co-creativity challenges   288
Some questions for marketing   289

10: Key Principle No. 7: Letting Go   291
What a score!   293
The limits of my powers   295
The loneliness of the touchline   295
What Carwyn did and didn't do   297
The loneliness of the manager   297

The company as machine   298
Reducing the human element   298
Children of the lesser god   299
Another point of view   300
Human remains   301
Interaction businesses   302
A different kind of job   302
Back to the drawing board?   304
So what can you do?   306
More human physics   306
Crisis, what crisis?   307
Let them all talk   308
Talk with the talkers   310
What do they talk of?   311
And finally . . .   312
As inside, so outside   312
The end of management   313
Some questions for marketing   314

Part Three: Making Sense of the Herd

11: Conclusions   317

Life, the universe and giant aquatic reptiles   319
Seeing things differently   320
Conclusion 1: Our species is first and foremost a social one   321
Implication 1: Stop thinking and talking with words that conjure the 'I' perspective   321
Conclusion 2: Individuals are unreliable (if not largely irrelevant) witnesses   322
Implication 2: Ignore them   322
Conclusion 3: Interaction is everything; interaction is the 'big how'   322
Implication 3: Understand the how-mechanic and use it   323
Conclusion 4: C2C, not B2C   323
Implication 4: Get the system to work for you   323
Conclusion 5: MIC vs. MVC   323
Implication 5: Rethink targeting   324
Conclusion 6: B2C communication, not information transmission   324
Implication 6: Rethink communication as action   324
Conclusion 7: Word of mouth is the most powerful sales tool   325
Implication 7: Make WoM the real goal of all actions and not just WoM campaigns   325
Conclusion 8: Be more interesting   326
Implication 8: Find your beliefs and live them   326
Conclusion 9: Co-create   326
Implication 9: Learn to be a great co-creator   326
Conclusion 10: Letting go   327
Implication 10: Rethink 'management'   327

Postscript   329

And it's goodnight from him . . .   329

Endnotes   331

Index   341

Foreword

Thomas Edison didn't know how electricity worked.

His best guess was probably that electrons sort of rolled along a wire, taking some sort of force from one end to the other. He had a vague sense that this wasn't true (and it wasn't) but he never really had the time to investigate that deeply because he was busy inventing light bulbs and phonographs and creating a vast business empire.

He had a model in his head for how electricity worked, which was good enough to get a lot of things built and invented. With his inventive sprit, his persistence and his genius for spotting opportunities he built entire industries through trial and error and a dogged pursuit of what seemed, on the whole, to work.

This got him a long way. He created much that was useful and interesting, but without pausing for reflection, without examining his assumptions, without changing his mind about everything, he couldn't get any further. He couldn't invent television or the transistor or computing.

And I suspect you can see where this analogy is going . . .

What Edison built

. . . because I think the last 50 or 100 years of marketing and advertising have been quite a lot like Edison. Industries have been built, methodologies have been codified, conventional wisdom has been institutionalized. But every practitioner has always had a vague sense, in the back of their mind, if they bothered to think about it, that they really have no idea what they're doing. Peel back the layers of accreted thinking about brand awareness and 'opportunities to see' and usage and attitudes and it's clear that all we have are lots of competing theories, a bunch of well ingrained habits and vast squadrons of trial and error.

This is OK. This has gotten us somewhere. This has created some useful and interesting things as well as lots and lots of crass and pointless ones, but it's stalled, the consensus is falling apart, the old solutions don't seem to fit the new problems and famous admen shout that advertising is dead to everyone who'll listen.

The web-enabled, digitally empowered, brand-savvy consumer cliché of the futurists' recent past has arrived and they're not willing to buy our old act. We need a new model. We need to think differently.

The kind of book we need now?

Mark Earls might be the solution. Or at least a bit of it. Because Mark is a new sort of communications thinker and he's written exactly the kind of book we all need now.

(And to explain why, I'm afraid I have to resort to a list, because I've spent the last three years of my life blogging and I find I simply can't write in proper coherent paragraphs anymore.)

1. Hats off to Mark for writing a book with some big theories in it. You don't see much of that these days. Most of the 'revolutions in marketing' books you get nowadays are just very long business cards. They tell you how badly wrong everyone else is getting things (particularly big, old businesses and big, old brands), they offer quite thin solutions (normally 'hire someone very like me') and they give a couple of examples the author worked on. Plus some Nike ones. These books are more about tactics than strategy and more about tools than thinking. This is all right as far as it goes. But if we're going to go beyond improving light bulbs and start inventing television we need some new, grand theories. Mark is shooting for this. So hurrah!

2. He doesn't assume brands/marketing/whatever is a white Western phenomenon, and he helps us think about a world where communications are created everywhere, not just consumed everywhere. Indeed, as business globalizes it's very possible that Western I-centric ways of working are exactly the wrong ways to be building great brands and that the unthinking assumption that we'll be doing creative industries and they'll be doing call centres is short-sighted and foolish. Why spend all your money trying to get individualistic Westerners to collaborate properly

when many of your prospective employees have grown up in more naturally collaborative *we*-centric cultures?

3. He draws ideas and inspiration from every imaginable intellectual discipline and philosophy including anthropology, psychology, ethnography, rugby and pop music. He draws on personal experience and business case studies. He recognizes that whatever turns out to be 'the way that brands etc. work' it's unlikely to be clear and simple. It's going to be complex and messy and it's going to cut across boundaries of professional discipline, intellectual tradition and marketing agency silo. If like me you're all surface and no depth this makes for a brilliant read, skimming from one slightly understood topic to the next. And if you're more of a detail merchant then this book'll make a fantastic stepping-off point for exploring all kinds of obscure but fascinating stuff.

4. He writes well. There are pictures. There are jokes. As marketing people get more and more post-literate it's nice to be able to recommend a book people'll be prepared to read.

And that's it. Read this book. Think about it. You don't have to swallow it whole, but if you're going to be any good at your marketing, branding or communications job in the next 20 years then you need to question your assumptions about how stuff works, not just where to spend your media money. And Mark's provided a great place to start. Hurrah for him!

Russell Davies
Open Intelligence Agency
(Formerly of Weiden & Kennedy & Nike)
www.russelldavies.com

Acknowledgements

This book is really David Muir's fault. And not mine.

When, in 2002, I asked him what I should write a Market Research Society conference paper about, he advised me not to think harder about what I had called our 'herd nature' in my first book;[1] indeed he told me to drop the idea. There's not much mileage in that line of thinking, he explained. Instead, he suggested I ponder the technical market research implications of the rise of 360 (in the round) communications.

Being more than a bit contrary, I did precisely the opposite to what David suggested. This stubbornness on my part did not stop him introducing me to the wonder of decision markets or helping me see other connections in the disparate fields I was crossing.

Along the way a number of other people have helped me, debated the things I was struggling with and often pointed out interesting evidence for the core idea of this book and its application to the worlds of business and marketing in particular.

As ever, my good friends, David Wood of Leo Burnett and Peter Wells of Nilewide, have both been inspirational conversational partners; Adam Morgan a great encouragement as ever. Domenico Vitale and the US AAAA planning conference committee have repeatedly given me the chance to work out my thinking in public. My Ford Motor Company client, Murat, also encouraged this line of thinking. As did the Market Research Society – particularly Kevin Maclean, Ginny Valentine and Wendy Gordon. Mark Sherrington, Russell Davies, Paul Feldwick, Chris Forrest, Robin Wight and Nick Kendall have all said very nice things about the herd idea and encouraged me to make it a book. Tessa Graham introduced me to some interesting folk and bought me lots of pink wine. And many of my Ogilvy friends have helped, too: Paul O'D, Rory Sutherland, Mark Oldridge, John Shaw, Bernardo Geoghegan, Colin Mitchell, Rob Hill, Gary Leih and

Robyn Putter have all made encouraging noises. My creative partner, Paul Smith, has been incredibly tolerant of my obsession – even though he has often admitted he only half-understands what I am on about. Something I only half-believe. Roderick White of Admap and Judy Lannon of Market Leader have both respected the line of thinking in their magazines and encouraged me to articulate it further. And the boys and girls from Naked and Howies were a delight to interview and talk with.

Lots of people have had their evenings (and other dayparts) ruined by my herd obsession. My sister Ros, C, Sara, Liz, Trems, Mikey, Merry, Quancey, James, Sam, Kieron, Sox, James, Hilly, Cronky, Nick, Stephen, Kirsty, Carl, Trigg, Jori, Crispin and lots of others. These brave folk have continued to encourage me to write, write, write. Thank you also to Jon, Gay, Tom, Sannchen, Hendy, Fiona and the boys who continue to treat me like a 'mensch' and not like a monomaniac.

And thanks to Cecilia for the original cover concept and Jon for the curiously simian likenesses. And Sara for helping prepare the manuscript and do the illustrations that were beyond me in the latter stages. *Big Shout* to Chris and Tim and the team at Antidote (http://www.antidote.co.uk) for their cover and other identity design work: you did fab things with neither time nor money to work with. Last but not least the Big Shorts themselves – 2-3-4 – you have provided some wonderful distractions as well as one or two powerful insights into mass behaviour (without I suspect any knowledge of doing so).

Big thanks again to my editor Claire Plimmer and her team who have again been extraordinarily patient and helpful to this most unreliable author.

But my biggest fan, biggest supporter and biggest inspiration in the writing has been the lovely Louise. I hope that the finished product makes you as proud as you had hoped it would do. Whatever you think of it, this book would be much – *much* – the worse in every way without you.

Thank you.

Introduction

If I am an advocate, it is for discoveries about human nature that have been ignored or suppressed in modern discussions of human affairs . . . Why is it important to sort this all out? The refusal to acknowledge human nature is like the Victorians' embarrassment about sex, only worse: it distorts our science and scholarship, our public discourse and our day-to-day lives.

S Pinker[1]

At the 'cellotaph'

A friend of mine recently returned to Britain from a long period working abroad to find the country visibly transformed. Not in the way that politicians would have us believe – a rich and varied multicultural nation, which leads the world in science, innovative public services and principled engagement with our peers – but instead, as a nation of people who *say it with flowers*.

Government statistics tell us that in the last 10 years crime has dropped and yet at the same time every road in every town has been transformed again and again into what *Private Eye* magazine has called 'a cellotaph' – that is, a temporary roadside floral memorial to the victim of a traffic accident or a violent crime. Some of the tributes consist of little more than garage-bought carnations, wrapped in garish cellophane; others are more elaborate in the time-honoured East End genre, spelling out the name of the dead individual with some greeting ('goodbye dad'). Some become elaborate shrines (what the Mexicans who have a much longer tradition of such things – and I guess a much higher incidence of fatal road accidents – call *descanos* as in 'interrupted journeys'); others remain simple and unprepossessing, yet at the same time moving.

One, opposite Camden Town tube station, was still tended daily, months after the murder of 19-year-old Ohmar Mahir. What struck my returning friend was the sheer ubiquity of the floral tributes when, a decade ago, the sight would have been – if not unknown – then certainly rare.

Indeed, in the last 10 years, these shrines have blossomed and seeded themselves across our land, like the vigorous Chinese buddleia (or butterfly bush), which wriggles into the cracks and forgotten corners of our tarmacked country. Or perhaps more like the more inventive and colourful American-influenced graffiti that now springs up overnight on any blank wallspace in our cities: today's 'tags' are not the monochrome scribbles of the teenage gossip-mill and the toilet wall, but increasingly inventive visual street-art. Indeed, several 'taggers' are recognised as authentic artists by the art-world. One, Banksy[2] enjoys world-wide success as a social satirist and provocateur, as well as a curated artist and illustrator. At first, there were only occasional examples of such public wall-art to be found in urban locations; now, they are everywhere.

So how are we to explain this kind of thing?

Our explanations of such examples of mass behaviour tell us a lot about how we think about human behaviour. They reveal our underlying beliefs and models of mass behaviour: the ideas we use to explain mass behaviour (and to shape it). The floral tributes themselves are a particularly interesting case which casts light on the way we think about other social phenomena.

What's certain is that the tributes are not new. Some commentators trace the roots of mass floral tributes back through history to show how common they really are. After all, the UK's military veterans have been trooping down Whitehall with poppies in their buttonholes, to leave wreaths to the fallen dead of two World Wars every Remembrance Sunday for three generations or more. I have visited the shrine in Barnes to the glam rock star, Marc Bolan, at the tree into which his girlfriend crashed their mini, one wet night (Figure I.1). But such floral tributes have not just been for soldiers or celebrities. In 1912,[3] eight boy scouts from Walworth drowned when their boat sank on a trip to Kent. The result was a mass outpouring of grief in East London. Flags were flown at half mast. Churchill himself intervened to ensure that the bodies were brought back up the Thames in a naval vessel, which was met with floral tributes from huge crowds, with much weeping

Figure 1.1 *Marc Bolan cellotaph reproduced by permission of Tom Mattey*

and sobbing to boot. So maybe the phenomenon is not so alien, after all but this view raises some other issues, such as why are cellotaphs everywhere now?

Other social commentators take a different approach. They have sought to explain the cellotaph phenomenon by making it an indication of some big long-term trend (or BLTT), or *an indication of what we've become* as Blake Morrison[4] puts it. It has been seen as a sign of the 'feminization of Britain' or of our increasing mawkishness or indeed, bizarrely, a sign that the class system is somehow in its final death throes (the largely working-class nature of many of these tributes is undeniable but I suspect that this is more to do with the fact that there are more street deaths among the working classes than anything more sinister). In other words, these are explanations based on the notion of mass behaviour as something that is the result of outside forces acting on individuals (whether it's 'historical processes', something in the air or even something in the water!).

Other explanations choose to trace the trend back to the enormous out-pouring of public grief at the death of Princess Diana in August 1997. During the days and weeks following her fatal accident, the nation seemed convulsed by a grief mania; people started to lay flowers, first a million blooms in the grounds of her London home, Kensington Palace, then more and more around the country, at the funeral and finally at the family home of Althorp. This is an example of thinking about mass behaviour being the result of some external traumatic event. What you might call the Macmillan theory of mass behaviour (the former Prime Minister was once asked what caused governments to fall – his answer was 'events').

Not everyone was caught up in Diana-grieving; many people remained untouched by the floral madness. I remained similarly unaffected by Diana's 'tragic demise' (as the tabloids and the Diana-bloggers would have it) but was aware of the stir it was associated with among the population. And I recall vividly how confused I was by what was going on: ordinary sane people apparently doing strange things with tears and flowers. I quizzed a number of friends including one – then a high-flying advertising executive – as to why she and her personal assistant had given up their lunch hour to 'make their pilgrimage' to Kensington Palace. Her response was simple, 'I want to . . . you know, *be part of this* . . . to show my respect, too . . . with the others.' Another friend chose to camp out with his young family just to have a good view of the funeral procession.

Bigger boys made me do it

This is where we seem to get a little clearer about the real mechanics of mass behaviour. At the peak of Diana-grief mania, the Cambridge-based literary magazine *Granta* complained of the 'floral fascism' spreading through the country – by which I think they meant the social pressure to take part in public grieving. Others bemoaned the pressure to conform in other ways; my father in his own way loudly refused to become sentimental about some 'thick (and dead)' Princess.

This is what I think is the important lesson for those of us who try to make sense of the kaleidoscope of human behaviour which we observe around us: that it is not driven (as the likes of Karl Marx, Naomi Klein or Vance Packard would have us believe) by powerful extra-human forces like economics or brands or by traumatic events (although these may have a part to play) but instead, *by other people*. Individuals do not do what they do largely on their own volition, but through the influence of others. That is the heart of the model of mass behaviour that this book proposes.

So the floral commemorations – the cellotaphs – made by mothers and fathers of children cut down before their time in road accidents or drunken stabbings are not individual acts. Nor are they the result of some mass brain-washing by the florist trade or of garage forecourt marketers. They are an example of the enormous influence each of us has over the others in our lives. Not just those close to us, but those we have never met and never will – people whose behaviour influences other people's behaviour which then in turn influences ours. People just like us.

Terrible as the story behind each floral tribute is, the phenomenon itself illustrated on railings, lampposts and traffic lights throughout the UK serves to reveal a deep and long-hidden truth about human nature which those of us in marketing, in management and in government would do well to embrace: *we are a we-species who do individually what we do largely because of each other.* As my childhood excuse ran, 'Bigger boys made me do it.'

A book about mass behaviour

This book is intended for anyone who tries to change the behaviour of large numbers of people – of customers, employees or private citizens. It is not a self-help book – although I have learned a lot about myself in researching and writing it. Nor is it intended in any way to challenge the professionals who help individuals bring about change in their lives.

No, this book is not about individuals and individual behaviour; *it is about mass behaviour.*

Why is this important?

Marketing, management, public policy and service delivery are not really about factories or hospitals or finances or service level agreements (SLAs) or satisfaction measures or indeed any of the other things we feel more comfortable with and find easier to measure. Rather they are (or should be) about human behaviour. But not about individual behaviour – all organizations need to serve and harness the talents and efforts of large numbers of people: customers and staff and citizens and so on. All three are concerned – or should be – with mass behaviour and how to anticipate and shape it.

Mass behaviour is hard to change

As any psychotherapist will tell you, individual behaviour is very hard to shape; mass behaviour is even more difficult. The evidence speaks for itself.

When governments report on their policy successes, they struggle to do so convincingly. Be it the uptake of a new welfare benefit or an initiative to reduce street crime or improve health service provision, ministers and civil servants almost always end up having to be creative with the numbers to evidence change on a mass scale.

When the sharp-suited bankers celebrate another big merger deal, they're clearly not aware of the dim chances of the deal being a success (or maybe the financial rewards for doing the deal help them ignore the truth); one source suggests only one third[5] achieve the synergies that the dealmakers and the management promise the shareholders. Over the longer term, the numbers are even more worrying. Another source[6] suggests that between 50% and 60% actually destroy shareholder value (as opposed to building it or making no difference).

For those of use who work in advertising and marketing, our inability to create long-term changes in customer behaviour is repeatedly disheartening. While there are some notable exceptions to this rule that are acclaimed all around the world – the Apple iPod being one of the most high-profile of recent years – these remain exceptions rather than the rule. Even if we accept a lesser ambition of keeping customer behaviour the same (as the London-based academic, Professor Andrew Ehrenberg suggests), it is hard to demonstrate that this lack of change has had anything to do with our efforts.

This perhaps explains the obsession with relationship marketing in recent years, be it in its simple form or the more exciting e-based versions or indeed the wholesale reorganization of companies around the CRM principle (customer relationship marketing). Those with some kind of vested interest as the blueprint often present the latter for the future of marketing. Again the facts are beginning to reveal a less than glorious success. For all its internal intellectual consistency, for all its rigour and measurability at an individual level and for all of the commonsense axioms behind the approach, CRM turns out not to be the roaring success that it has been claimed to be. Forester suggested some six years ago that while two thirds of vendors thought their CRM projects had been a success, only one third of their clients thought so. Clearly somebody's not on the ball here. They can't both be right about the success or otherwise of this latest marketing fad.

And things are getting worse, not better: the latest research suggests that most of the money paid to CRM consultants, IT manufacturers and software companies has failed to bring about the significant changes in mass behaviour – inside the company or with its customers – that the vendors promised. The blame for this failure is often[7] attributed to the greed of the software vendors trying to sell solutions to a problem that might not exist, or even by some in the discipline[8] to the oversimplification of the theory which drives the technology and practices. It is just much harder to change mass behaviour than we thought.

Bad theory, bad plan. Better theory? Better plan?

In this book I make a simple and challenging claim: we will find it much easier to change mass behaviour if we start from first principles; if we go back to basics and develop a better conception of humankind; if we abandon our existing ways of thinking and accept that we are not a species of independent, self-determining individuals, whatever our brains and our culture tell us (see Chapter 2 for more detail on the curious illusion of 'I').

Most of our behaviour is – like the floral cellotaph phenomenon – the result of the influence of other people because we are a super-social species. A herd animal, if you like.

I believe that this is important to get your head around, because as Stephen Pinker points out in the introduction to his *Blank Slate*, our failure to acknowledge the truth about human nature distorts our attempts to understand human behaviour and frustrates our attempts to change it. Bad theory = bad plan = ineffective action.

What I have called 'herd theory' is not some flighty or floppy idea – an assertion without support or evidence. A number of advances in the medical and behavioural sciences are beginning to reveal the profound truth of our herd nature. From the newer disciplines of modern neuroscience, econophysics, evolutionary psychology and network geometry it is becoming clear that we seem to be uniquely built to be interactive and interdependent herd animals – we are so extraordinarily gifted at human–human interaction and the results of this interaction have shaped our world and continue to do so for the future.

The promise this insight holds for those of us who try to change mass behaviour is enormous. Imagine if we could tap into this underlying power of human nature to bring about the changes we seek – in business, in marketing and public policy! However, be warned: while this book will use a host of examples by way of illustration, the ways in which we can use the insights to change mass behaviour are still being worked out and there is a great deal of distracting noise, particularly around the idea of word-of-mouth marketing (see Chapter 6).

Old news?

But maybe this rethinking of mass behaviour is not such new news. Africa has long known that human beings are a we-species; the pan-African notion of Ubuntu has helped South Africa migrate with relatively little pain from minority to majority rule in a decade. The Truth and Reconciliation Commission is just one of the policy initiatives that the governments led by Mandela and Mbeki have deployed to bring this about. Desmond Tutu has developed a social Christian theology based around the same idea. The same thinking is also being deployed in war-torn Rwanda to bring about peace and there is some debate about how to apply this notion to post-Troubles Northern Ireland.

But this is not merely an African truth: the same conception of human nature lies at the heart of many oriental cultures. Richard Nisbett's[9] collection of cross-cultural studies shows how the same conception of humanity underlies many oriental cultures. 'We' is more important than 'I' to people who grow up in environments that are more collective; it shapes how such people see the world in profound and interesting ways. And it provides a point of comparison for those of us who grew up in an individualist, 'I' culture: it reveals that our conception of humanity shapes our own view of the world. It challenges our blind acceptance of 'I'.

I and the other

Maybe this is not such a novel insight to those of you who know the psychotherapeutic canon. Close reading of the greats of psychoanalysis and psychotherapy make it quite clear that they have known this about ourselves all along but we have chosen to ignore it. Sigmund Freud was in many ways the arch individualist – his major clinical concern was quite rightly for individual patients; he phrased much of his writing in terms of the individual and their neuroses. However, he is very clear that what he called 'the Other' lies at the heart of his view of the individual sense of self and determines much of our behaviour, for good or ill. Indeed, in his later works Freud and his colleagues (e.g. Erich Fromm) struggle (with mixed success) to find some kind of synthesis of the individual and the group or society.

We cannot escape the *Other* – parent, sibling or stranger. Freud seems to have been right about the fact that most of our unhappiness comes from mislearning the rules of interaction with others and doing so very early on. Others such as Alice Miller[10] have shown the importance of early interaction with others in an individual patient's later dysfunction without the use of some of the Freudian constructs which have since been questioned. More recently, longitudinal studies exploring Bowlby's attachment theory have allowed us to see how long-lasting these effects are. Those who make less successful attachments early on are indeed more likely to struggle with attachments later. It is not by chance that most people's experience of psychotherapy is talk about their childhood.

Moreover, recent advances in neuroscience are allowing us to understand more about the social applications of brain function (how the brain changes on interaction with others and quite how much of our brain function seems designed to enable us to thrive in the social contexts which make up so much of our lives). At the same time, the discipline of social psychology (hidden to many since the post-war period, due to ethical issues around studies on human subjects created by researchers like Stanley Milgram – see Chapter 5 – and the difficulties of testing hypotheses) is now being revisited by a number of generalist writers and the pioneering work is being reinterpreted and reapplied to today's questions around mass behaviour.

Market research and me

By contrast, the commercial world and in particular market research is obsessed with the individual (some £2 bn is spent every year in the UK in understanding what individuals think and do) and while most of the money is spent on individual interviews, the focus group has become incredibly popular in recent years. But don't go thinking that the focus group somehow accesses our herd nature and that what is said in this format is somehow more accurate than the unreliable ask–answer methodologies such as opinion polling.

It is increasingly widely acknowledged that a large part of the appeal is the impression of the truth being revealed by so-called real people – you watch them come in off the street, you ask them questions, you watch and listen to what they say and that clearly is that. Real people have revealed to you what they do, why and what they are likely to do next. And you get the impression of what the rest of the real people out there (sic) might be like.

There's a new kid in the market research block who takes things further, whose ready adoption reveals our underlying commitment to the idea of individuals as self-determining machines: 'neuromarketing' uses brain-scanning techniques, which were originally developed to map the brain and observe the physical correlates of our mental experiences, for something really important and worthy (not): to measure individual responses to examples of product design and advertising!

Ethical, statistical and scientific quibbles aside, what strikes me is the excitement in market research circles that the vendors of these techniques have caused. And the reason why seems clear enough: here, at last, is a technique that claims to be able to 'lift the lid' on individual human heads and show us what is really going on to shape behaviours. Just as witch doctors and mediums have done for centuries and indeed the father of modern qualitative research, Ernst Dichter, promised with his motivational research in the 1940s.

Here at last is the means to see inside the heads of customers (and fiddle with them). Which of course misses the point entirely, because we are not discrete, self-determining individuals; we do what we do largely because of our interaction with – and under the influence of – others. And mostly without realizing it.

We're all individuals – I'm not

Underlying all of the individualist agenda is a really interesting cluster of misunderstandings about ourselves and our brains. I will spend some time and space to discuss them in Chapter 2.

For example, we tend to think of individuals as concrete and well-defined units of humanity. Units that decide for themselves what to do. As Descartes spotted in his *cogito*, the key to this is our experience of continuous consciousness – our individual sense of ourselves. I don't wake up this morning thinking I am somebody else; I know that I am Mark and the same Mark I went to sleep as (only normally slightly clearer-headed, another day older but none the wiser). Sometimes on waking I am momentarily confused as to where I am or what I am doing but I – like most folk – tend to look at my continuous memories as an indication of who I am.

But on another level, this common-sense argument is misleading and you don't need to be an expert in cognitive psychology or neuroscience to work out why. We all know our memories are wildly unreliable – they change in content and emotional charge according to when and how we recall them. Recent debates at Earls Towers have confirmed that I too am subject to this weakness. And my girlfriend also.

Our memories are not like a computer's file retrieval system, locating and retrieving simple digital data chunks. Memories are not just units of factual information and retrieving them is never 100% accurate.

We suppress things we don't want to think about or feel uncomfortable processing actively and – as every page of a recent compendium[11] of ways in which the human brain deceives us shows – we change our memories, cognitions and beliefs to fit into our existing schema of things. Sometimes we even imagine things that never actually happened . . .

Understanding the *how*, not just the what

Let's be clear why this insight into our human nature is so powerful *in practical terms* . . .

Once we recognize that we are only interested in *mass behaviour*, and not just in the idiosyncratic individual, the truth about our herd nature becomes really useful. It not only enables us to describe the *start point* (mass behaviour) and the *desired outcome* (mass behaviour) better than other frameworks, but it also *explains the mechanics* of mass behaviour change (or lack of change – most substantial businesses spend a good deal of time and effort protecting what they have and keeping their customers just where they are).

If we understand the *hows* – how the roadside floral tributes came about and are sustained – we should also be able to explain any number of other mass phenomena and put that insight to work in changing mass behaviour. For example, how did an unknown band from Sheffield, the Arctic Monkeys, manage to get a brace of number one records without the machinery of record companies and distribution deals? Why do football crowds sing and why do they like it so? How did text messaging take off in the UK with little or no marketing hype? How did one man spark a mass movement by asking passing visitors to 'Join me'? If we can understand these kinds of behaviours, we can go about changing other large-scale group behaviours with greater hope of tangible results.

That said, this is not meant to be a theoretical or academic book. It seeks to explain and convince you of our herd nature and shows how it can be applied to building more effective change programmes for all kinds of mass behaviour. It uses tangible examples from all spheres of human activity and from many different parts of the world to illustrate the key points.

What the book will cover

Because this view of human nature runs contrary to our individual experience and the culture in which most of those who read this book have grown up, I think it important that I don't rush into practical applications of the theory too quickly. I think it's important to have a good long think about human nature and what is known about it *before* we move on to practical applications.

The notion of humankind that underlies what I call 'herd theory' runs so counter to what we experience and what we are taught that I have decided to spend three whole chapters assembling the evidence for 'we' and against 'I'. Some of it will be familiar to certain readers, some to others but I think it's worth laying the whole piece out in front of you. If you just wanted a few marketing case studies to copy out then I'm afraid you'll find the early part of the book disappointing and perhaps a little heavy-going. However, I believe that any intelligent general reader should be able to grasp the evidence and the implications. That said, I have also included some questions that these new facts raise for marketers and business leaders generally – perhaps these will help you apply the evidence and the ideas to your professional life.

After making the case for what Pinker calls 'the truths about human nature that have been ignored (and) suppressed', the book then starts to build a new approach to understanding and changing mass behaviour built around seven key principles. I'll attempt to spell out how each challenges some of our most dearly held ideas and practices in marketing and business. Here goes . . .

Part One – A 'We-species' with the illusion of 'I'

Chapter 1 collects the evidence from a number of fields for seeing our species as first and foremost a herd animal – the ultimate primate, a 'super-social ape'.

Chapter 2 explains why each of us has the opposite impression in our daily lives and how this impression is largely an illusion.

Chapter 3 examines the reasons why it is that we in the West have not appreciated our true human nature, the blinkers of our cultural ideology of individualism. Other cultures' views of what it is to be human reveal the oddity of our Western received wisdom of what it is to be human.

Part Two – The seven principles

Once I have established the facts about our 'we'-nature, I'll then start to apply it: start to build a different model of mass behaviour and how to change it. For simplicity's sake, I have divided this into seven key chapters, each explaining the background and application of one of the seven principles of herd marketing.

Key Principle No. 1: Interaction

In this chapter I'll explore how mass behaviour is neither the result of some Borg-like communal brain nor the sum of individual thinking, but rather the result of interaction between individuals within a given context.

Key Principle No. 2: Influence

In this chapter, I'll show how *influence* (rather than persuasion) is the key to shaping mass behaviour and how this leads us to rethink the notion of 'targeting' (who to focus on in our attempts to bring about change).

Key Principle No. 3: Us-talk

This chapter will examine the most visible (but by no means the only) influential behaviour within the herd, what is commonly termed 'word of mouth'. I discuss what it is, how to measure it and how powerful a tool it really is. Also, I will try to work out whether this has always been the case or whether the lack of trust in many aspects of modern life is making it more important. I also warn of the traps of much of today's word-of-mouth marketing, by distinguishing between 'endogenous' and 'exogenous' word-of-mouth behaviour.

Key Principle No. 4: Just believe

This chapter explores the most important tools in generating human–human interaction, influence and word-of-mouth, both in terms of communication programmes and product and service design. At the heart of this lies the notion of personal belief or purpose. I will show how beliefs create a different, better performing business than cold-eyed financial management. An interesting one, too.

Key Principle No. 5: (Re)lighting the fire

This chapter deals with a situation that many of us face: in most organizations the fire of belief and purpose seems to have gone out (if it ever flared). Here I show how the same principles of belief, making it personal and aligning behaviour to belief can be applied to mature businesses to bring about changes in mass behaviour.

Key Principle No. 6: Co-creating

This chapter suggests that if businesses and organizations are to thrive within this herd world, they are going to have to learn to change their stance towards their customers, staff and fellow citizens and learn how to *co-create*.

Key Principle No. 7: Letting go

In this chapter I show how the herd approach requires a different approach to leading and shaping change. I use this personal approach to make some bigger points about how companies need to change their stance towards customers and staff. But most of all, I will encourage you to let go of the twin illusions of certainty and control.

And last of all, I have attempted to conclude with a summary of the herd theory approach to mass behaviour and to spell out some of the main applications for marketing and business leaders.

How to use this book

This book pulls together learning from different practitioners and theorists across a wide range of disciplines, both academic and commercial. As such it is never going to be complete or comprehensive; indeed, it would be wrong for me to claim that it was, given the co-creative way that it has developed and will continue to do so. However, I have tried to highlight what it is you need to rethink and do differently if you want to consciously take advantage of the power of the human herd.

Of course, I could be wrong about all of this. That's up to you to decide. At the very least, I hope to make you think for yourself. I will try to provoke you and challenge you with practical issues about behaviour change. I have included some questions that each chapter or topic has raised for my colleagues and friends (at least those kind and interested enough to read what I have written).

And hopefully this tangible character will provide you with a way of making the kind of change you want to see a reality. Remember, you may be reading this book on your own but you are not alone – there are many, many others out there who are already having similar thoughts and are reading this and similar books and thinking similar thoughts to you. What if you could work together to make change a reality (and not just a bonus-able objective)? Why not try? It's what we were made for – and the source of all our strength and power as a species.

Here are some websites that might provide you with the kind of collaborators who might just be able to – if they all push together – move the odd mountain or two.

http://www.pledgebank.com
http://www.join-me.co.uk
http://www.peaceoneday.org
http://www.wearewhatwedo.org
http://www.guerillagardening.org
http://www.antidote.co.uk

Part One

A 'We-Species' with an illusion of 'I'

1

The Super-Social Ape

What this chapter will cover

The true nature of mankind is that of a super-social ape. We are programmed to be together; sociability is our species' key evolutionary strategy; we feel happier with others; our brains develop through interaction with others and when our brains don't develop normally this often robs us of key human skills. When they develop properly we have the most amazing capabilities to live together and create things together.

Interdependence is and ought to be as much the ideal of man as self-sufficiency. Man is a social being.

Mahatma Gandhi

Tea and kindness

Danny Wallace is an unlikely cult leader. He's of average height, wears glasses, has no track record of ambition or fantasies of world domination and – by his own account – little or no charisma; his speechifying is anything but riveting or rabble-rousing. And yet he has created a cult (or 'collective' as he prefers to call it) of thousands of smiley people around the world who willingly pursue an agenda which runs right against contemporary mores. What's more they all seem to share a kind of sickening niceness that conjures up the brainwashed of Waco, Texas.

How did it all start? Back in 2001 Danny attended the funeral of a great-uncle he barely knew, Gallus. As he flew to Zurich to attend the rites in a language he barely understood (Danny's Swiss-German had not really thrived as he grew up in London), he did not suspect that his life (and those of people he'd never met) would change. During the course of the endless reminiscing about the life of the lately departed, all conducted in the local dialect, he thought he heard something really strange. Did somebody mention Uncle Gallus and a commune?

Yes, his grandmother confirmed, a commune. But a failed one.

It turned out that Great-Uncle Gallus, stout Swiss burgher that he was, once became so disillusioned by the small town politics of Monzwang (population 1,000) that he decided to set up his own town on a patch of land he already owned. Idealistically he hoped to start the perfect community from scratch. Unfortunately, only three of his fellow citizens saw the attraction of the idea and Gallus never pursued it beyond the initial invitation. That said, from the reaction of the family gathered at his funeral, everyone seems to have thought Gallus mad and still felt more than slightly embarrassed by the whole situation: 'Another one of Gallus' crazy ideas.'

Now this is the sort of anecdote that all of us would like to be able to tell to our friends down the local pub or bar – 'I can top that last story. My great-uncle (yes, that mad Swiss one . . .) well, he tried to start a cult . . . but failed.' If the social value of this story crossed Danny's mind, he was careful not to make too much of it. Indeed, Danny didn't really do much with the thought at all, apart from telling his long-suffering girlfriend on his return to London. And then he pondered a bit more, while hanging out in his flat. And then on a whim he acted.

Advertising works

He put a simple text advert into *Loot*, the newspaper that consists of nothing but adverts for second-hand cars, sofas, house-clearance services and accommodation for rent. This is what it said: 'Join me. Send a passport photo to . . .'

And then he sat back and waited to see if he would garner the same level of indifference as his great-uncle. Probably, he thought to himself. After all, he hadn't actually said what people might be joining or what they would get out of it.

The first response was telling; it came from someone in my own London Borough of Camden. A very normal-looking fella from his passport photo. Who enclosed a menu from a local Indian takeaway restaurant. Fair enough. Nice thought. Someone prepared to be friendly and share at least one of his favourite things in whatever this new movement became. Maybe the whole idea of building a different kind of community wasn't so bad. Then, on examining the menu more closely, Danny noted a curious niceness in the restaurant that made the gesture slightly spooky (but still nice).

> We are proud of our chefs (!) and our management (!!). We are proud that you the customer choose us to satisfy your appetite.[1]

So the restaurant people must be quite nice, too. Not many companies are both truly proud of their people and grateful to their customers (at least not until you've given them a lot of money and even then rarely so, certainly if Anthony Badouin's *Kitchen Memoirs* are at all accurate).

Even more advertising works

And from there things sort of snowballed. A flimsy little website and lots of personal recommendations soon led to some 4,000 passport photos on Danny's dining table. As with many things in life, success brought stresses and strains. Soon Danny was feeling that he ought to give the organization some purpose, some meaning. More and more joinees (as he called them) were happy to join in, but more and more of them wanted to know what Danny as Leader wanted them to do.

This was tricky, as Danny hadn't really thought about the answer to this question. But he had to work it out quite quickly. As he comments:

> Now, I don't know if you've ever started a cult, but one of the first things you have to do is decide whether to use your powers for good, or for evil. You will already have realised that I decided to work for good. And it was working.[?]

Following Danny's decision to get the collective to work for good, cups of tea and pints of beer were bought for strangers, biscuits offered, heavy shopping bags carried. All across the country.

Join-me was born. And with it the Karma-army, an army dedicated to tea and biscuits and RAoKs ('random acts of kindness'). Danny was overwhelmed again and again by the power of the idea – a simple email led to hundreds of joinees turning up on London's Oxford Street for 'Karmageddon' (a meeting of the collective which included folk from all over the country and – as seems to be required for these kinds of things – one rather jolly Dutchman. The Belgians went ape for it – the Leader found himself on prime-time TV – the Norwegians, Australia and even the USA have felt the power of tea and niceness; and every day at www.join-me.co.uk new joinees are welcomed and electronically hugged by old hands. Try it and see the reception you get.

We want to be together

The curious thing about this phenomenon is not the story of Danny's great-uncle; nor is his stumbling into a leadership role for which he feels himself most unsuited. No, the curious thing is that all of these people were so happy to join him. And are still keen to join and take part in this little community.

Equally odd but just as heart-warming is the 'guerilla gardening' movement. Originally a form of political activism[3] for those fighting against both big business and state neglect of the poorest areas of New York City (the Chico Mendes Garden in Little Puerto Rico, NY, is perhaps the most famous), guerilla gardening activities have taken both a hard-line approach (on 1 May 2000,[4] thousands of guerilla gardeners descended on Westminster's Parliament Square as one of many protests against global capitalism that took place that year – you may remember the green Mohican that Winston Churchill's statue developed), and much gentler, less confrontational ones.

One such group is Britain's own Guerillagardening.org – a loose collective, which shares much the same enthusiastic niceness as Join-me. This jolly crew – all shapes, sizes and ages – identify rundown sites around the UK and descend on them in the dead of night to clear, dig and replant 'dead' areas in Britain's cities. From building sites to central reservations, from communal gardens in rundown estates to planters on derelict streets, the motley crew that are the British guerrilla gardeners transform – for free – the urban world around them. Partly, of course, because they just love gardening; partly, of course, because they enjoy the challenge (it feels kind of heroic). But most of all because other people enjoy it, too. It's good to do this kind of thing together. It's great to be together and have something to do together. *Together.*

These kinds of communities run directly counter to what we tell each other about the modern world. We are individualists now, my client Pat reminds me when I tell him of my herd theory. We all want to be recognized for ourselves, we don't want to belong, he avers. The modern world is fragmented – the old ties and structures that held our lives together are crumbling. Family, church, states – all of these seem to have much less influence on us than ever before. And the Henley Centre seems to confirm the trend is getting stronger if anything. It has asked a simple question for over 20 years:

Do you think the quality of life in Britain is best improved by:
a. Looking after the community's interests instead of our own?
Or
b. Looking after ourselves which ultimately raises the standards for all?

From 1994 to 2000, the overwhelming majority of British respondents chose option a; but since then, things have changed. This year, for the first time in a decade, the majority chose option b.

A few years ago one of the USA's leading trend spotters wrote a book called *Bowling Alone* based on this very thesis. In magazines and on TV, we are encouraged to believe that everyone is seeking their own unique happiness, their own customized life, the way of living that works uniquely for them. In our private lives, the self-help/amateur therapy voices encourage us to do so in hundreds of kooky ways.

And in marketing, we've fallen for this hook, line and sinker. As Roderick White puts it in Admap:[5]

> For the last 20 years or so, virtually every commentator on marketing, advertising and consumers has been saying that, along with their media habits, today's consumers are more individualistic, more fragmented, less easy to categorise.

We all know that customers are more picky and more demanding than ever before — everything needs to appear to be tailor-made to suit each individual and as a result, the notion of mass-customization in jeans, trainers and skin-care have all taken off in management meetings and marketing plans. In the last few years marketing has been passionate in pursuing (with the help of computer software vendors and the management consultants) the illusory goal of the one-to-one relationship with all its customers or all the customers it wants to have (see Chapter 5 for more details on the illusory notion of one-to-one). Everywhere you look in the modern world it seems we hear the same message: We are all individuals pursuing our own interests. But is this correct?

Say what you see

When anyone in business or government thinks about the Internet, they tend to see a set of channels through which messages can be sent or products sold. This is wrong. The Internet was founded on the basis of sharing and community; that's why we users like it. While it is possible to intervene in the online world and indeed send messages to individuals from some central source, it is fundamentally not a 'channel' in the sense that TV or newspapers are — it is not a conduit between us and them. In their enthusiasm for all things 'e-', commentators and vendors pretend to us that it is, or that it will replace other channels. This is also wrong. (That's spelt w-r-o-n-g.)

Their excitement also leads such folk to make an even more fundamental error in talking about the Internet (the same is true of mobile telephony fans and their technology): they talk as if this kind of technology has changed us – half-human, half-mouse-pad or some such. 'Cybercitizens' or 'digital consumers' or the 'digerati'. Or some such nonsense.

On the first Goldie Lookin Chain album,[6] the Welsh Rap Collective satirize this fantasy in their song 'Half man, half machine' – Eggsy believes he has transformed himself into a robot. But there is one human in Britain who has made himself at least a bit cyber. Professor Kevin Warwick of the University of Reading has had microchips inserted in his body to monitor his physiology and to enable him to interact automatically with his environment at the university. For most of us the truth is very different and will continue to be so, even for Kevin. Whether or not we are heavy users of the Internet, this technology is revealing us as who we have always been: *a species whose prime feature is its social nature.*

Danny and all his Joinees demonstrate this. So do the other similar force-for-good communities (like www.pledgebank.com on which individuals pledge to do something like write letters to MPs or give up chocolate but only if say 10 others join them).

A we-species

We are programmed to be together. We will move mountains to be together; albeit not necessarily within the old forms and structures but do it we still do. At heart, Join-me and Pledgebank and guerilla gardening and the whole of the Internet tells us we are a 'we-species' and not an 'I-species'. We are community-minded and not selfish as certain political thinkers would have it; community-minded in this most important sense – we are a community species: we want to be together; we are made to be together; we are made by being together and we are made happier by being together. Most of the enormous achievements and technologies that continue to shape our world are the result of our ability to co-operate together. Indeed, without this we would be just another evolutionary curiosity.

Even when we think we are being most individual in the way we present ourselves through the fashions we wear and the way we cut our hair, we are conforming to this same truth. Exactitudes is an ongoing photo project started by Dutch photographer Arie Versluis and stylist Elly Yttenbroek in 1995. The two tour the world taking pictures of individuals from social groups wherever they are to be found and get individuals to pose in identical poses. They then display shots of these individuals in grids of 4 x 3, so that the similarities are clear. The tattoo section (reproduced at http://www.needled.com) shows that even when we think of the most individualist of fashions – having someone draw on your body – the individuals are clearly doing what other individuals are doing and not being 'different' and unique. Our efforts to be individual are ultimately in vain.

Morevoer, if you visit their home site www.exactitudes.com, you will get the instant impression of our species as a truly herd one. Page after page of similar poses, from all around the world. While there is variety, it is of a very superficial and misleading kind.

Our social nature also works on us in another important way: the mere symbolic presence of other people regulates our behaviour. It's long been recognized that human eyes have a very powerful symbolic effect on individuals, often at an unconscious level. In a recent series of experiments,[1] Melissa Bateman and team at Newcastle University found that contributions to their own psychology department coffee-room honesty-box were increased by nearly three times when a photocopied picture of human eyes was placed near or on the drinks price list. In another experiment by Harvard researchers Burnham and Hare[8] on the subject of altruism in group-based games, half the subjects were exposed to a picture of a cute, big-eyed robot and they contributed 30% more to the collective pot than those who hadn't seen the robot picture.

This deep truth about *Homo sapiens* is something we in the West have long denied. It is uncomfortable and frightening. In fact, it's something that we have made taboo (see Chapter 3 for more details) in order to ignore it. But it is the truth about who we really are and this truth is becoming impossible to ignore for much longer.

Are we stardust?

There are lots of ways to make yourself feel better about yourself. Being called 'Stardust' by the (oddly Simian) singer Ian Brown (the former leader of the Stone Roses) just makes me feel, well, a little sparklier than I was. Your local neighbourhood guru might have the same effect on you. Another way is to deny things about yourself that you don't like or want to think about.

I suggest that we have not liked to think about ourselves as first and foremost social animals since the Enlightenment because it clashes with some other things we want to think about ourselves or permit ourselves (see Chapter 3 for more on this). Stardust is but one of our excuses.

In our minds we have separated ourselves from the rest of the animal kingdom and particularly our closest relatives (the great apes) in order to feel better about ourselves. King Kong is *bestial* but we are *civilized*; chimps are cute if they behave like humans but brutish and violent if not. As Katherine Hepburn remarks in John Huston's *African Queen*, 'Nature, Mr Allnutt, is what we are put in this world to rise above.' The result is a great loss to our understanding of ourselves: we fail to see quite how close we really are to chimps and gorillas (but chimps in particular) and how similar we really are. Instead of accepting – as all primatologists readily do – that as primates we are social animals first and foremost, we find other means to distinguish ourselves from our 'lesser', less evolved brothers and sisters and more distant relatives.

Some have used the idea of an immortal soul or our ability to exercise free will to separate us from the beasts; others focus on our thinking abilities. Only humans are properly intelligent they say, forgetting that tests which measure human intelligence might not be so good at measuring chimp or dolphin intelligence, not least because the test papers get a bit too soggy and chimps have difficulty holding the pencil. Others follow the literal word of the book of Genesis to remind us that only Adam was made in the image of the deity ('out of clay' is a good thing?). In C.S. Lewis' Narnia tales, this arrogance is turned and twisted into a tale in which four ordinary, middle-class, priggish children from wartime Finchley are the natural rulers of a land of talking creatures. To a curious lack of challenge from its inhabitants. I was in Finchley recently looking for today's versions of the family – I found the priggishness but little evidence of actual superiority. What I saw were human apes (albeit dressed in tracksuits, fur coats and corduroy).

The successful ape

It *is* true that our little offshoot of the chimpanzee clan has come to enjoy a tremendous advantage over the rest of the pack, our primate cousins included. A curious little bundle of primate genetics, we seem superbly adapted to the environment in which we have found ourselves; indeed we have begun to shape the environment to an extent that no animal has done before.

Our population growth has been phenomenal – *in little over 10,000 years we have gone from around a million or so to several billion humans.* Some of us are even waking up (finally) to the fact that we have the fate of the planet and all its life forms in our curious little paws. But does that make us superior to our cousins? I'm not sure.

And actually it's quite hard to insist on the differences. The same kind of brutality we observed in the jungle was also to be found in European cities – uncontrolled bestial (yep, that thought again) violence and destruction and cruelty. In the 20th century, 160 million human beings lost their lives to the actions of other violent humans – through war, genocide and political oppression.

So have we got the whole picture? Are we really so distant from our close genetic relatives? Is it really so long ago that we parted company? And if not, does this not unpick our attempts to distance or elevate ourselves from other primates? Might it not show that we have much more in common with them than each of us would like to think? That we, too, are a social ape but one of the most extraordinary and remarkable kind? And that this is the most important truth about our curious little creature, which has taken over the world?

Homo or Pan?

Early this year[9] a team of geneticists at Georgia Tech in Atlanta led by Soojin Yi have confirmed what many of us have long believed, that chimps and men are much closer relatives than accepted wisdom has it. They compared 63 million base pairs of DNA from different species – each 'base' being a letter in that species' genetic code. This has allowed them to look at what is called the 'molecular clock': that is, the speed at which the genetic code evolves. The analyses show that even though the two species split from a common ancestor between only 5 million and 7 million years ago, the speed at which they evolved apart is very much slower than for other primates. This means that humans and chimps – both *Pan troglodytes* (the common chimp) and *Pan paniscus* (the bonobo or pygmy chimp) – are much closer to each other than anyone has thought (at least for a while). Another research team at Wayne State University in Detroit, MA, had previously found a similar level of closeness: 99.4% or the most critical DNA sites in both species are identical. Yet another has suggested that while we separated some 7 million years ago, we reunited briefly around 2 millennia later.

These findings have reignited a centuries-long debate about whether the two represent separate genera (*Homo* and *Pan*) or whether they should be considered as members of the same family. In 1991, the science writer Jared Diamond called humans 'the third chimp' but the belief goes back to much earlier attempts at classification.

In 1775, when chimpanzees were first named, their physical and behavioural similarities with humans led the classifiers to place them in the same genus – *Homo* – as mankind. It was some 40 years later in what seems to me to be a fit of early Victorian self-aggrandisement that chimps were pushed out into their own genus, *Pan*. As one eminent evolutionary biologist puts it, 'In terms of life on Earth, chimps and humans are really not that different to each other.'[10]

Whether we put chimps into the genus *Homo*, or humans into *Pan*, seems to be of little import. Either route would certainly encourage us all to show more respect to these close cousins and thus provide rather more protection for what are endangered species by any measure.

The big point for us though is this: if we and chimps are so close, what of our chimp nature do we need to open our eyes to? What kind of species is a chimp or bonobo? For if we are of the same kind, something around our social nature may prove to be our characteristic feature and not perhaps our intellect or our immortal soul.

When I grow up

As children, my brother and I were transfixed by chimps, inspired no doubt by TV shows that we watched, shows such as *Daktari* (with Judy the chimp and Clarence the cross-eyed lion) and of course endless reruns of old Tarzan movies on TV and at the Saturday morning cinema club in suburban Kingsbury. While I wanted to become a vet or a zookeeper or really anything that would bring me into daily contact with them, my brother took things further. Much further. For nearly six months he was convinced he was a chimp (how insightful is that for a four-year-old?). Hours of pleading and endless negotiation by my mother led him to accept that chimps do indeed eat more than just bananas. But not much more.

So I have long had an amateur interest in primatology – the study of primates. I devoured books like Desmond Morris' *Naked Ape* which detailed the behavioural, psychological and sexual behaviour of chimps. Jane Goodall was another favourite. More recently, in my desire to learn more about human behaviour en masse I have scoured the works of the likes of Frans de Waal, Robin Dunbar and others and developed a much clearer picture of what kind of creatures we (both chimps and humans) really are.

Primates are social

What is clear from all of these erudite sources is that primates are first and foremost *social creatures* – this is our core evolutionary strategy, the thing that enables our type of animals to continue to reproduce.

But why would sociability be useful to our species? Why is it useful to any creature? There seem two broad ways in which being a social animal affords us some protection from predators: first, a social animal is able to divide responsibilities for watching out for predators. More eyes and ears mean better alarm systems (incidentally, this alertness to predators seems to lie behind our tendency to see things from a negative point of view and to activate our flight or fight system). Second, it provides each individual with a great deal of active support – both within the species and in contact with other species. Chimpanzees have been known to band together to chase lions and leopards up trees to protect each other. So being a social animal is core to our species and both humans and chimp are very good at it.

By this I mean much more than short-term alliances that hyenas or lion packs can show. Chimps develop close and long-term relationships with each other (largely through grooming) in order that social bonds are strong enough to protect each other. Being a successful chimp means carrying around a lot of information about other chimps, one's relationship with them and their relationship to each other. And doing so over a long period of time. De Waal describes returning to Arhnem Zoo many years after having worked with one particular chimp and being greeted enthusiastically by her as an ally.

This is why descriptions of chimp life are very much like our own. Alliances are built and nurtured and sometimes abandoned, too. Allies bring with them responsibilities and duties as well as benefits. Sometimes, it is difficult to do what is expected; sometimes we just do the wrong thing by mistake. Of course, in chimp society, things can get very scary as the social power shifts (chimps are actually very violent when necessary and not just the cute tea-drinkers of the TV ads of my youth) but we shouldn't mistake this for the true story about ourselves. Our other close cousin, the pygmy chimp (or bonobo) are by contrast rarely violent with each other. They solve social tensions through sexual means in any combination: male–male, female–male and female–female.

Without a social group to protect and nurture it, individuals of all three species feel distressed and show it (our body chemistry often supports our species' evolutionary strategy). They show similar changes in cortisol levels (the stress hormone) and are highly agitated. What worse punishment can any chimp/human impose on another than separation from its peers (as in prison, or in the extreme, solitary confinement: as a child, being sent to your room, or as an adult being blanked or sent to Coventry)? This physical response to being alone suggests how important our social nature is to us, but the truth about us is more curious still.

Why the *naked* ape?

So, if we are so closely related, then why are we virtually hairless (of course in some cases like my own, human males lose hair where they want it and gain it where they don't)? Why are we the *Naked* Ape?

Over the years, many interesting answers to this question have been sug- gested but few of them make much real sense when exposed to daylight. For example, some have suggested that we stopped needing body hair in profu- sion when we stood upright and walked across the savannah on two legs. Now, the lovely Louise has the most magnificent hair – long and curly and slightly red. As she walks along the beach, it certainly does a much better job than mine in protecting her scalp (even if I had the same amount of hair, hers would do a better job because redheads have thicker hair than those of us who are dark, both bigger follicles and more of them). Yet she still ends up burnt on back, front, legs and feet if she doesn't wear her factor 30. More- over, the disadvantages of bipedalism are legion: back pains, the difficulties of childbirth and so on. So being bipedal doesn't seem to be much of an explanation.

Sexuality

Desmond Morris, the author of the classic book[11] on this subject suggests that it is all to do with reproduction: we are hairless in order to show our genitals off or to make sure our partners see our genitals and our secondary sexual signalling areas (such as our chests and faces).

Now there are some curious things about human sexuality. For example, the pleasure that we gain from it – although we are not alone among our close relatives in enjoying that evolutionary benefit because bonobos are extremely good at social sex. They do it all the time. Equally, the pair bonding that human couples experience through a combination of oxytocin and vasopressin in our brains is the result of face-to-face sexual play. The same chemicals are involved in both mother–child bonding humans but in other primate social activity also. It is worth pondering for a moment how close human adult sexuality is to mother–child interaction; and what this tells us about our underlying nature. And our nakedness.

The infant ape

But the best explanation for our nakedness I have come across is this: *humans are a neotenic mutation.*[12] That is a variation from the traditional stock that only ever reaches the infant form. It is if you like a backward step which gives the creature some evolutionary advantage.

The best-known example from elsewhere in the animal kingdom is to be found in the rivers and lakes and pools above Mexico City: the axolotl or water salamander (*Ambystoma mexicanum*) (Figure 1.1).

While most amphibians such as our own frogs, toads and newts go through three life stages – egg, larva (e.g. tadpole) and adult – some species under certain conditions get stuck at the larval (or tadpole) stage. Low levels of iodine (an essential element for animals to make thyroxine hormones, necessary for growth and development), or random genetic mutation are both associated with neoteny in amphibians. Axolotls are curiously ugly creatures that spend most of their time in water (as you'd expect of an amphibian). Although they have rudimentary lungs, they breathe largely through the gills that they retain to maturity and are able to breed both within the species and with the closely related Tiger Salamander.

Figure 1.1   *Axolotl*
Source: http://homepages.indiana.edu/~pietsch/memory-optics.html
Reproduced by permission of Paul A. Pietsch, Indiana University.

Domestic animals such as dogs are another example of neoteny. It is now clear that dogs and wolves are genetically very close – the same species, in fact (they can still interbreed). The difference is that we have selectively bred our domestic animals for peaceful co-existence; in doing so, we have chosen the infantile behavioural characteristics.

To see the truth of this insight into humans, please consider the highly scientific illustration in Figure 1.2. On the left is me and on the right an infant chimp. See how both of them are largely hairless, with relatively high leg-to-body ratio, with flat faces and large eyes. What you can't see is that both of us have a neck that joins the skull at the back.

Now look at the larger creature who has us both in his hands – the adult chimp. This clearly illustrates the difference between the two of us and him. We are the infant form; he the adult.

So why *naked* then?

In order to accept neoteny as a sound hypothesis, we need to be clear what evolutionary advantage it might give us to be the infant ape. Some have seen our long legs as the basis of the key advantage of our bodies being as they

Figure 1.2 *The infant chimp?*
Reproduced by permission of Jonathan Tremlett

are. As the forests cleared and the savannah opened up, so the argument goes, having long legs proved an advantage in that it allowed us to run faster to chase our prey and escape predators. However appealing this may seem, the proposers of this theory have clearly never had to catch a chicken. Nor have they seen how fast chimps can run on all fours (over 100 metres none but the greatest Olympic athlete could outrun a chimp). And it is over this kind of short distances that predators make their attacks. Moreover, bonobos can also walk very well on two legs (as well as four). So the argument seems to run into the ground pretty quickly.

Clive Broomhall, the architect of the recent version of the infant mutation theory, provides a much simpler and more convincing argument. The infant mutation is advantageous because of the social capabilities it brings. Infant chimps are much less violent than adults and happily live in larger groups. In other words, being already of social ape stock, the infant mutation that is our species has been selected for its ability to live even larger and more complex lives. Being a neotenic mutation enables us to be *the social ape par excellence*.[13]

The brain of a social ape par excellence

Robin Dunbar's team of researchers have provided some further evidence for this theory. They measured the size of primate brains and the size of the groups in which they normally lived; and found that there is a very high correlation (see Figure 1.3), but that humans have brains nine times the size you would expect for our body size.

Our brains are extremely greedy – in the first years of life they consume up to 60% of our energy intake and continue to take up to 25% of our energy despite weighing only 2% or 3% of our body weight. This is partly because

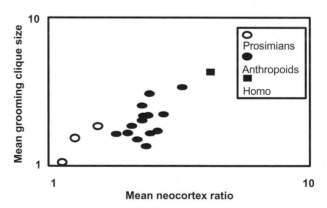

Figure 1.3 *Group size and neocortex size in primates*
Source: R. Dunbar (1998) The Social Brain hypothesis
Evolutionary Anthropology: Issues, News, and Reviews Volume 6, Issue 5, Pages 178–190
Published Online: 7 Dec 1998. Reproduced by permission of Robin I.M. Dunbar.
Key: The square is *Homo sapiens*. Species sampled are: *L. catta, L. fulvus, Propithecus, Indri, S. Sciureus, C. apella, C. torquatus, A. geoffroyi, A. fusciceps, P. badius, P. entellus, P. pileata, P. johnii, C. campbelli, C. Diana, C. aethiops, C. mitis, E. patas, M. mulatta, M. fuscata, M. arctoides, M. sylvana, M. radiata, P. anubis, P. ursinus, P. cynocephalus, P. hamadryas, T. gelada, P. troglodytes, P. paniscus*

our brains develop much more after birth than with other primates. Indeed, we are born some 12 months premature relative to other primates (those of you who have given birth to a human child or are planning to should think carefully about that. Ouch!). It is only in the first few years of life that our brain develops to its adult form and enormous complexity of wiring. This state of affairs would seem to be the reason for the pair-bonding miracle discussed above. A huge impetus needs to be given to our species (particularly the males) to ensure that children are provided for as they slowly, slowly develop into apparently independent adults.

How others shape us

It used to be thought by developmental psychologists (following Piaget) that we all develop naturally through certain predetermined stages, but this is increasingly being challenged as more is learned about our early years and what happens. Indeed, primatologists are playing an important role in describing what this account misses about the really important role of others on our lives.

It now seems that other people have a prime role in shaping each of us. From our very earliest moments after birth others shape our brains – physically as well as emotionally. Human and chimp infants both emulate the faces and noises they see around them and both respond to other infants' cries with disturbed behaviour.

Most of us continue to do just this throughout our lives. We mirror other people's body language and tone of voice in order to interact successfully. When you next go into a bar, watch how people mirror each other (or choose not to . . .). In every aspect of our lives we copy each other or differentiate ourselves from others in behaviour, clothes, accent and opinion. More of this later, but the truth is we start to become who we are through copying others[14] – each of us is a unique creature on this earth with a unique sense of who we are – with, by and through other people. Those of us who do not have sufficient stimulation early on develop brains that are less *plastic* (flexible and capable of taking in new information) than those that receive the right kind and level of stimulation. Essentially, they are less smart, less able to learn and adapt. Also, they are more fearful. They are less successful humans.

The other side of this – as Chapter 4 details – is that copying behaviour leads to 'herding' patterns of behaviour in groups of humans. That is, through the interaction of copycat individuals a crowd (or market) can develop strikingly consistent behaviour without any agreed or planned intention to do so.

One theory to explain why this emulation response is quite so strong in humans is that we are born so premature but with so much to learn to thrive and survive in our complex social environment that emulation – the copycat strategy – is a particularly useful way to learn how to live in our world. Andrew Whiten[15] of the University of St Andrews argues for this point of view. 'Because humans have massive cultural complexity, children need to learn quickly how to do many, many things, and they can modify techniques later if need be', he says. 'Imitation is quicker because it provides a ready-made solution to the problem.'

Another line of thinking is that the more social interaction we have, the more we learn. Carel van Schaik has studied our redheaded cousins, the orang-utans of Kluet Swamp in Northern Sumatra, for many years. He has identified the important role of social interaction in promoting intelligence: the Orangs he observed in the fertile Kluet Swamp had much greater social interactions than those in the nearby forests; at the same time their problem-solving abilities and their ability to invent and to deploy tools to do so was much greater (the reason why the swamp has such a high Orang population is that it is a fantastic foodstore). As he puts it,

> Without strong social – that is, cultural – inputs, even a potential wunderkind will end up a bungling bumpkin as an adult . . . animals that are intelligent are the ones that are cultural: they learn from one another innovative solutions to ecological or social problems. In short . . . culture promotes intelligence.[16]

How we make each other unhappy

Social interaction in our developing years is not purely a positive factor. Freud was not wrong in proposing that what others do to us in infancy and how we respond to it will shape our future life for the worse.

However, more recently Alice Miller and John Bowlby[17] have separately argued a rather more credible mechanic for how this happens. Both place importance on our primary care relationships and 'attachments'. In particular, Bowlby suggests that it is the nature of the attachments we have and develop early on that will determine our emotional health later. Indeed the latest longitudinal studies[18] (looking over decades rather than months) would suggest that he is spot on: those who have sound early relationships are much more likely to have a successful relationship history through their lives and vice versa. And those who have unsuccessful early 'attachments' are much more likely to live a life full of unsuccessful relationships.[19]

If you examine your own life and your own circle of friends and relatives, I'm sure that you will see that this is largely true. Of course there are always some exceptions and other reasons for these patterns, but these need not worry us; the important thing is that in many ways we become who we are for good or ill, largely with and through others. (Remember this phrase: 'We become who we are with and through others', when you read Chapter 3).

The social brain

Our brains seem to have developed to give us enormous advantages as social animals – some cognitive psychologists go as far as saying cognition is essentially a social act. We perceive the world of other people and other things and do so through the lens of our relationships with others. Certainly, there are certain phenomena that can only be described as social thinking that our species excels at.

One example is what is known as 'distributed memory' – that is where a group together remember better than an individual can. We see this most often in the kind of family gathering that Danny Wallace attended. Think of his aunts and other relatives recalling the exploits of the would-be cult leader, Gallus. Every long-standing group, be it family-, work- or friendship-based, will demonstrate the same phenomena. Every couple does too.

But the most remarkable thing is our ability to interact with each other – largely successfully – without much obvious thinking going on. Consider Oxford Street in the heart of London. Everyday something like 100,000 people traipse along it but there are very few human-on-human accidents (despite the banning of private cars there are still a few human–machine incidents everyday). This is made possible by something called the mirror neurons – specialized neurons that allow us to interpret without conscious thought the intentions and likely behaviour of others. These were named by Leonardo Fogassi of the University of Parma, who dubbed them 'mirror neurons' because they fire both when a primate makes a movement and when it watches another animal make the same movement – our brains seem to fire whether I or you do the action. There is some debate within neuroscience as to whether these belong rightly within the cognitive or motor systems (many experts believe that 'both' is the correct answer) but the important thing to know is that mirror neurons enable us to read the intentions of others; they enable us to understand – without any complicated calculation – what the intention of our social peers is and thereby to interact more successfully. And mirror neurons serve other purposes, too; these are the same parts of the brain that allow us to feel sad in sad movies and afraid in scary ones. It is also believed by some that this is why we want to move our feet and bodies to copy the movements of dancers at a performance we might see. (For more on mirror neurons see below.)

Another amazing feature of human social intelligence has been demonstrated by the experimental evolutionary psychologists, Leda Cosmides and John Tooby.[20] Their research has been conducted over 25 years and with all kinds of societies around the world from hunter-gatherers to American bankers. Essentially, their research shows that in every kind of human society ever studied, however good the individuals studied might be at logical reasoning, our abilities to spot cheating – that is the ability to think correctly about how someone has behaved dishonestly in social exchanges with others – is constant. From the !Kung San people of the Kalahari to hunter-horticulturalists in the Amazon and to educated and uneducated societies in more developed economies the numbers are much the same. We are very good at interacting and keeping the score in our interactions with others.

The sound of the crowd

For a while before she met her charming husband, my friend Christine was often stuck for a date on Valentine's night. But in many ways this was a good thing as it allowed her to spend time with her first love, Arsenal FC.

So it was that on a damp February evening in 1988, she found herself standing at the Clock End of the old Highbury Stadium watching a friendly between her boys and the French youth team, then managed by the great Michel Platini. At that time, Highbury was not the cosmopolitan place it is now (it seems half the French national team play for the 'Gooners'). No, for the crowd of North Londoners 'abroad' was beastly and so were all foreigners.

So it is curious, that within 30 minutes of the start, the entire stadium was ringing to a song sung in French. As so many football chants do, it cast doubt on the referee's parentage but in a humorous manner: '*Qui est le ba(s)tard dans le noir?*' (who is the b . . . in black?). Admittedly, this is not very good French grammar. Nor is it particularly insightful, being sung tunelessly, over and over. However, what strikes me about this phenomenon is the speed with which the song was taken up and sung together. And the good feelings that Christine and her fellow die-hard fans report.

No song sheet, no rehearsals, no choirmaster, no piped music to lead the crowd on. Nothing 'made' them do it. They learned from each other, they copied and they joined in. Without thinking.

The empathetic ape

Emulation and empathy are not just human phenomena. They have also been identified to be operating in our non-human cousins. De Waal[21] tells a story of a chimp who, hearing the plaintive cries of an injured sparrow, risks her own life to climb down into the moat around her enclosure to pick up, calm and then release the bird. Primatologists' anecdotes are full of the empathy that their subjects show them over long-term relationships.

I was particularly touched by the story with which Dunbar opens his most influential book: he describes being groomed by a chimp, how after his initial anxiety he feels the nimble fingers scattering over his bare skin until a slight imperfection is found and scratched so that an incredible feeling of well-being floods over him.

All of us benefit from friendly physical contact with others; the same feelings that Dunbar describes are to be had from any hug or embrace. And again our brain chemistry is changing when this happens; we feel good because our brain is flooded with natural opiates, or endorphins. What else lies behind the enormous value of hugs and stroking in intimate human contact? Some people suspect that this lies behind some at least of the efficacy of many alternative medicines. For example a recent BBC TV series conducted a clinical trial on the power of acupuncture in managing osteoarthritis of the knee. They created three double-blind cells (that is groups of patients who were randomly allocated to the three groups): drug treatment only; drug treatment and acupuncture; drug treatment and 'placebo' acupuncture (that is using a needle which does not penetrate the skin because the point withdraws like the blade of a stage sword). While the highest claimed improvement was among patients in the second group, the third group (the placebo needle group) showed a significant improvement. Largely, it is suggested, because of the tactile human contact.

One friend of mine is addicted to the kind of massage found at health spas; I am sure from my own experience that these work the same way. We need the touch of other people to feel good. It is no surprise that the sex life of the infant ape mutation – us – is full of tactile sensations of all sorts. Our bodies take great pleasure from the touch of another.

Language and stroking

Ah, you may argue, this is all very well but what distinguishes us from the other apes is our language skills. They cannot talk or communicate quite in the way we can, spinning argument and adducing evidence as you are doing, Mark.

True. But consider the origins of language. It is now widely accepted that human language abilities have evolved directly out of stroking and grooming[22] behaviour in other apes. No wonder that most of what is communicated when you and I meet face to face is through our body language and our tone and intonation. Very little comes through the content of the words. No wonder either that what we say to each other is largely about relationships – Dunbar and fellow researchers have recently shown that what is remembered in gossip (as it passes from mouth to mouth) are the things of social value. That is, who did what to whom and what the social implications of this are. So even the thing that you might want to cling to as a superior skill or ability that separates us from the apes is rooted first and foremost in ape social behaviour and indeed just appears to be a very top-of-the-range version of picking nits from each other.

The loneliness of autism

All of us are in some way or other a mutant; every one of us is a unique variation on the shared genetic code of our parents and their parents. Each of us varies slightly from the norm because every time genes are copied from parent to child something is lost in translation. But rarely does this cause us any real problems in life because few of these variations result in significant or damaging variation in the species' normal, physical form and function.

However, there are many ways in which our brains can fail to develop as they should do. One of the most common (in the popular imagination at least) and certainly one of the most upsetting to parents is autism. Leo Kanner in Baltimore and Hans Asperger in Vienna independently described this devastating developmental disorder, and named it from the Greek word for 'self' – *autos*. Autism can coexist with other malfunctions (such as Down's syndrome) but it is generally understood as an inability to interact or empathize with others.

Diagnosis[23] is now much more systematic with the USA having a 10-point system (see Table 1.1) and the UK a seven-point one, but the heart of the diagnosis relies on social interaction.

Frequently, the symptoms develop some time *after* birth – parents and clinicians often note some behavioural difficulties at two years or beyond. It is not at all uncommon for what seems to be a normal child actually to go backwards in their development and this has led some to point to childhood vaccinations as a key causal factor (although this is widely discredited now following an examination of both the proposers' research design and larger-scale studies and meta-analysis of the literature). It is generally recognized by the experts that many factors (both environmental and genetic) may be involved in prompting the condition but that doesn't make it any less distressing for parent or child.

Table 1.1 Summary of the DSM-III-R criteria for autism (USA)

- Qualitative impairment in reciprocal social interaction (e.g. lack of awareness or feelings for others, no or impaired imitation, no or abnormal social play etc.)
- Qualitative impairment in verbal and non-verbal communication and imaginative activity (e.g. no mode of communication – babbling, gesture, mime or spoken language; markedly abnormal body language – facial expression, body posture etc; absence of imaginative activity – e.g. no role playing, no interest in stories about imaginary events etc., marked impairment in ability to initiate or sustain conversation with others, tendency to monologues)
- Markedly restricted repertoire of activities and interests (e.g. stereotyped body movements like hand flicking or head banging; preoccupation with parts of objects or their characteristics or unusual objects; marked distress over changes in trivial aspects of environment; insistence on routines and preoccupation with narrow interests)

Source: Adapted from Baron Cohen and Bolton

An autistic child or adult is locked into a curiously private world, a world in which other people are incomprehensible and confusing both in their intentions and their behaviour. (Note that it is not always the case that language skills are absent.) An autistic person finds it difficult to fully participate in the world as we know it because they cannot interact successfully with other humans; they cannot benefit fully from our species' core evolutionary advantage. They may become obsessive in their behaviour (the hero of the award-winning novel, *The Curious Incident of the Dog in the Night-time*,[24] cannot eat food of different colours; the son of a friend insists on reciting and memorizing all the car licence plates that they pass on the way to school) but this is thought by some experts to be a psychological defence mechanism. It is an attempt by the individual to bring order to a world that is confusing and scary by describing it or behaving in it in an understandable manner. When these defence mechanisms are challenged (for example when the obsessive behaviour is denied or interrupted), the result is high levels of stress, just as in a chimp exiled from its group.

Given the central feature of the condition is an inability and/or unwillingness to interact successfully with other humans and an inability to 'read the minds' of others, it is no surprise that in recent years a number of neuroscientists have suggested that it is the result of malfunction of the mirror neurons which help us interact successfully with others and read their intentions. The Indian-born neuroscientist Vilayanur Ramachandran[25] was one of the first to propose this view. His intial study ingeniously deployed the fact that one component of a brain scan, an electroencephalogram (EEG), the mu wave, is blocked whenever someone makes a voluntary movement such as moving their hand; the mu wave is also blocked when that person watches someone else do the same thing.

By comparing the mu waves in EEGs of autistic and non-autistic subjects, Ram (as he is known) and his colleagues were able to show that mu suppression occurred in the non-autistic subjects when they watched hand movement *but* also when they moved their own hands. By contrast, the EEGs of the people with autism also showed mu suppression when they moved their own hands, but not when they watched other people's hands moving. Others, such as Mirella Dapretto[26] of the University of California, Los Angeles, and Andrew Whiten, have since provided more support for this view with their own studies.

Compare and contrast the lonely, unempathetic world of the autistic person with the Join-me gang or Christine's football crowd: people more like you and me. The latter are all highly skilled social animals who choose to be together and who feel better together. The absence of a key function in our brains in the former group serves to underline the powerful importance of our social selves. In an important way, autism reveals the truth about who we really are. If we were not a social animal of such sophistication and so deeply programmed to be together, our lives would be very different.

Collaboration: the keys to the kingdom

Collaboration is an extraordinary gift that our ape forebears have given us. Chimps show quite remarkable collaboration in their daily lives – the long-standing alliances between individuals that are created through mutual grooming provide security and safety within what might otherwise be a violent shifting social environment. Chimps and bonobos get enormous practical benefits from collaboration – sharing food sources, childcare, education and training and so on.

We have tended to think of mankind otherwise. In the West, at least, we tend to see humans as creatures driven by their own individual needs and desires. This, the anthropologists and sociologists tell us, is the reason why religion and ethical teachings are so important in our culture. 'Do unto others . . . etc.' is just one exhortation of this sort. But underneath, human beings are selfish and self-serving, aren't they? Otherwise, why would we need to have these ethical imperatives beaten into us? Indeed, classical economists tend to assume that this individual selfishness is key to our nature. Adam Smith's hidden hand is essentially a way of expressing this – in pursuit of our own individual interest, each of us interacts with other humans.

But is it really true? Well certainly, the great figures of the English industrial revolution whom Smith so admired were a tight-knit and interdependent group of Quakers who built the businesses that changed the way we make and sell things; they were very much a collective lot. And the exchange of goods that all trading peoples have pursued for generation after generation assumes that the other guy is not going to rip you off. Walk round any market any where in the world – from Calcutta to Camden – and there you will see this in action. And you see it in family groups, in businesses and in team sports. Is this tendency to collaboration just a cultural response to our genetic pursuit of self-interest or is it something that we are programmed to do anyway? Something that we have taken to new heights?

Self-interest and collaboration

It's undeniable that crime sometimes pays. Sometimes you can do the wrong thing and get away with it and end up better off. Less seriously, sometimes it is better in the short term to be selfish, even if not criminal. Some in the West (and many on the Right) argue that this is a much bigger truth. Rational individuals guided by logic will always seek their own interest first (according to Hobbes without the protection of contracts and laws to enforce them, each of us would be 'prey'). It is undoubtedly true that in the real world, people cheat and lie and deceive each other every day. But is this the norm? Is it even in our nature, as some of Adam Smith's apologists would have us believe?

This has long been a big question about human nature that has framed political debate and thinking about how to organize ourselves. The big questions here are: Is it better for a social animal like ourselves to pursue Hobbes' self-interest or is some form of collaboration more advantageous? Is it in our nature? Is it advantageous for us, if we are programmed to spread our genes?

Game on

To get to grips with this cluster of questions, we need to understand what is called 'game theory'. This was largely the invention of the great mathematician, cardsharp, playboy and latterly member of the Manhattan Project team, Johan von Neumann. His interest in poker and other games was more than social; he was first and foremost interested in the way people behave within the confines of games and what this could tell us about other forms of behaviour. If Von Neumann laid the groundwork of game theory, it was Merrill Flood, of the West Coast RAND Corporation, who created its most famous game: the prisoner's dilemma.[27] This simple mathematical model has been used by moral philosophers and psychologists, mathematicians and political theorists as the means to understand behavioural strategies between two or more players.

In the simplest and original version, the prisoners are two in number. Both have been arrested for the same offence, and both are given the same offers by their jailers. If one agrees to testify against his colleague to secure his conviction then the testifier goes free but the convicted prisoner gets a long stretch. If neither agree to testify, then they both get a sentence but shorter than in the first case. If both testify against each other then the sentence for both will be middling, not as long as in the first case but not as short as in the second case.

Imagine you are one of these prisoners: what would you do? Should you testify or not? If you work through the percentages, the rational thing to do is always to testify. This gives the best outcome in the majority of cases – if you testify and the other doesn't, then you get off free; if the other testifies and you do too then you both get a middling sentence. So from a rational point of view it's not much of a dilemma at all really (even though I spent several wet afternoons as a philosophy undergraduate arguing that there were dilemmas buried here).

The issue for a social animal – and this is where the problem really starts to get some traction on human behaviour – is that the dilemma is true for both prisoners, so both are driven to testify if they act rationally. Which ends up with both being sent down and being badly off.

Game over and over

This becomes really interesting when you play the game over and over, over a period of time. Here communication becomes possible – we learn from how the other party behaves. We learn to understand their likely moves, the probability of them defecting or not; and this enables us to make sounder decisions about our own actions than the simple isolated rationality. We are able to act on some more rounded view of the individual to whom our fate is tied. This is much more like our social life. If we know how the others that make up so much of our everyday environment are likely to behave then we can make much more useful decisions for ourselves.

Put another way: iterative plays allow us to *collaborate* with the other prisoner – to act in a manner that maximizes our individual interests which are so tied together by the situation. If I cheat on my neighbour by dumping my rubbish in his front garden, he has plenty of opportunity to retaliate. Most of us in business know that if we cheat on our suppliers or customers, they are likely to leave sooner or later. Put more mildly, if we fail to deliver what we promise, customers (or voters) can walk; if we don't pay the bills that our suppliers send us, they will – if they can – follow suit.

Collaboration across the nation?

But is this really how collaboration emerges in the human species? Psychologists have explored this in innumerable forms – changes to the rules, the penalties and rewards and assuming different kinds of personality in the players. All the time, it's true that one-off defection can pay – the temptation to defect is always with us. So what is the best strategy? What would be the best way to play in real life?

The eminent economist, Robert Axelrod,[28] devised an experiment to come up with an answer for this. He asked professional game theorists to propose the best strategy for a round-robin game of prisoner's dilemma. Each player was to play all the others and the total aggregate score of all these games would indicate the winner. The *strategy* was essentially a set of rules for interaction: e.g. always cooperating no matter what the other guy does (this turns out to be a pretty poor strategy). Of all of the 14 entries from psychologists, economists and mathematicians, the winner was perhaps the simplest. Anatol Rappaport suggested 'tit for tat' (TFT). This starts with co-operation but then defects if the opponent defects in its first round. If however, the opponent co-operates then TFT mirrors this. So, as a strategy for the game, TFT takes advantage of opportunities for collaboration but punishes defectors. TFT rarely gets exploited for more than one round.

But that doesn't mean that TFT is the best strategy for all situations – if you are faced by an unconditional collaborator, unconditional defection is a better strategy (the suckers won't punish you and you can keep on winning). The reason why TFT won Axelrod's game is because it profits from most situations, not because it is better at all.

It seems to be important[29] that TFT is essentially a 'nice' strategy – that is it doesn't defect first, assuming if you like the best in the other party. Eight of the top 14 strategies in Axelrod's original game were 'nice' strategies. But also it doesn't let defectors profit for long. Of course, subsequent versions of Axelrod's game revealed improved variations on this strategy: for example GTFT (generous TFT) gives defectors several goes at defection before punishing them.

And of course, TFT can be a disastrous strategy, locking opponents into an endless cycle of retaliation (think of the Sicilian blood feuds, which persist for generations long after the original offence). Equally, TFT has a major flaw in that it assumes that the data we collect about other players is accurate, that a defection is always deliberate and intended, rather than just an error (think of the US's problems interpreting Soviet Russia's foreign policy acts and how close this brought us all to mutual destruction). That said, collaboration and co-operative approaches do tend to end up on top – if you play the game long enough. Some have even produced evolutionary simulations that suggest that populations with collaborative tendencies will tend – over many generations – to come out on top.

But beware: we don't need to turn this into some ethical principle in nature (although it is easy to read this quality into such a simple strategy). The fact is that a number of unthinking (and therefore unethical) organisms follow these kinds of rules of interaction (such as monkeys, bats and even fish), which suggests that whatever ethical gloss we put on our own behaviour, collaboration has a functional root in social animals. More importantly, it does suggest that the strategy of rational self-interest is not in the best interest of the social ape.

Learning from each other?

Of course, most of the experiments and games described so far suggest that spending time together enables us to learn to build trust and encourages co-operation. But we've since learned that collaboration doesn't need repeated exposure to the same individuals in order to emerge. Two Swiss economists Ernst Fehr and Simon Gaechter[30] demonstrated that collaboration can emerge even when players don't interact frequently with each other. They split their volunteers into groups of four, gave them some investment cash and set the game rolling. Each group member was invited to stake all their funds on an investment and the return would be proportionate to the total investment that each group (not each member) made. In other words it was in the group's interest if all members participated and not if certain individuals held back – the spoils were divided according to investment made. What's different about this game is that the groups were changed after every play – thus depriving individuals of the ability to learn from each other directly. Co-operation did emerge at a low level, but was much higher when the notion of punishment for non-cooperators was introduced, even though the punisher stood to gain little from doing the punishing (he or she would not play with the defector again).

How collaboration built the world

So what has all this game theory shown us?

First, collaboration of some sort seems to be a sound strategy for social animals for the short, medium and longer term. Second, it seems to bring some evolutionary advantage (bounded collaborators tend to deal with most other types of players really well over the longer term). And thus third, the strategy of non-cooperation (acting purely on self-interest) may be of short-term value in many situations (e.g. it can take over a population of total collaborators with ease) but it certainly is far from ideal for most situations.

As Adam Smith himself put it,

> How selfish soever man may be supposed, there are evidently some principles in his nature which interest him in the fortune of others, and render their happiness necessary to him, though he derives nothing from it except the pleasure of seeing it.[31]

And this might just be the final piece of the jigsaw of our super-social ape: not only are we designed to be a super-social creature; not only do we make each other through interaction from our first moments after birth; but also we have taken these social skills and tendencies[32] and created over many generations a remarkable collaborative creature using our peculiar social gifts. This collaborative tendency (whether you follow the explanatory path of genetic or cultural transmission) has enabled us to master and shape the world in which we live; and at the same time given us the keys to our own destruction.

Shirts – the work of many hands

In his remarkable book, Paul Seabright[33] describes the miracle of economic activity that our collaborative species has created. He shows how one simple piece of consumer activity on his part (buying a shirt) involves the collaboration of thousands of people across the world, very few of whom had or will ever meet or learn much about each other. But collaborate they did.

> this morning I went out and bought a shirt. There is nothing very unusual in that; across the world, perhaps 20 million people did the same. What is more remarkable is that I, like most of these 20 million, had not informed anybody in advance of what I was going to do. The cotton was grown in India, from seeds developed in the United States; the artificial thread . . . from

Portugal . . . the collar linings from Brazil . . . the machinery . . . from Germany; the shirt itself was made up in Malaysia (and of course) engineers in Cologne and chemists in Birmingham were involved long ago.

Of course, no one individual had the overall plan (there is no international shirt tsar ensuring that Paul and others around the world got what they wanted). Nor was Paul ever part of the reckoning. But through collaboration, or 'trade' as we call it, the miracle was made possible. Paul got his shirt, in the size, fit and colour he wanted, in the shop he went to, on the day and at the time he went there.

It is because we are collaborative at heart that trade can function at all. Thanks to modern communications and logistics, international trade can flourish at lightning speed. And this gives us the means to shape the world in which we live. New techniques and technology can be shared and transmitted around the world now in moments. Early humans had the ability to learn from what they saw around them in their peers and their enemies *and to share that back* – this lies at the heart of our success as a species.

Without it – we would just be quite clever social apes. But with it, we are able to shape our world to such an extent that we hold its fate in our curiously soft paws.

Summary of this chapter

This chapter has traced some simple truths about our species, *Homo sapiens*. We are not a separate branch of creation from chimpanzees but very, *very* closely related and thus have much more in common than we might like to think.

- Like chimps (and the more peaceable bonobo) our essential evolutionary strategy is to be a social animal. This shapes our brain and our body.
- Like chimps, this means being empathetic and seeking the company, support and affection of others.
- Like chimps our brains are developed through interaction with others. Our lives depend on it so we feel good with others and bad without.

The difference between us is *not* that we are a more individualistic species but the opposite. Evolution has selected this body and this brain in order to make us an even more successful social animal than our cousins. The ultimate social ape if you like.

An ape that is programmed to really collaborate with others, both kin, friends and strangers. Here lies our strength and the means by which we have created mastery over our environment to such a degree that we are the first primate to be able to destroy ourselves by destroying the world in which we live.

Questions to ponder

- Why does it seem to me otherwise? Why does it seem to me that I have control over my thoughts, feelings and behaviour? Why does it seem to me that I do what I do because I decide to do it? (Chapters 2 and 3)
- We may be social animals, but how does mass behaviour actually arise? You've described the origin and the capabilities of our social skills but what is the *how* that explains behaviour such as the cellotaph? The how behind the football crowds singing and Danny's mad collective? (Chapter 4)

Questions and issues for marketers

- What does the social nature of our species have to tell us about the creatures whose behaviour we want to change? If this is our prime characteristic, then it must be within the social context that our brand or project is to be understood. How does it feel to know that social issues are the important ones – not your brand?
- How could you harness the power of our social connections to bring about change? What does this say about media thinking and the value of private over public media?
- How can you understand the different social contexts in which our customers and employees live and interact? To what extent do current market research techniques reflect this?
- What does this view imply about our obsession with precision and targeting? Does it make sense to pull individuals out of the groups in which they live?
- How could you apply the learning about emulation and mirror neurons to attempts to change behaviour?
- If there is no 'shirt tsar', what does that tell you about the way we tend to think about our role as managers and the degree to which we like to pretend we are in control?

2

The Illusion of 'I'

What this chapter will cover

Why it is that it seems to each of us that 'I' is the place to look to understand human behaviour? Modern neuroscience and psychology reveal that much of our experience of ourselves is illusory: things don't work the way they seem to. Our memory isn't a photographic file-retrieval system; it is inherently unreliable. Our will isn't what drives our action; the sense of willing often comes after the action starts. Even our subjective experience of our own consciousness is largely an illusion.

Don't part with your illusions. When they are gone you may still exist but you have ceased to live.

Mark Twain

Stage illusions have long fascinated me. Particularly those from the golden age of 19th-century magic. Part of this is I'm sure due to the fact that I grew up in a London still prone to the occasional visit of its ancient fogs and mists. Of bitterly cold winters. And a lot of Dickensian sightseeing. And these things seem to conjure the age of the great illusionists for me.

I am constantly surprised how many things we have in common with our Victorian forebears despite the fact that our modern lives are in many ways so different from theirs. The Victorians were simultaneously fascinated by rationality and science and at the same time subject to any number of crazes about the supernatural, just like us. Sir Arthur Conan Doyle for example, pillar of the rationalist community and creator of the super logical detective, Sherlock Holmes, was at the same time a frequent séance goer. Similarly, as the Victorian theatre reached new peaks of technical brilliance, the spiritualist movement blossomed in and around it. Indeed, many of the best performers of the era deliberately mixed the two together. The Davenport brothers – one of the most important acts to emerge from the young country across the Atlantic – used this convergence of opposing worlds to much effect. Their most famous illusion was that of the 'séance box' into which they tied themselves and then performed any number of unusual pseudo-supernatural tricks.

Pepper's ghost

Perhaps the most elegant illusion of the era, however, was the simplest: 'Pepper's ghost' managed to give the impression of a 'real' ghostly figure on a stage, through a combination of mirrors and lights. The technique was not Pepper's invention but largely the work of a Liverpuddlian engineer and inventor, Henry Dircks.[1] His other inventions seem relatively straightforward by contrast – he patented things such as a sewing machine, a fire escape and a way of preparing vegetable extracts. But the ghost machine appeared to be something new, not least because it depended on a knowledge of mirrors, lenses and refraction to project an image of an illuminated human figure from below the stage on to the stage itself. The figure could materialize and dematerialize at will; depending on the brightness of the light used to light it up. Veritably, ghosts – of which the Victorians were inordinately fond – could walk the boards.[2]

Dircks seems to have been unsure of what to do with this particular new idea so far from his usual sphere of work. He presented the idea to a meeting of the British Association for the Advancement of Science in Leeds in 1858 to little interest. Undeterred, he pressed on; he took his idea to London, to the Coliseum and the Crystal Palace where again he failed to find the enthusiastic response from theatre owners in the capital. The problem – which Dircks himself played down – was that while his invention could create a huge range of effects on the stage, it depended on a complete reconstruction of the theatres for which he intended it. The illusion depended on two things: first a plate of perfect glass between the audience and the stage and second, the audience being sat above the stage. This allowed the illusion of the ghost to be reflected back to the audience and to appear to be on the stage, rather than essentially in the orchestra pit.

It wasn't until Dircks presented his work at the Royal Polytechnic Institution in 1862 that he found someone who could make the most of it. That man was John Henry Pepper,[3] 'Professor' Pepper according to the Polytechnic's billing. A tall, grave man with waxed moustache and sonorous voice, Pepper had been on the staff of the Polytechnic for 14 years before the day that Dircks turned up with a model of his invention. As he peered through the model's sight holes he saw the 'ghost figures' appear alongside the other, more solid figures that Pepper had seen before. Pepper was shaken.

With a few minor tweaks, this would definitely bring the audiences in! And make Pepper's reputation for sure.

On Christmas Eve that year, the first of Pepper's ghosts appeared on stage at the Polytechnic in a scene from one of Dickens' Christmas tales, 'The Haunted Man'. A skeleton slowly materialized out of thin air to terrify both actor and audience alike. The latter in particular were so captivated that Pepper chose not to go through with his initial plan to explain the illusion to the audience. And Dircks chose to accept £500 for the idea, a payment he was later to regret (penning 102 pages in his own defence without once mentioning the name of the professor). Very rapidly, the British (and later French and American) audiences abandoned the previously popular magic lantern shows and flocked to see ghosts walk the stage.

What does Pepper's ghost tell us?

Illusions can be very compelling. They must be if they are to work. They work by giving us the impression of one thing happening when in fact something entirely different is really going on. They give us the sense that what we want to believe is occurring, when in fact it is not. The Victorians really wanted to believe in their ghosts so they were content to believe in Pepper and Dirck's illusion.

So it is with our view of our own nature, of what it is to be human, of how our own behaviour arises. We would like to think (for reasons I will explain below) that each of us is in control, is self-determining and the conscious agent of our own lives; That what I do, I do because I choose to; that the 'I' I experience every day is still essentially the same 'I' as it was yesterday and 10 years ago. I don't question the content of my memories. All of us would like to think that our memories are accurate – like informational Polaroids – records of things that have happened in our lives. And when we recall these memories, that they are accurately recalled, that they are somehow independent of our emotions, both then and now. And even that when we recall something it must have happened.

But none of these things is true. This chapter is concerned with the illusions of ourselves with which we comfort ourselves: partly those due to the way our brains are designed – we are meant to have these illusions; somehow they are important to maintain; partly they seem due to the culture we in the West grow up in, because the East and Africa have a different take on these truths (see Chapter 3 for more details).

Why is this important? Simple. It's because these illusions get in the way of us seeing how we really are and thus prevent us from developing a sound model of mass behaviour. And thus going about changing it.

As Stephen Pinker[4] puts it, 'The refusal to acknowledge human nature is like the Victorian's embarrassment about sex: it distorts our science and scholarship, our public discourse and our day-to-day lives.'

I woke up this morning . . .

. . . and found that I am still Mark, the same Mark in fact that went to bed last night. The same thoughts are running round my head. The same view of what today might hold (well, perhaps slightly fuzzier to start with). And the same set of memories and knowledge of others in my life, my friends, my family. The same worries about contracts and deadlines and what seem to be accurate memories of the movie I saw last night – A Cock and Bull Story. And as I reflect, I'm sure that of the two actors, I still prefer Rob Bryden to Steve Coogan, just as I did before the film. I get a call from my boss and we pick up where we left off two weeks ago; neither of us suspect that the other is significantly different. I decide to get back to him later and get on with writing this chapter.

This is a good practical example of the kind of argument from experience that many use to justify our sense of 'I'. Not just the great philosophers (for example, Descartes uses a similar approach in his *cogito*), but each of us, when challenged, will accept that though our bodies age, lose or gain hair, put on or lose pounds, we are still the same because of how we experience our minds. If we have ourselves tattooed or our hair dyed, does this change us? No, it is the continuity of our mental facilities that delivers us proof each and every day that we are ourselves.

But am I right to trust such working proofs, such common-sense argumentation? Can I trust my sense of continuous identity? Can I trust the memories that make up that sense of identity? Can I trust the sense of 'I' that comes from feeling I have decided what to do? Can I trust the sense of 'I' that comes from experiencing my thinking and feeling in any way? The answer is 'sometimes' – and I have to do so in order to function in the world – but the subjective experience of my memory, my sense of willing things and my experience of my own consciousness are actually bad guides to what really happens in my life and my behaviours. And thus are very bad things to include in any model of mass behaviour.

What it is – oh, I forgot

Our memories are notoriously unreliable. We all know that as individuals we can forget things (where *are* my house keys this morning?) and that certain conditions and substances can make this worse. I know that different people have different memories of the same event (what good domestic row fails to expose this truth?). But it is not just around the edges that our memories are unreliable – they are not reliable in the way that we like to think about them at all. They are not information-file retrieval experiences, like a computer has.

I used to be very good at exams. I used to be able to memorize facts and dates and arguments and regurgitate them at will. Some 20 years after studying Roman military history, I found myself reciting my own notes on Marius' military reforms while stuck in a traffic jam outside Rome, although I wish I recalled everything this well nowadays.

But it is a mistake to think of memory as a data-storage and retrieval system alone; indeed, very little of its function seems to be usefully described this way. I blame all those computer scientists who infiltrated the psychology faculties of the 1950s and 1960s for preserving this informational view of memory in our culture.

Eternal sunshine and spotless minds

The only Jim Carey movie I have actually enjoyed watching – *Eternal Sunshine of the Spotless Mind*[5] – has as its premise the thought that it might be possible to avoid the pain of the end of a relationship by having all memory traces of your ex removed from your brain. An intriguing premise for a movie but not actually very good science.

Memory is not some computer function or like a factual Polaroid of an experience we have had – even though it seems to be. Like most other mental capacities, memory is the result of a distributed system in our brains. There is no simple 'module' of the brain in which memory resides; a large part of the brain is involved in memory functions. Neurons across our brain are connected to each other in memory and each time the memory is recalled a slightly different memory network is activated. And the emotional flavour and the *facts* – what actually happened – are distorted and changed each time we recall them, depending on the emotional context of the recalling.

This means our memories are essentially flexible and at the same time misleading. What we remember happening is not by any means what happened; what we remember feeling is not by any means what we actually felt. Even though it seems as if we did. This applies both to small events and to the terrible traumatic things which damage individuals, often beyond repair.

False memories

Perhaps the most extreme example of false memories is to be found in the field of clinical psychotherapy. In the last 20 years a host of cases have emerged into the public domain in which an individual *recovers* a memory of childhood sexual abuse which they had previously *suppressed*. A number of therapeutic techniques can deliver this recovered memory – hypnosis, regression, guided visualization and so on, and some misguided therapists seem to make a living out of seeking out these memories. That is, they approach the other symptoms (depression, anxiety) through the lens of suppressed memories of abuse.

Certainly, sometimes the recovered memory of the abuse is accurate – there have always been people who abuse their own children, a truly dreadful crime – but the psychotherapeutic professionals have now woken up to the unreliability of 'recovered memory'[6] and have had to issue guidelines to their members and to the public. For example, in 1993 the American Psychiatric Association stated, 'It is not known how to distinguish with complete accuracy memories based on true events from those derived from other sources (i.e., invented or suggested)'[7] And the British authorities reflect the general caution in what are sometimes presented as memory-enhancing techniques:

> Practitioners are advised to avoid engaging in any 'memory recovery techniques' which are based upon the expectation of past sexual abuse of which the patient has no memory. Such ... techniques may include drug-mediated interviews, hypnosis, regression therapies, guided imagery, 'body-memories', literal dream interpretation and journaling. There is no evidence that

conscious-altering techniques . . . can reveal or accurately elaborate on any past experiences.[8]

Very often the alleged *abuser* is challenged publicly and legally – and very often the alleged abuse is vehemently denied. Both parties clearly believe their own memories of events but neither agrees on the factual content. The Canadians put this simply: 'Psychologists acknowledge that a definite conclusion that a memory is based on an objective reality is not possible unless there is incontrovertible corroborating evidence.'[9]

The same is true of our everyday memories. They help us live our lives more successfully, however inaccurate they are.[10] As super-social apes living in highly complex social environments, we need memories to carry around in the form of working beliefs about the world and our fellow inhabitants, however rough and ready those memories might be, because without them, we can never keep up with what is going on around us and react quickly enough.

Monkey see

However, this same inaccuracy is also found in our perceptual abilities. We see only what we want to see, what we expect to see – unlike many animals (and it is suggested by Temple Grandin,[11] autistic people) who see everything in detail. We are not the high-precision scanning units that our experience tells us we are. Our eyes can and do regularly deceive us (and this is what stage illusionists regularly exploit in their audiences).

Daniel Simons of the Illinois Viscog (visual cognition) Lab has demonstrated this time and time again. As he and collaborator Christopher Chabris put it,

> We have all had the embarrassing experience of failing to notice when a friend or colleague shaves off a beard, gets a haircut, or starts wearing contact lenses. We feel that we perceive and remember everything around us, and we take the occasional blindness to visual details to be an unusual exception.[12]

But it's not. Our brains constantly screen out visual information that is irrelevant to the task in hand, to what we are concerned with at a particular time but we get the sense of it being otherwise. *'The richness of our visual experience leads us to believe that our visual representations will include and preserve the same amount of detail.* In other words it seems to us that we perceive the world in great detail, but our visual systems screen out what is unimportant for us. (Just to be clear: it's not that our eyes don't receive the data; rather it is our cognitive systems that edit the data out).

Simons' best-known demonstration of this is known as 'Gorillas In Our Midst'. In the experiment, a videotape of some students playing basketball is played to subjects. Subjects are split into three cells: those instructed to watch one team or another; those instructed to count the number of passes; and those given no instruction. What Simons and Chabris found is that only the latter group spot to any degree that halfway through the game, a student in a gorilla suit walks right on to the court, beats its chest and then walks off again. How could we miss something so obvious, you might ask.

Because we aren't looking for it, that's how. We're looking for something else.

But it seems to us otherwise. It seems that our perceptions are comprehensive and precise (we don't get a red flashing light or an alarm going off to tell us that we're missing something – not literally, at least).

They are not. This 'inattentional blindness' – as Simons and Chabris dub it – reveals another illusion in our experience of our minds.

Lazy minds

Our minds are *lazy*, and not the finely honed data-processing devices they seem to be. Our minds constantly deceive[13] us to protect us from having to think too hard.

Perhaps the greatest exponent of this 'lazy minds' view is Daniel Kahnemann. Though a psychologist, he was awarded the 2002 Nobel Prize for economics, so profound and useful has his lifetime's work been.

In essence, Kahnemann has demonstrated through a host of practical experiments that our day-to-day thinking is nowhere near as rational and considered as it seems to us and as we would like to think. Instead he proposes a two-stage model that suggests a number of simple operating principles of our minds (Figure 2.1).

- We are approximate (we use rules of thumb or 'heuristics' such as 'familiarity' – does this look like something I know? – to simplify our perception and thinking about the world).

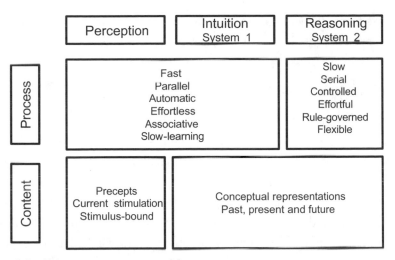

Figure 2.1 *Kahnemann two-stage model*
Source: Daniel Kahnemann. Reproduced by permission.
The Bank of Sweden Prize in Economic Sciences in Memory of Alfred Nobel 2002 Copyright The Nobel Foundation 2002

- Most of our thinking and perception is intuitive (individually we mostly don't know what or how it operates).
- We rarely do any calculation (even if we are good at it – one famous experiment[14] showed how doctors and patients are equally bad at calculating probabilities of survival).
- All of this is driven by emotion – how we feel in a given situation.

The importance of this model is not just its ability to explain some of the sillier things we do – even the smartest of us. For example, the American mathematical genius John Allen Paulos[15] lost his shirt on WorldCom, because despite his extraordinary gifts he fell victim of the cognitive biases inherent in the design of his brain rather than *do the math* as they say. In his painstaking confession, he describes how he falls victim to these quirks of the human mental process, one after another, from framing biases, substitution biases and on and on. An intriguing cautionary tale indeed.

It also explains a lot about our success as a species. We can take in and process enormous amounts of information about the context we find ourselves in, about other people's intentions and any threats or rewards in the environment, without having the backing of NASA's computing system, which is what would be required if we thought about things as much as we imagine we do – sifting all the data individually and consciously. No, our approximation is very efficient, even if it does get us into trouble sometimes.

Don't think too hard

But the other reason why Kahnemann's work is important is because it unpicks the old enlightenment idea of *Homo economicus*, the rational and calculating individual. This, I'm sure, is the real reason that the Nobel Committee honoured Kahnemann.

As regards most of our behaviour, we don't think nearly as much as we'd like to believe we do. By that I mean, we just act without any real conscious deliberation going on. No benefit-trade-offs; no utility calculations. No, most of us go through most of our lives just living them, rather than thinking about what to do next. Indeed, we would not live much if we calculated this kind of stuff all of the time.

Say you and I are driving down the road. We chat happily about who's doing what to whom among our group of friends; I turn the radio down to hear you better. I can manage to do this and drive at the same time, very safely, despite the complex motor function involved in doing so. I barely pay any attention to the process of driving or what lies on the road . . . until something catches my eye and my attention is suddenly focussed on a child chasing a ball out from behind a parked car. Everything else – you and our conversation – is forgotten as I slam on the brakes and avoid the child. My heart is pumping faster and my entire body is on alert (cortisol is likely to be pumping around my system which is why I feel so clear-headed and slightly sweaty!). Of course, having stopped I will swear heartily at how stupid the child has been but soon enough my heart and body will return to normal and we will pick up our conversation. I will no doubt apologize to you for the sudden jolt of stopping. Now at no time did I decide to do anything rationally. I just saw a situation I recognized (or thought I did) and acted accordingly. My whole body was involved in this and not my rational mind.

Retelling the story

Of course, I might well recount the story of how I bravely avoided a child's death to you or someone else, with the sense that I did decide to do something (something vaguely heroic perhaps) but that is largely an illusion. The reality is different.

The retelling may itself be important; there is a wealth of evidence that we change our account of events to match both what other people might be interested in or what we want them to think of us, but also of what we want to think about ourselves.

Leo Festinger's notion of cognitive dissonance would suggest that we often resolve any conflict between our beliefs and behaviour to match our behaviour. Should a project fail we change the story of the project that we tell ourselves to protect our view of ourselves (unless we are prone to depression, in which case we might well find ourselves taking too much or all of the blame for the outcome). Should you get fired from a job, you transmute your beliefs and feelings about the company and its suitedness to you and your skills in order to make it work for you. If a relationship doesn't work, we do something similar. I remember an ad for Bovril from my childhood in which a girl gets stood up by her boyfriend. She is left crying in the rain outside the cinema where they were due to meet. Afterwards, warmed and cheered by the beefy brew, she decides she didn't really like her boyfriend after all. 'He had a big nose', she remarks. Not something she might have thought beforehand.

Put more simply still: attitudes tend to change after behaviour, not before. This is a fundamental challenge for one of the most widely held assumptions of most of those who collect, report and use market research data about mass behaviour for commercial organizations. Not only with regard to our private lives, but in business we also tend to assume that each individual (say a customer) thinks, decides, then acts.

Thus we worry about what people think and the opinions they have. Models of behaviour change which support this way of thinking such as AIDA (awareness-interest-desire-action) still have a lot of currency in the business world (particularly among market researchers who should know better and the more naïve marketer and politician). Certainly the witnesses will tend to support the point: if you ask the individual consumers whose decision-making processes we are seeking to influence they will tend to support this thinking-before-doing version of the story (who would in all seriousness admit that they bought something without thinking and then got to like it after the fact? Particularly something that costs a lot of money, like a car). And they will adjust the memories of what they went through to make sense of the behaviour at the same time.

Our memories of our actions are often unreliable. The truth seems to be that each of us brings our attitudes and accounts of what happened into line with what we've just done. Do-rethink-believe, if you like.

Professor Andrew Ehrenberg has noted this effect in marketing data in any number of categories and markets; people tend to adjust what they say about a brand depending on whether they are heavy users or not. They tend to think better of a big brand than a small brand because that is the brand they buy. As he puts it, 'I have to think my girlfriend attractive, after all she is my girlfriend.' (I'd also suggest that this is because other people think she is, too, but more of that in later chapters.)

As you'd expect, this reinforcement loop seems to keep big brands big, and small brands small. It doesn't prevent big brands from losing share but it does give them a real advantage.

The big when

So far we have seen a number of illusions that our minds create for us. Our memories of our actions are highly changeable and unreliable, our perception of the world is much less precise and comprehensive than it seems and we change our opinions to reflect our behaviour (rather than the other way round). But there's another important illusion that reaches to the heart of our experience of 'I'. The sense you have of making a decision – even to do something very simple, say waggle your finger or move your hand – is misleading itself.

Benjamin Libet of Harvard University has spent his entire research career showing us that the experience of deciding something actually follows the brain activity that starts the action. That is, we sense our own volition after our brain starts the action. His latest book[16] provides a compendium of his repeated attempts to explore and measure the phenomenon first exposed in what is now named after Benjamin himself.

The Libet test wires respondents up to brain monitors and galvanometers that record the electricity on the surface of the skin. Very often (for example as described by Susan Blackmore in *Conversations on Consciousness*[17]) the movement to be investigated is waggling the finger. Respondents are told to watch a moving dot that monitors time and report the time they decide to move their fingers.

Libet noted that what he called the 'readiness potential' in the brain – the brain getting the motor system to start movements – starts some 550 milliseconds before the movement itself. However, respondents only noted their intention to wiggle some 350 milliseconds later, still 200 milliseconds before the movement but after the readiness activity in the first place. Of course, it could just be that the 350 milliseconds difference is due to respondents' slowness in monitoring and reporting themselves. Libet claims to have disproved this.

Why is the Libet delay important? First, it suggests that our notion of the individual decision being at the start of a chain of events that eventually result in willed action is wrong, at least in simple actions. The non-conscious mind seems to be doing the heavy lifting in making actions happen, not the 'I''s volition. Second, because it opens up the possibility that our view of ourselves deciding to do things is plain wrong.

Daniel Wegner[18] of MIT goes further than Libet. By examining the examples of when we do things we don't think we are willing (such as succumbing to repeated invitations to take another piece of pie), and when we think we are willing something but don't do it (such as telling our boss he or she is wrong), Wegner suggests that the illusion of volition is often just that (in particular, he underlines the importance of social influences on individual behaviour, which often occur without us realizing it).

However, he goes on to suggest – following Isaiah Berlin's[19] dictum on the subject – that this illusion is 'essential to being human'. We need, he suggests, to feel as if we are deciding things in order to survive the complex groups in which we live and we can, he allows, actually decide things and do them, but all too rarely.

The illusion of consciousness

Beyond the doubts around our memories and our sense of deciding things, it is now our own subjective experience of consciousness that is being called into question by a number of neuroscientists. I should note that the whole topic of our subjective experience of 'I' is a hot topic among those brainy types who study how our brains work. In a famous paper delivered at the first Tucson conference on consciousness, the long-haired Australian neuroscientist David Chalmers described it as the 'hard problem' of consciousness studies. The name has stuck.

We currently know very little about how this aspect of our sense of self arises – we know some things about how it is altered and with what effects through the study of pharmacology (the discipline that Britain's leading neuroscientist, Susan Greenfield, first cut her teeth on). But a consensus is emerging.

The first thing to be said of what we do know about consciousness is that it has no locus, no obvious or single physical seat (in the popular imagination there is some little homunculus situated somewhere in our brains, some tiny controller if you like).

> Each of us feels that there is a single 'I' in control. But that is just an illusion that the brain works hard to produce . . . the brain does have supervisory systems in the prefrontal lobes and anterior cingulated cortex, which can push the buttons of behaviour and override habits and urges. But those systems are gadgets with specific quirks and limitations; they are not implementations of the rational free agent traditionally identified with the soul or the self.[20]

Perhaps things are just a little more complicated. Perhaps consciousness, like memory, is a distributed brain function. While some – like the late Sir Francis Crick – insist that the 'neural correlates of consciousness' *are* there to be discovered, Dame Susan Greenfield's point of view is that we are a long – long – way off doing so. Her current subject of study is 'the particular physical state of the brain that always accompanies a subjective feeling'. A modest but practical ambition for further study in this area.

A more radical way to approach the question is to acknowledge that it may have its basis *in and beyond* the brain (rather than just inside our heads). Many neuroscientists conceptualize the brain in terms of the entire nervous system, which feeds and interacts with the organ that we like to think of as the 'seat of consciousness'. Some strange experiences have been reported by a minority of heart-transplant patients whose personality changes to match that of the heart donor.

In more quotidian examples, each of us *feels* different in different situations – sometimes anxiety can show itself in our digestive functions, sometimes it shows itself in other parts of our body. Perhaps consciousness is a whole-body phenomenon?

Second, it's undoubtedly true that it's hard to pin down the roots or home of consciousness – the physical mechanism, if you like. It's even harder to explain what we mean by the subjective experience itself except in a circular kind of common-sense way ('It's the feeling of being conscious', for example). But perhaps this is something for the philosophers to help us with. Thomas Nagel's[21] famous 'What is it like to be a bat?' paper still shows quite how hard it is for us to grapple with describing the experience of consciousness to each other. It's like trying to grasp a bar of soap.

Third, there is a lot of evidence to undermine the common-sense view of consciousness as consisting of a continuous stream of mental experience. Not only is this not true over most nights – only some sleeping states qualify under any useful definition as conscious – but it is clear that the common-sense view fails to account for a number of things. Susan Blackmore uses the example of listening to another human voice to make the point that the stream itself seems to make sense in retrospect of things that don't make sense as we experience them.

> You need to hear several syllables before the meaning of a sentence becomes unambiguous. So what was in the stream of consciousness after one syllable? Did it switch from gobbledygook to words halfway through? It doesn't feel like that, it feels as though you heard a meaningful sentence as it went along. But that is impossible.[22]

Fourth, our consciousness can also be misleading in other ways: our minds can create very believable illusions of something happening which is not in fact happening. The well-known phantom limb syndrome that amputees report is one such example. Wegner describes curious visual tricks using mirrors that can create the sense of somebody else's arm, or a prosthetic, feeling like your own. Another is what Blackmore calls 'the cutaneous rabbit';

> If a person's arm is tapped rapidly, say five times at the wrist, then twice near the elbow, and finally three times on the upper arm, they report not a series of separate taps coming in groups, but a continuous series moving upwards – as though a little creature were running up their arm.

No, consciousness is best understood as an unreliable experience of ourselves – at least intermittently, an illusion.

Some go further still, (the primatologist Dunbar being a notable proponent), asserting that a sense of self is an essential tool in our super-social species, with its whirl of social interaction and alliances. It helps ground us. Illusion or not, it helps us live in the highly complex groups we normally do. Others such as Dennett have suggested that consciousness is a by-product of other brain functions: not the prime evolutionary adaptation we imagine it to be.

We know that individuals of our species function much less well in our world when they have faulty or malfunctioning sense of self. If our memories are faulty – if we cannot retain a history of the members of our group and ourselves and on what basis we should interact with them – we will become anxious because we cannot successfully interact with these other individuals on whom so much of our lives are built.

If our sense of self is damaged in other ways – say through depression – we will find it hard to continue to operate successfully in our natural habitat: the company of other people. Let's examine this negative aspect of 'I' – a malfunction of our sense of ourselves – as it is often the case that the malfunction reveals more about what the proper function is or should be (just as the discussion of autism in the previous chapter shed light on the social brain found in non-autistic individuals).

Depression and the distorted self

Depression can be the most awful prison for the individual, either in the anxious form or the more solitary isolated form. Nothing tastes the same, nothing seems to offer any comfort, and nothing seems to offer any hope. Curiously, many of the greatest names in our history were serial depressives, Winston Churchill being perhaps the best known. He named his condition 'the black dog'. Those that are close to the depressed individual are particularly vulnerable because the individual is changed radically – many partners of depressive patients comment as if their loved one has actually disappeared.

So what is this condition and how is it caused? Depression is primarily a cognitive malfunction with real roots and effects on their brain chemistry (i.e. each influences the other). On the one hand, it is a condition in which our view of ourselves in absolute and in relation to the world is negative and our self-esteem low. On the other hand, it is rooted in a malfunction of the brain. Neurotransmitters that help send messages between synapses don't function as they should and this disrupts the brain's internal communications.

Frequently, it is accompanied by other changes in our bodily function too – sleep is disrupted, libido damaged and our immune system suppressed.

Some sources suggest that depression has become more common in recent years, having doubled in the last decade, but part of this at least may be due to the improved knowledge among medical practitioners and the fact that drug companies have a drug for which they need to better define a condition which it treats. Estimates for the incidence of depression are frightening[23] – at any one time between 7% and 12% of men and 20% to 25% of women have diagnosable depression. Other estimates suggest that at any one time one in 10 adults in the USA is suffering from the condition. Others suggest the numbers are higher still.

In trying to make sense of the condition, some see the onset as a necessary and logical response to circumstances and the individuals' mindset, when the former changes so that the latter no longer works. The psychologist Dorothy Rowe is one proponent of this view. Others see it more from the point of view of unsuccessful rules of thumb about oneself and the world which were learned in childhood: the post-Freudian Alice Miller is one such. She identifies grandiose depression as a result of attention-seeking patterns established when a child is not given the right kind of attention or love by a parent. Initially, the psychotherapeutic community ridiculed her hypotheses but now they are widely accepted. (See Chapter 4 for more on rule -based interaction in humans).

Treatments

There are a number of treatments documented for the condition, including drugs which aim to rebalance the brain chemistry, but increasingly cognitive behavioural therapy (CBT) is seen as the treatment of choice particularly by those authorities who have to pay for the treatments (not least because its effects are measurable, it can be administered within limited time periods and it is relatively cheap). Others make claims for more traditional psychotherapy to treat depression but, given the nature of such treatments, it is hard to demonstrate the impact except through anecdote. Most experts acknowledge the need for the right mix of pharmacological and talking therapies that will vary by individual.

Given that I am arguing for viewing our species as a social creature of a particular sort – a super-social ape – it is perhaps interesting to note that the physical symptoms of depression (see above) are also to be found in chimps and other social mammals. The individual skulks around, is listless and isolated (and more prone to disease).

Some (e.g. Leahy) have suggested that depression represents an extreme version of what is necessary to keep groups functioning successfully: group politics would never survive if we didn't have some abiding sense of where we stood on the social hierarchy and felt our subservience strongly and continuously. And *felt it physically to make sure we complied.* Another point of view (the social status theory) suggests that depression is necessary to a group's continued functioning in difficult times. Depressed individuals take up less food, require less attention from the other members of the group and yet continue to contribute to the group's safety-in-numbers security strategy.

Depression could be seen as a social malfunction, caused partly at least by the context in which the individual lives and his or her individual means of interacting. I was once told that when the original anti-depressant (Prozac) was taken to China for clinical trials, the local Chinese doctors were bemused that only one member of a social group should be dosed. In Chinese medicine, 'depression' is often seen as a condition of the individual but often as a sign that the group is malfunctioning. Perhaps, as you read on through the next chapter, you might think this not so far off the mark. A similar hypothesis about schizophrenia was made 40 years ago by the radical psychiatrist R.D. Laing (although that has now been largely abandoned by his peers who are more interested in the pharmacology of mental health).

Whatever the truth of this particular hypothesis, it seems insightful to see the social aspect of depression. Anecdotal and government data both suggest that it seems to be one of the significant complaints of the modern era. British GPs report that it is perhaps the most common presenting symptom in their surgeries. Many blame the rise of individual housing rather than collective living over recent years. One study[24] in Germany suggests that depression has increased by 70% in the last few years, due to economic and political uncertainty – and the data from the poorer parts of the USA would suggest that the figures are similarly stratospheric there. As the context of our lives becomes less like that to which we are suited – or if you like there is a mismatch between the environment we live in and the one we are designed for – so depression grows. The less we live in a world that is super-social, the more we are prone to depression.

Summary of this chapter

So far, I have tried to show how so much of our common-sense argument for individuals being the best place to start in thinking about our species is undermined by the gap emerging between what we believe about the mind and the brain and what scientific advances tell us. Much of our own experience of our lives is illusory. Let's revisit each in turn.

1. Memory – the memories which provide us with a continuous sense of self are often illusory and downright unreliable as a means for understanding what an individual has done and why. We have little access to the truth about our motivations or what we or others have done. The sense that we do have access to this stuff is largely illusory.

2. Decision-making – the sense of making decisions before we act is often (if not largely) also illusory. Few decisions are made in the way we would like to believe. Very little calculating is done – we tend to work intuitively and without realizing it. Volition – the act of willing – is largely an illusion and often created afterwards. This leaves us open to the influence of our instincts and other folk.

3. Finally, the sense of 'I' – our subjective sense of being conscious beings – is often also largely an illusion. There is no 'I' in the sense that we would like to think of it; no place in the brain where executive decisions are made, no little controller; no one in command. The stream of consciousness is not a constant feed. It is prone to all kinds of illusions. And in itself it may be just a pleasant mirage that helps us survive the social maelstrom of human society.

It is important to acknowledge these illusions, because if we don't we find ourselves examining the illusion of our own experience again and again as we try to look at the social creature we really are. We slip back into the experience of what it is to be me in the world and this will distort our model of human behaviour. We keep trying to slip 'I' back in. Consciously or otherwise.

And illusions they are – helpful – but illusions nonetheless. While it seems to each of us that 'I' is the locus of human behaviour – whether I am acting as an executive trying to change mass behaviour, as the object of somebody else's mass behavioural experiments or as a private citizen living my private life surrounded by other individuals – this is itself an illusion. A damn good one that fools billions of people every day. But an illusion better even than Pepper's ghost.

Issues arising

For us in the West, there is a bigger problem: our culture teaches us to see the world this way, in terms of 'I's and not 'we's. If you were born and raised in Asian or African cultures, or indeed in a traditional Mediterranean one, then you may not struggle so. But those of us from Northern European cultures (including Australia and the United States) are stuck in a world of 'I'. And this is what the next chapter will explore.

Questions and implications for marketers

1. Memory is unreliable. Why do we put so much credence into the accounts of individual humans of their own lives in say, market research? Why do we believe what consumers and employees tell us they remember? What could we do instead?
2. Individuals are approximate, not precise. Why do we persist in pretending that they calculate benefits or calculate much at all? How can we take account of the 'intuitive' thinking ('I feel this is the one for me') and harness it to bring about individual change?
3. Most decisions are not made in any way that our models of decision-making would support. Most people make sense of most of what they do after the fact rather than before. How can we redirect our marketing efforts to help them do this, rather than waste it on 'changing their minds' before the fact?

3

'I' vs. 'Us'

What this chapter will cover

The rest of the world sees us as a 'herd' species; the Asian perspective, Ubuntu and Africa. Collectivism and interdependence. The Latin school of society and consumption. Our fear of the madding crowd. The culture of 'I' and our preference for individuals, experts and individual heroes. Individualism as a largely Anglo-Saxon ideology: roots in the Renaissance and Enlightenment. Why Mrs Thatcher was both right and wrong. How individualist ideologues actively shaped social psychology and our tools for understanding mass behaviour. What this means for business and market research and our existing approaches to changing mass behaviour.

The white man regards . . . individuals . . . (as) . . . tiny
organisms with private lives that lead to private deaths:
personal power, success and fame are the absolute measures of
values, the things to live for. This outlook on life divides the
universe into a host of individual little entities that cannot
help being in constant conflict thereby hastening the approach
of the hour of their final destruction.

Policy statement, 1944, of the Youth League
of the African National Congress

A blast of hot air

I remember very clearly my first steps on Indian soil.

I arrived at the airport in Goa exhausted after an overnight charter flight (and that surreal two-hour midnight stopover in Bahrain). I remember that after the usual chaos that surrounds a baggage delivery for tourist flights to any holiday destination, my sister and I marched through immigration and passport control to the seething crowds outside the swishing automatic doors. And the searing bright light of India.

I remember my first overwhelming experience of Indian crowds, armed with bright-coloured, chrysthanthemum garlands and equally bright saris, all keen to welcome anyone – or so it seemed – to this exotic enclave of tourism in the vast subcontinent. Outside, I remember, cows ambled past the terminal building seemingly unconcerned by the fuss; to them, such things are commonplace and nothing in the eternal cycle of birth, death and rebirth. But most of all, I remember the wall of heat that tore in through the terminal doors – a heat so strong and dry that it quite took my breath away. I will never forget that moment, that sensation, that hot dry air hitting my nose, throat and lungs. And the heady feeling that it gave me.

So it is when we encounter any other culture. So many things seem familiar but so many others so strange. Some of it can seem unsettling, some of it just weird. But the modest traveller recognizes that the main function of travel is to help us discover ourselves. It is by understanding and accepting the differences in other ways of living that we see our own more clearly than before. Indeed, this process can help us realize which ideas that guide us are no longer useful to ourselves and which we wish to retain.

This chapter argues that we in the Anglo-Saxon world have got it wrong. Most of the rest of the world conceptualize our species as first and foremost a 'we-species' and this affects not just how they think but also how they behave. By contrast, we are stuck behind the lens of our 'individualist' ideology and this – even more than the design of our brains – is one of the key things which prevents us from embracing the truth about our curiously naked simian selves: our herd nature.

Travelling for real

Of course, anthropologists travel for a living. They peer inside cultures to which they do not belong in order not just to understand the surface behaviours but also the underlying points of view about how the world is. One recent study I came across was of the role of the wolf in different human cultures, which revealed all kinds of interesting assumptions that we carry around with us. In almost all human cultures, wolves have an interesting liminal cultural value; that is, they have come to represent the danger of everything that lies just outside the safety of civilization, in the Dark Woods, real or symbolic. Norway is in the grip of a national debate about the culling of 25% of their native wolf population (of some two dozen individuals) – those working in the icy wilderness see this as a necessary safety precaution; those in the cities as a crime against our natural world. Whatever the rights and wrongs (and anthropologists try to avoid thinking about rights and wrongs), the debate reveals an awful lot about the assumptions that each group has about themselves and their place in the world.

Increasingly, psychologists are having to do the same kind of cross-cultural analysis. It is not far from the truth to suggest that most of what we know in the different fields of psychology is based on middle-class white (and often American) psychology students; even methodologies are rooted in assumptions derived from local cultures. For example, both psychologists and primatologists have long presumed that intelligence was an individual function. This is one reason why chimps (and some human subjects) were deemed to be stupid – they performed badly on traditional individual IQ tests. It was only with the advent of Nick Humphrey's[1] social intelligence theory that the definition of useful intelligence was considered properly and allowed to influence methodologies used to measure it in human and non-human species. We now have a much greater appreciation of the incredible powers of intelligence that primates use to interact successfully.

So, cross-cultural studies can reveal very different ways of seeing the same thing, depending on which culture one starts from. They help us see what is culturally determined and what is not, what is illusion and what is true.

One who has done more than most is Richard Nisbett. His massive compendium of cross-cultural psychological studies[2] provides a really interesting set of evidence for the thesis that we in the West think differently from our relatives in oriental cultures.

We think in terms of individuals and causes; they think in terms of groups, relationships and systems. For example, Nisbett reports a case of so-called mall-rat massacre (the kind of tragic event which is the result of a disaffected teenager taking his parents' semi-automatic weapon down to the shopping centre), conducted by a Chinese–American high school student. Nisbett notes that the Chinese language newspapers in the town despaired of the community. What has gone wrong with us that such a thing should happen? What have we done to get to this terrible place, they wailed. English language newspapers meanwhile traced the psychopathology of one evil individual, speculating on how early the evil of his soul had been revealed.

Nisbett sees this as indicative not just of different cultural mores, but *of different ways of seeing the world.* In other words, he is suggesting that our culturally received notions act like filters or lenses on how we actually see and interact with the world around us; the culture we grow up in changes the way we think. He notes the evidence for our Western overconfidence in identifying causal relationships between events and the corresponding but opposite bias in Chinese subjects. They are underconfident in identifying causes of things, not because they are stupid or lacking in some way. Rather, it is because they see the world in terms of systems with multiple variables, instead of one with simple, single, cause–effect characteristics. Nisbett uses the evidence of how mothers play with infants to suggest that this cultural worldview is transmitted at a very early age, and reinforced thereafter. In a study of Korean–American and European–American mothers and children, he notes that the play between Korean–American mothers is about relations between the two; the play in the European–American families tends to be about objects, their characteristics and differences between objects.

Beware Greeks

His underlying thesis to explain these differences is bold (if not entirely without challenge): our Western culture derives from the merchant and sea-faring culture of ancient Greece. Difference and separation were important. Ideas that would later shape our Western world, such as democracy and rights, emerged in this lively and multicoloured context. Logic, rationality and rhetoric were key skills and these were shaped by the society in which they emerged. By contrast, he suggests that Chinese mainstream culture – Confucian – is the product of an environment where homogeneity not heterogeneity was the norm. Few people travelled outside their village; few strangers were ever seen, so difference never became so important. By contrast, mutuality and interdependence were essential to the survival of those living within that culture.

(On this subject, it is interesting that while Chinese intellectuals probably exceeded our own for some millennia, Chinese logicians never managed to come up with what logicians call 'the law of the excluded middle' – one of the primary principles of classical European logic. That is, that a thing – say, this book – cannot have a characteristic and not have it at the same time. Something cannot be both A and not-A. Without this tool, much of the Western tradition of argument and rhetoric is redundant. Most of the articles you and I read or write would not stand up; the practice of science as we know it, with its hypotheses and verifications, would be unimaginable; until quantum physics and the uncertainty principle came along, that is.)

Whatever you might think of this broad-brush explanation of the difference between what Nisbett calls Greek and Confucian cultures, the phenomena which it seeks to illuminate – the different ways that people from the two cultures tend to think and behave – is striking and holds good in many fields. I know from my own experience how hard it is to get opinions from focus groups with Thai or Chinese consumers; they don't seem to have the means to air differences; it doesn't seem proper. By contrast, in the West you just have to switch on your tape recorder and most people will tell you their opinion (at length, even if you haven't asked for it). And disagree with the next person. Violently.

Ubuntu

It is not only Asian cultures that challenge our Western focus on the individual. People who grow up in many African cultures tend also to think of the collective, of humans being group animals and not members of an individualist species. The word 'Ubuntu' is to be found in both Zulu and Xhosa and it shapes so much of African life.

Ubuntu means 'shared humanity' or 'humanity towards others'. At heart it is recognition, as Archbishop Desmond Tutu puts it,

> [That] my humanity is caught up and is inextricably bound up in yours. A person with ubuntu is welcoming, hospitable, warm and generous, willing to share, open and available to others; affirming of others; does not feel threatened that others are able and good, for they have a proper self-assurance that comes from knowing that they belong in a greater whole and are diminished when others are humiliated or diminished.[3]

While individuals can be said to have or exhibit Ubuntu, the real meaning is more ideological; it represents an imperative to action (as the Zulu proverb suggests: *umuntu ngumuntu ngabantu* (a person is a person only through other persons). Ubuntu explains both the sharing-out of resources in many African cultures (and the enormous portions of food served to guests by even the poorest hosts) and equally the sense of solidarity that keeps communities going through even the worst of times.

It is easy to read this as some floppy, hippy-ish statement of mutuality and loving and sharing; easy to underestimate the distance between the former colonial overlords and their subjects in their view of humanity. The quotation at the top of this chapter, taken from the 1944 ANC policy statement, reveals the depth of conflict between Ubuntu and our Western view of things. Again it is only by understanding others' view of ourselves that we see who we really are and how we see ourselves. Let's consider it again.

> The white man regards . . . individuals . . . (as) . . . tiny organisms with private
> lives that lead to private deaths: personal power, success and fame are the
> absolute measures of values, the things to live for.[4]

Tiny organisms. Private lives. And private deaths. Not the whole truth, you
might think. But not a million miles from the reality of life in a modern
Western city.

At the same time, it is not hard to see how the collectivist political analyses of Marxist Leninism and the imposition of military dictatorships have
found such a fervent welcome in post-colonial African culture and politics.
Though neither are the same as Ubuntu, both share the fundamental belief
in our interdependence and mutuality as opposed to lionizing the individual
as the ultimate unit of human behaviour.

Peace and reconciliation

That said, the application of the essentially African idea of Ubuntu has
played a central political role in helping South Africa avoid the terrible mas-
sacres that other post-colonial countries on the continent have endured
along the road to majority rule. The transition of regimes has been approached
with much more than just a handing over of the keys to the drinks cabinet.
Desmond Tutu, Nelson Mandela and latterly Mbeki have all led policy initiatives based on this central idea. Probably the most important of these, in
terms of the peaceful transition of this richest of Africa's nations into a
multicultural country, has been the Truth and Reconciliation Commission,
which Tutu himself chaired for several years, despite his day job.

The commission harnessed the sense of our shared humanity to heal the
wounds between the different groups in South African society, not just
between black and white, but between all the different sectors, whatever had
been done by one to another. Tutu again:

> To forgive is not just to be altruistic. It is the best form of self-interest. What
> dehumanizes you inexorably dehumanizes me. [Forgiveness] gives people
> resilience, enabling them to survive and emerge still human despite all efforts
> to dehumanize them.[5]

The programme – now applied to other conflicted countries, such as Rwanda
and latterly Northern Ireland – has five stages that are deemed necessary to
achieve lasting reconciliation.

1. Acknowledgement of guilt
2. Showing remorse and repenting
3. Asking for and giving forgiveness
4. Paying compensation or reparation as a prelude
5. Reconciliation[6]

Many psychotherapists and relationship experts will tell you that something similar is also needed if individuals in our world are to come to some lasting resolution of their differences. Something very different and much harder than the 'cheap forgiveness' that Bob Hoffman[7] derides (by which I think he means 'just forgetting' or other such one-sided statements of forgiveness).

That South Africa still has its troubles is not surprising; it is a vibrant country with many have-nots jutting up against some of the richest haves on the planet and not some paradise on earth. In particular, poorer and less skilled members of the former ruling Afrikaner group often still find it difficult to swim in the post-reconciliation nation. That said, it is hard to deny the fact that the nation is in many ways more united than its neighbours, more at ease with itself and its place in the world; it has avoided the post-colonial bloodbaths that so many of its neighbours, such as Robert Mugabe's neighbouring Zimbabwe, have suffered. Apart from the hard work and commitment of those leading the process, it is to the idea of Ubuntu that much credit for this is due. When a *rainbow nation* (as Mandela describes it) can unite under one flag and sing *Nkosi Sikelel' iAfrika* together, what you see is a nation largely healed by its own idea of Ubuntu. At least for now.

Wo die Zitronen blühn

And it seems that it is merely in cold climes of Anglo-Saxon Europe and among our offspring across the water that 'I' is privileged above 'We'. Southern Europe – for centuries a strange and exotic place where 'the lemon trees bloom' as Goethe had it – has a different assumption about how to understand human nature.

A group of sociologists and market researchers from the Mediterranean countries (and some Scandinavian ones) have joined together to propose a *Latin* (as opposed to Anglo-Saxon) view of society and consumption. Its most famous advocate in the business world, Bernard Cova[8] of the European School of Management, Paris, suggests the model shown in Figure 3.1.

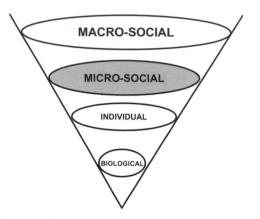

MACRO-SOCIAL	**Aggregated actors** Cultures, generations, genders, social classes, lifestyles
MICRO-SOCIAL	**Concrete actors** Interactions, practices, tribes, subcultures
INDIVIDUAL	**Single actor** Individuals, subjects, cognition, motivation, the unconscious
BIOLOGICAL	**Need** Nutrition

Figure 3.1   *Cova's funnel model*
Source: Levels of Observation of Consumption (adapted from Desjeux, 1998)
Desjeux, D. (1998), 'Les échelles d'observation de la consommation', in Cabin, P., Rochefort, R., Desjeux, D. et Nourrisson, D. (Eds.), Comprendre le Consommateur, pp. 37–56, Sciences Humaines, Paris. Reproduced by permission of Bernard Cova.

In contrast to the individualist model, Cova's insistence is that all pertinent human behaviour happens in a social context – be it consumption, mating or religion. Equally, he contends that it is only within moderate-sized groups that social contexts really exist. While you and I may both watch football, if you live in Madrid and I live in London, we really don't share the same social context (of course, the Internet is changing this to a great degree but only to the extent of making it possible to have a social connection with others without geographical closeness).

This is why he concludes that the Anglo-Saxon attempt to understand human behaviour, either at the very micro level of idiosyncratic individual psychopathologies or neurological and biological reality, or at the macro level of society at large (or both – this is the essence of the standard social science model) is necessarily misplaced. Instead he recommends the 'tribe' or social milieu in which we live as the correct place to study human behaviour and consumption in particular.

To someone dwelling in a Mediterranean culture this makes tremendous sense. Even Mediterranean city life is tribal; that is, life is lived out in medium-sized groups, rather than as individuals or as parts of a larger society. But the same is true of the inhabitants of a huge Anglo-Saxon city such as London, even if we don't notice it – the reality is that even when I am not on a plane flying to a meeting in some distant city I live a 'tribal life'. That is, I have significant interaction with only a relatively small number of individuals. My London may be spread out over the entire city, but it consists of a number of small geographies that I visit, while ignoring the others (which will not be the same as my neighbour's London).

Try this trick for yourself to see how true this is of modern urban life in the West. Take a piece of paper and put a cross in the middle of it to represent where you live. Now mark the places you visit regularly – for shopping, entertainment and work. Don't forget the friends and relatives you visit. Join each of these with your home by using a line from each back to the centre.

Now look at the whole picture. What you have is a personal geography – your personal London, Manchester, Frankfurt or New York. Or some synthesis of all three.

Studying consumer tribal behaviour

While Cova's model has its roots in the reality of the experience of Mediterranean life, its validity is not limited to that specific location or some preindustrial idyll. Indeed, being a management expert, Cova identifies a number of examples of social behaviour which business might find interesting – from the rise of inline-skating in France to the faddish adoption of low-tech cameras such as the LOMO (Leningradskoy Optiko-Mekhanicheskoye Ob'edinyeniye). More recently,[9] Cova has also shown how the same mechanisms can deliver similar behaviour on lower-involvement fast-moving consumer goods (FMCG) products (such as spreads).

This enables him to formulate a clearer definition of the *tribe* as the social context in which we consume. He draws the following distinctions between what he calls 'postmodern' and 'archaic' tribes to make this clear (more traditional social groups such as you might find in what we call 'primitive' societies).

1. Ephemeral vs. permanence
   Ephemeral and non-totalizing groups. Archaic tribes were permanent and totalizing.
2. Plurality vs. exclusiveness
   A person can belong to several postmodern tribes. In an archaic tribe a person could only belong to one tribe.

3. Conceptual vs. tangible
    The boundaries of a postmodern tribe are conceptual. They were phys-
    ical in the archaic tribes.
4. Feelings vs. kinship
    The members of a postmodern tribe are related by shared feelings and
    (re-)appropriated signs. Members of archaic tribes were related by kinship
    and dialect.

Beyond marketing

This makes a lot of sense to those of us who work with the consumerist
behavioural phenomena of exciting or talkworthy brands. Cova is surely right
to suggest that much of modern consumer behaviour is social in nature. We
do it not just in a social context (tangible and immediately present or over
distances) but *for social reasons* – that is the object or activity is the means
for a group or tribe to form or interact. This also echoes a lot of what Douglas
Atkin describes in his study of cult brands – brands which have developed
a cult status (like Apple, and Ford's bestselling pickup) seem to serve an
underlying social need within each individual (just as religious cults do): a
need to belong. The real draw is probably not the brand but . . . other
people.

However, Cova goes on to provide a useful warning against the arrogant
assumption of many in the new media world who want us to believe the
perverse notion that any brand can build a community around itself. He
notes that, as Shakespeare put it, each of us plays many roles: for Cova,
postmodern tribal membership is fluid and changeable (both within the tribe
and between tribes). Modern social life is for most of us a constant movement
from group to group; most of us play different roles within the group at different times.

Some, like Alan Moore,[10] are prepared to accept that only a handful of
really interesting brands can do this but a lot of the rest of the advocates
keep trotting out the 'brand community' website proposals which companies in their blind arrogance and selfishness (see Chapter 5 for more on businesses' selfishness) want to believe. Even Cova's own Nutella example is the
exception rather than the rule here. But the truth is real human life is based
on other humans and not on brands. Marketers would do well to remember
this.

Far from the madding crowds

Why is it that we in the West find our herd nature so uncomfortable? On my first day in India, once I'd grown accustomed to the heat, I found the sheer numbers of people that crowd the streets quite disconcerting, which is why I, like so many other first-time visitors, found India such an overwhelming experience. Despite being a sports fan and thus accustomed to being in large crowds, I felt totally overwhelmed. I felt panicked and anxious for quite some time.

It is undoubtedly true that we in the West larder a feast of fears about crowds; fears which are very near the surface. If you Google 'crowd (or mob) psychology', you get a bunch of descriptions of the negative side of crowds.

The swirling irrational and violent nature of crowds is always to the fore and it is – within our culture at least – almost always taboo. Not just in our grandmother's moral tales which exhort us to 'be a man', to 'stand up for ourselves', to 'rise above the crowd', but also in street violence, political demonstrations, stock market bubbles and religious zealotry. Mob thinking never has a positive value in our culture; it represents everything that we dislike and feel uncomfortable with. Indeed, it is often seen to be an example of our animal selves. Ralph Waldo Emerson suggested that 'The mob is man voluntarily descending to the nature of the beast.'

No, our fear of the crowd is to be found everywhere: in our art, our politics and our institutions. Juvenal and Milton both railed against the stupidity of the mob. Both in Ancient Rome and Ol London Towne, the mob were a spoiled and dangerous crew to those more enamoured of philosophical reflection than realpolitik. Shakespeare's Coriolanus is in effect a meditation on the tension between the individual and the crowd. While the eponymous hero is by no means presented as a role model, the play pre-echoes much of our own distrust and dislike of the crowd. Coriolanus ends up as the rejected creation of 'the beast [sic] /With many heads'. As ever with Shakespeare there is no simple moral here – he is on the side neither of the mob nor the individual; Shakespeare is no simple proto-democrat. He makes his citizens of Rome into a convulsing and unpredictable mob and thus a cruel and unreliable master for any man. 'He that depends /Upon your favours swims with fins of lead' (i.e. with difficulty).

Rudyard Kipling's, 'if . . .' – the poem inscribed above the entrance to Centre Court at Wimbledon – is not just a call to 'meet with Triumph and

Disaster /And treat those two impostors just the same'; it also recommends holding your own line and ignoring the crowd –

If you can keep your head when all about you
Are losing theirs and blaming it on you;
If you can trust yourself when all men doubt you,
But make allowance for their doubting too.

And generations of sensitive reflective writers have from medieval saints to romantic poets have encouraged us to escape the crowd and its dangerous and noisy influence, to meditate and reflect on our own individual thoughts.

The politics of 'I'

In many ways, this notion of 'I' has proved politically useful for its proponents. In *The Blank Slate*[11] Stephen Pinker shows how the notion of human brains being *tabula rasa* (i.e. without innate ideas) was – true or not – an important part of the argument against the old order of kings and clerics; it turned a man born a slave into the peer of kings. Hereditary privilege becomes untenable if you accept that the day we are born we are all alike; inherited powers, status and riches become merely something men have made, rather than *natural* or *god-given*.

Just so, the individualist assertion that 'I' is the basic unit of our humanity proved useful in arguing for freedom from the old social order. The founding fathers of the United States used 'I' to justify their freedom from the English Crown, and the great 19th-century reformers such as Wilberforce and J.S. Mill used 'I' as a plank in their arguments for changes in the abolition of slavery and the broadening of the franchise to first men and then women. (Mill is fantastic on the latter argument – saying only that it makes as much sense to deny women the vote as it does to deny men who just happen to have red hair.)

The collective mind

When it comes to thinking about crowd behaviour from a more academic or pathological point of view, things have been no more positive. The classic

19th-century text on crowd behaviour (*The Madness of Crowds*[12] by the French social psychologist, Gustave le Bon) proposes that crowd behaviour should always be distrusted because something weird happens when a crowd forms.

Le Bon suggests that individuals who join a crowd experience some kind of hypnotic effect from the crowd and become subject to a sort of collective suggestibility which makes them prone to the influence of madmen, charismatic leaders and other members of the crowd. Protected by the anonymity of the crowd, individuals abandon their rational selves and personal responsibility and commit all kinds of terrible acts that alone they might never have contemplated; indeed, acts that they would normally condemn.

A near contemporary of Le Bon's, Sigmund Freud, wrote his *Mass Psychology*[13] as a response to the Russian revolution and the rise of the right in Austria and all over the German-speaking world. Like so many of his cultural forebears and his American and British colleagues, Freud saw the degree to which crowds are susceptible to manipulation by charismatic leaders such as priests, rabbis and politicians as a very real danger in tolerating the crowd behaviour, a key source of his dislike of crowds.

One of the most avid fans of Le Bon's work was a young Austrian, Adolf Hitler. *Mein Kampf* is built heavily on Le Bon's theory of the crowd. Later Hitler's PR guru, Joseph Goebbels made much use of Le Bon's thinking in his design of both the structure and content of Nazi Party meetings (as revealed by a curious record of the 1927 Nuremberg Rally[14]). The way the country was galvanized and driven into conformity through propaganda derived from Le Bon's thinking. Emotions, repetition, mutual hypnosis and the mask of anonymity are all put to work in stirring up crowds. Even the choice of night – and flickering torches – seems to be part of the plan. Much the same toolbox was deployed by Soviet Russia (and to a lesser extent by the other wartime Allies).

The founder of modern public relations Edward Bernays (actually a relation of Freud's) codified this for the business world in his classic studies such as *Crystallizing Public Opinion*. Rather cynically he notes that while education and propaganda have

social and moral implications . . . the only difference between [them] really is in the point of view. The advocacy of what we believe in is education. The advocacy of what we don't believe in is propaganda.[15]

Even in its weaker forms, crowd behaviour is still taboo. The modern notions of peer-pressure and group think are either culturally stigmatized (stupid and vulnerable individuals such as children and the poor are vulnerable, so should be protected from them) or simply seen as signs of moral failure (the Butler and US Senate reports on the road to the second Gulf War accused both British and American governments and their advisors of 'group think', to much disdain from the media).

No such thing as society[16]

It is no surprise then that we in the Western world distrust the crowd. And those who can manipulate it. And we despise propaganda be it political (when we spot it) or commercial (which we can't avoid).

We'd rather stick with our liberal Enlightenment view of self-determining individuals, of the rational man (and woman), of the goodness of the individual, than let ourselves be exposed to the wild seas of crowd emotion. Equally, we find the strictly collectivist ideologies of revolutionary socialism and fascism highly suspect. Inhuman. Illiberal. Intimidating.

By contrast, we continue to focus more and more on the individual, both in the way we structure our societies and in the way we guide our individual lives. We obsess about individual rights, on individual wealth, on individual happiness. The ultimate expression of this ideology is Margaret Thatcher's famous declaration, 'There is no such thing as society, there are only individual men and women and families.'

Is the rest of the world so wrong?

What do you think? Remember that Le Bon, Freud and Bernays are products of our Western culture rather than independent authorities to be trusted whatever. It is undeniable that the we-species view of mankind has garnered a lot of votes outside the West. Can they all be wrong and we be so right in our general conception of human nature and human behaviour?

Have we failed to see things as the rest of the world does? Is it ignorance or willfulness? Is it that our brains work differently or are we just a different kind of human?

No, my belief is that the rest of the world is right in its basic analysis. The herd part of human behaviour is very real – however frightening. The difference between us and them, between Anglo-Saxons and the rest, is not biological but cultural. As Richard Nisbett suggests with his Korean–American mothers studies, we are taught to see human behaviour through the lens of individualism from the very earliest moments of our lives. The culture in which we all grow up and in which we learn to see the world as those around us do teaches us to think 'I' rather than 'we'. The tides of assumptions that flow around us, all day, every day, shape our world (or our perception of it and ourselves anyway).

'I' ideology

So let's be really clear. Our culture in the West has, since the Reformation at least, been rooted in *individualism*. The printing press allowed large numbers of individuals to read and interpret Scripture for themselves, rather than remain subject to the intellectual and religious control of the priestly elite and their interpretations. And as the priestly caste repressed those who made their own minds up in the more conservative parts of the old world, the deviants themselves fled to the new one. This is why individualism has become more prevalent and more central in the culture of protestant nations, like the Anglo-Saxon countries and particularly in the United States than in the old Catholic or orthodox cultures.[17]

As Professor Robert Farr[18] notes in his description of the origins of social psychology, individualism has become so central to Western culture that it has become *transparent* – we no longer really notice it; we take it as a given truth about the world.

In itself, this is a key aspect of Durkheim's original definition of ideology: something that we take as a given truth. Consequently we pretend to ourselves that it is not an ideology after all. Instead we see it as a fact, a simple and unremarkable truth about how the world is. By contrast, we assume that non-individualist ways of thinking are true ideologies. This is perhaps why we in the West have been swamped by a wave of 'End of . . .' books and papers in recent years that crow over the decline of the collectivist ideologies and systems such as Soviet communism. Take a bow, Francis Fukiyama . . .

How social psychology got individualized

Individualism *is* a cultural ideology and it does pervade and shape our way of seeing the world. This is particularly true among those academic

disciplines that should know better, such as the social sciences. Farr makes
the point very clearly that the social sciences have been 'Americanized': that
is, turned into individualist ways of seeing our humanity. In particular, he
identifies the Allport brothers (F.H. and G.W.) as leading perpetrators.

One a behaviourist, the other a cognitivist, together they shaped the discipline which should tell us most about our herd natures, social psychology.
Through official handbooks and textbooks over 50 years, their beliefs shaped
how subsequent generations of social scientists thought about human behaviour. F.H. Allport's 1924 textbook *Social Psychology* states bluntly:

> There is no psychology of groups which is not essentially and entirely a psy-
> chology of individuals. Social psychology . . . is part of the psychology of the
> individual, whose behaviour it studies in relation to that sector of his envir-
> onment comprised by his fellows . . . Psychology in all its branches is a science
> of the individual.[19]

G.W. Allport's definition is similarly individualist:

> With few exceptions, social psychologists regard their discipline as an
> attempt to understand and explain how the thought, feeling and behaviour
> of individuals are influenced by the actual, imagined, or implied presence of
> others.[20]

Equally, F.H.A.'s model of mass behaviour defines public opinion as an individual thing – ignoring the person-to-person interaction that the social ape
thesis I have outlined in Chapter 1 suggests.

> The term public opinion is given its meaning with reference to a multi-
> individual situation in which individuals are expressing themselves, or can be
> called upon to express themselves, as favouring or supporting (or the disfa-
> vouring or opposing) some definite condition, person or proposal of wide-
> spread importance, in such a proportion of number, intensity, or constancy,
> as to give rise to the probability of affecting action directly or indirectly,
> toward the object concerned.[21]

'I' research

From here a direct line leads to our practice of public opinion polling and
attitudinal surveys. George Gallup – the first great opinion pollster – employed
the Allports' thinking and methodologies to inform his own. Like most
market researchers today he assumed that individuals make decisions on their
own; their behaviour is initiated without the influence of others. This model

works so simply and seems to make such sense (particularly in cultural terms). We ask individuals what they think, what they do now and what they will do in the future; they tell us what they think and what they do and what they plan to do, and we count the hands and report the data back on this basis. As if it was objective truth.

Some users of this kind of data have begun to realize the real dangers of using opinion polling to predict future behaviour but not by any means all are aware of the weaknesses. Simon Clift – CMO and Group Vice President of Unilever's Personal Care Division – is one such. 'I just don't believe in predictive research. And we don't use it.[22]

But even Clift accepts the validity of the other uses of traditional market research to describe current or recent past activity as, to be fair, most of his peers in marketing or other business functions do. Market research assumes fundamentally that individuals make decisions about what to do on their own; this is what it measures. It rarely reflects the fuller context of human behaviour – it rarely bothers to consider the social context in which any behaviour takes place and the fact that almost all human behaviour is social because that is the nature of our species.

This should be no surprise. The tools we use reflect our underlying cultural assumptions. The tools provide details of the world as described by those cultural assumptions; we act on these tools and our shared view of the world is thus reinforced again and again. It is almost impossible to see beyond the ideologies that are the reason we struggle to lose our blinkers.

While the Allport brothers are both long dead and many other hands have fashioned the tools and ways of thinking that are now accepted and used unthinkingly, few have had a greater influence on how we in business see human behaviour as these two quiet studious Americans. The ideologues of practical 'I'.

Expert opinion

But the ideology of individualism reaches much deeper into our view of the world. We cling on to the notion that some individuals are better than others. Cleverer, more knowledgeable and well, just better.

We love experts – when there's a health scare we expect a government expert to tell us what to do. To tell us things are safe or not. And we experience a terrible disappointment when they get things wrong. We are angry with the weatherman who fails to predict a hurricane (as Michael Fish did for the great storms of 1987). Or the sports broadcaster who predicts an easy win before the (almost inevitable) drubbing of our favourite team.

In fact, prediction is an interesting example of how wrong-headed this trust in experts can be and thus how our individualism can tie us in knots in many novel ways. Be it in sporting events, interest-rate rises or elections, we expect the expert to be able to 'tip' correctly, to tell us what will happen. And not just when there's money riding on the outcome. (Do you think that betting would be so widespread across all human cultures if experts really were that good at predicting things? If they were, then they would be as rich if not richer than the bookies are!)

It has now been shown that together we are better at predicting the future than the best expert (or opinion pollster).[23] A bunch of American academic economists set up 'betting markets' (the so-called Iowa Electronic Markets) to study investor behaviour. Individual participants were encouraged to trade options on a future event (in fact they chose US presidential elections). The prices the markets agree on were then compared with what published forecasts (based on opinion polls) predicted. Just to exclude the possibility that the published data could not influence or contaminate the market, it was decided to compare only the opening market prices on the day a poll was published. Which gives the economists a lot of data points to crunch.

The results are striking. On three quarters of the days in which an opinion poll prediction was published, the opening market price prediction was significantly closer to the eventual result than the opinion polls. For election after election (five in all), including the 2004 one which was determined by some 50,000 votes in either Ohio or Florida, the experts – with all their data which aggregates individual predictions – are defeated by the collective act of guessing that is a market. And this holds true from the day the markets open (around the time of the party primaries) all the way through to polling day. Again and again. Over five US presidential elections and many others.

This use of our collective intelligence could present a major opportunity to change how we go about the business of forecasting and indeed the world of market research. But I know to my own cost how resistant we are to embracing the truth of ourselves. Having studied in great detail the validity of the IEM predictions and followed the market prices and opinion polls early in the 2004 US elections, I still couldn't bring myself to believe that 'we' could beat 'I'. Unlike my friend and colleague David Muir who – shrewd Scotsman that he is – ended up hundreds of pounds better off, as I didn't place my bet at the bookmakers.

That said, a number of companies have trialled the approach to predict phenomena such as sales demand for new printer products or resource requirements for manufacturing, but there is a great deal of resistance to the idea that together we can be better at predicting the future than the smartest or best-informed individual. There was a great deal of fuss[24] around the American Admiral Poindexter's attempts in the aftermath of 9/11 to set up a decision market to better predict the next terrorist attack on the USA and US interests. Some of the fuss was moral indignation (how could something as serious as national security be reduced to a game?). Some was merely dislike of the novel and new-fangled. Some of it again was just an instinctive but culturally determined insistence in the power of the individual. In business and in politics, we'd prefer not to believe that together we can be better than experts at working out what happens next.

Which is just as the bookmakers would like it – their business depends on our shared belief that each of us can somehow beat the market of money riding on the outcome (be it through insider knowledge, a firm grip on the form book, lucky rabbit feet or just a hunch). And the opinion pollsters, too. And the multinational companies who own them.

Heroes and villains, and other individuals

No, we prefer to listen to narratives featuring individuals acting on their own decisions and motivations: stories of heroes and villains. Of individuals with an excess of courage and/or of vice. We tell ourselves stories of the noble or evil individuals. We give prizes and brickbats to sort out those individuals who excel or fail.

Which gives rise to the interesting paradox at the heart of the culture of celebrity with which we are currently swamped. We watch, we read, we gossip together about the lives, loves and losses of the privileged few who live lovelorn lives in the glare of the paparazzi's flash bulbs. In order for this phenomenon to have any cut at all, we have to all know the individuals and at the same time be able to be interested in learning and sharing our knowledge about their lives. This is why the celebrity gossip website Popbitch[25] is so addictive. It is to the advantage of this guilty pleasure that legal restrictions lead them to pass on otherwise unprintable stories in the form of a question, such as 'which well-known TV kids entertainer . . . (insert deviant or arrogant or just plain stupid behaviour here)'. It makes it seem an even juicier and more believable titbit of gossip.

Curiously, we don't seem to notice the amazing collective intelligence behind celebrity culture – our individualist ideology has blinded us to this. It's as if we are dazzled by the latter-day Helens and Lysanders.

Unhappy feet?

Of course, there are many great things that individualism brings to our lives. From the individual homes we now live in to the choice in how we decorate them that our consumer culture makes possible; from the means to shape our lives to maximize our happiness through psychotherapy and divorce to the self-improvement manuals which encourage us to 'get the lives we want'; from the well-off lives we were born with to the social, political and physical identities we choose for ourselves (sex-change operations are a very curious Western medical phenomenon, aren't they?). Released from the shackles of repressive collectivism and archaic social structures and mores, we are able to do what we want when we want to, to watch what we want when we want to watch it, to eat what we want when and how we want it and even where.

But has it made us any happier?

The evidence would suggest not.

Everywhere we look in the Western world, as economic individualism seems to have triumphed so unhappiness grows and grows. People become more isolated – and not just the old and the infirm – and more and more unhappy. Doctors in general practice report that the single biggest symptom presenting in their surgeries is loneliness and the spectrums of depression that come with it. On both sides of the political divide, the remedy is an 'us' prescription: the right wants a return to so-called family values; the left talks about communities – communities of lifestyle, race or class. As the experience of post-unification Germany shows, being sufficiently wealthy to exercise individual choice doesn't make you any happier in the long run (not that the Stazi state is the answer, just so we're clear here). Happiness – and not as has been suggested, hell – is other people.

The curious tale of curious George

One of the many questions that was asked from Manhattan to Manchester on the cold grey morning of 2 November 2004 was 'How?'. How could G.W. Bush and his running mate have squeezed through? How, when the polls had been so close? How, when the turnout was so high, could he have garnered enough support to win through for a second term?

There are many reasons – some fault is to be laid at the doors of both the Democrats and their allies, both sins of omission and commission. What did the gay-marriage movement expect by putting their amendments on state ballots in conservative parts of the USA?

But the most powerful force in squeezing those extra few votes out of Florida and Ohio – the votes that guaranteed a winning margin in the electoral college – was people-power; the power of the herd. Recognizing that individual voters live their real lives in real social groups, and influence each other far more than political parties can, the GOP recruited some 7.5 million volunteer advocates, most way beyond the traditional party machinery, and provided them with the means to influence each other – printable poster downloads, suggestions for contacting radio and TV phone-in programmes and hints on how to raise the issues that matter to their local church groups and communities.

Curious that the great advocate of social individualism in apparently the most individualist country in the Western world should harness the power of the human herd to ensure his re-election. Part Le Bon, part Cova. But also part Goebbels.[26] 'Ideas find people to spread them. The more an idea spreads and reaches all areas of life, the more it becomes a worldview.'

I'm not sure the good citizens of Ohio and Florida who worked so hard for George and Dick would like to know that this was one of the sources of their programme to re-elect the Republican incumbants. Please don't tell them.

What this chapter has demonstrated

In addition to the illusory experience of our own lives that is created by the design of our own brains, we in the West also labour under an illusion of 'I' because of the culture in which we live. We are all brought up in a culture with an ideological commitment to the individual. Western culture remains an oddity among the great cultures of the world; most of them see humankind as a 'we-species' and human behaviour in terms of 'us'. We, it seems, are the odd ones out. Much of our understanding of ourselves, the means we have to shape our lives and the ways we choose to do so derive directly from this cultural ideology. Which is curious in itself – given that we have learned to see 'I' rather than 'we' through the means of other people.

Some questions

OK, so what if we are a we-species, what if we are programmed to be together and we become ourselves only with and through other people, and our culture is wrong to assert otherwise? How can this explain the kind of mass behaviour that managers and marketers alike are interested in? How can we build another way to try to engineer change?

Issues for marketers arising from this chapter

1. What are we to make of the tension between what consumers tell us about their desire to be seen as individuals and the reality of their social selves as revealed beneath the culture?
2. What do you do about the cultural biases which frame the way we and our customers see and describe the world? One important example is our overconfidence in tracing causal connections, in our attempts to understand both how things are and what caused them. How can you counter these?
3. To what extent does the Latin model help illuminate the types of mass behaviour you study?
4. What opportunities are offered by decision markets to improve our ability to predict the future?
5. What are the implications for you of adopting the African notion of humanity over the 'fragmented' Anglo-Saxon one?

Part Two

The Seven Principles of Herd Marketing

4

Key Principle No. 1: Interaction

What this chapter will cover

Interaction is the first principle of herd marketing. It is through the interaction of individuals with each other, based on fairly simple and often unconscious rules that mass behaviour arises and not through external forces or carefully rehearsed moves. We show how from a very simple model of interacting rule-bound agents, a sophisticated model of all kinds of mass behaviour can be built. Examples include: Mexican waves, crime in New York, and the Sydney beach riots of Christmas 2005. We review how this model differs from the traditional models, for clarity, and highlight the weaknesses of current marketing and market research models.

Interaction is what jazz music is all about.

Stan Getz

At the market

This week is half-term in North London. The sky is still grey but the temperatures feel as if spring is just around the corner. This morning as I walked along the canal towards the market at Camden Lock, I came across two or three groups of teenagers enjoying the freedom of the holiday – from school, from supervision and from school uniforms. They gather together, in the black t-shirts and hooded tops of rock rebels, the same the world over – their sub-Marilyn Manson shabbiness worn with the occasional Ramones or Clash button or t-shirt. Every day this week I have tripped over them in the same places, not doing much but just hanging out, chatting and learning to smoke and trying hard to look cool. And wilfully oblivious to old saddos like me trying to get past them. I smiled at them – as if smiling at my own teenage self – and they were all slightly confused. I think they think I'm supposed to scowl and make disapproving noises.

Apart from the disturbing echo of my own youth – I actually bought Ramones and Clash seven-inches when they first came out! – what strikes me is how alike they look, how they group together, how they all share that slightly grubby air of the middle-class adolescent who has discovered the sound of loud guitars. I ponder what they might answer, were I to interview them about how they look, why they come here, what they do.

I suspect it would be the same answer as some research I did a couple of years ago with drivers of the best-selling executive saloon in the UK, the

BMW 3 series. Many of them look alike (as if there is an accepted and easily identified executive styling handbook); each professed their individuality but all of them used the same terms to do so and the same air of affected self-confidence. All of them commented on the excellence of the engineering and the uniqueness of the drive quality to justify their choice (so maybe advertising has contributed to the success of these run-of-the-mill bits of German engineering). And all of them admired each other's choice of transport and the uniqueness that it signified.

This chapter will go beyond what people tell us about themselves and their motivations when they interact with each other to try to establish the simplest of models for mass behaviour: what matters most of all in understanding how the Camden kids came to be dressed the same, to meet at the same place to do the same thing, how the BMW drivers got to embrace their sense of individual uniqueness – all together. Because it is possible to build a sound model of mass behaviour without understanding the individual's idiosyncratic thoughts, motivations and self-justifications; to describe human behaviour using the same tools and framework that also apply to other (less self-aware) herd animals.

At the urinal

The single most important principle to understand mass behaviour is *interaction* – that is, mass behaviour arises from the interaction between individuals and not as the result of powerful external forces.

In Chapter 1, I explained how well equipped humans are for social interaction, how much of it we do and how strongly programmed we are to do so. We are the ultimate social ape. Most of what we do we do because of other people.

What do I mean by this? Well, the first thing to grasp is that most of our behaviour is conducted in the company of others – most of what we do has a social context (real or imagined) to it. To paraphrase the Nobel Prize-winning economist Thomas Schelling,[1] each of us responds to an environment which consists of other people responding to an environment which consists of other people and so on.

Perhaps it is best to start small and then, when you grasp the principle of it, to expand the approach to larger mass phenomena. Let's say we are out having a drink in a bar or a pub. After a while and a couple of drinks, you

Figure 4.1   *Urinals*
Reproduced by permission of Kieron Monahan.

go to the toilet for a pee. If you're a man this normally means using the urinals. Female readers should not feel excluded. I first thought about this on hearing my friend Tracey discussing choice of cubicles in the Ladies, so I believe the same principles apply. There are many mysteries of the urinals (Tracey and her chums were quite intrigued by what goes on), but this is the one I worried over: *What drives your choice of urinal?* Which one will you use?

For simplicity's sake, let's say there are only three urinals, A, B and C. And only one of them is occupied (see Figure 4.1).

Now, what follows is not based on hours of CCTV footage (I work in strategy, not security); nor is it based on formal research (I am not an academic) but I believe I can tell which one you will choose based on understanding the simple rules that you have absorbed over time. All I need to know is the answer to one question: *Which urinal was in use?*

How does this work? Well, I have observed that (British) men follow two simple rules in their use of urinals:

Rule 1. The one-space rule

If you can, leave a gap between you and the next guy (this means if someone is using urinal A, you go to urinal C; if someone is using C, you go to A; but if two urinals are in use, you go straight for the empty one), Figure 4.2.

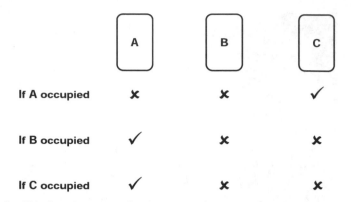

Figure 4.2   *Urinal usage options: the one-space rule*

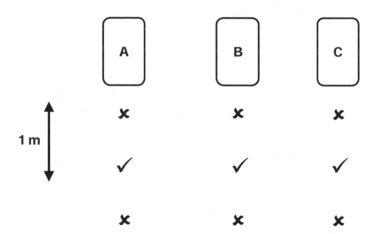

Figure 4.3   *When all urinals are in use: the one-metre rule*

Rule 2. The one-metre rule

If all urinals are in use, stand approximately one metre back (any more and you'll be loitering; any less and you'll come across as intimidating), Figure 4.3.

Of course, there are exceptions to these rules. For example, a vacant lavatory cubicle is often used to avoid proximity to others; it also seems to be the case that British men are looser with these rules as the evening wears on and the alcohol kicks in. And I have no data on the behaviour of other nation's menfolk so I cannot comment on their rules. However, the simple algorithm that these two rules generate results in incredible complexity in terms of all of the men who use the urinals in that location that evening. And yet it enables me to be pretty confident in guessing which urinal you used. Neat but perhaps not that useful – unless you are a urinal designer, I guess.

In the lecture theatre

Schelling's work was well ahead of its time; certainly the theory was much harder to demonstrate than it would be now, given the ubiquity of computers, both at home and at work in our modern world. It takes quite a few iterations to work out what patterns would emerge and whether you've got the rules right.

For Schelling this approach to modelling mass behaviour was central. He asserted that mass behaviour is the result of micromotives and interaction of the agents (hence the title of his groundbreaking work, *Micromotives and Macrobehaviour*); in other words that mass behaviour isn't different from individual behaviour, but it is the result of individuals interacting together based on fairly simple rules.

He claims to have been first inspired by watching how his students filled up the seats in the lecture theatres in which he taught. Most of us know never to sit at the front (at school, college or at comedy shows) because we are likely to be picked on by the guy at the front, so we avoid these.

Equally, most of us know that it's better to choose a seat with easy access if you're not sure you want to stay throughout the 'show', so many people would choose this. And most of us will prefer to sit next to or near our friends and acquaintances. However, while we'd probably recognize these rules, few of us would be able to articulate them to a researcher asking our reasons for choosing – indeed as Kahnemann (Chapter 2) suggests we are likely to use these rules of thumb 'intuitively', i.e. without much reflection, in deciding where to sit. While each of us will deploy these rules to a different degree (depending on the circumstances) and thus have our own idiosyncratic behavioural outcome, if we are trying to understand mass behaviour in the lecture theatre, we are best served by understanding the rules of interaction in general rather than looking at isolated individuals.

Just as in the urinal example.

Complexity vs. complicated

As Schelling was keen to point out, the patterns in the seating plan which these rules generate are rich and varied – given the number of choices available to each individual and the number of other individuals involved in the interaction, it is much harder to predict where each individual will sit in advance. However, the pattern of mass behaviour itself is fairly stable. We find fewer people at the front than you might expect if the distribution of individuals was rational (this is why lecturers are always able to advise latecomers that there are 'lots of seats down the front'). Ditto, people away from the aisles. We would also expect to see bunching together of individuals.

What this illustrates is the mathematical concept of *complexity* – one of the most important tools that science has developed to understand the modern world. We regularly confuse complexity with complicated – we talk of a complex problem when what we mean is a difficult one to disentangle; both of these words are used to suggest that we haven't really understood something. But here is a simple distinction: *A jumbo jet is complicated; mayonnaise is complex.*

By this I mean, a jumbo jet is made up of millions of tiny parts. If you only had the time, the patience, the skill and a good manual, you could take the plane apart and eventually put it back together again. Mayonnaise is different: it is a stabilized suspension – the result of the interaction of its ingredients (oil, egg yolk, sometimes mustard, lemon juice or vinegar and seasoning) and the way you add them to each other. You can't take mayonnaise apart to produce the original ingredients and then recombine them, as any amateur cook knows. So complicated is reducible and recombine-able; mayonnaise neither of these things.[2]

Here is an important lesson: *mass behaviour is inherently complex because it is based on the interaction of individual agents.* But we try to understand it as if it were complicated (i.e. reducible to individual component parts). This is why we find it difficult to understand mass behaviour.

Complexity as a way of seeing the world

Modern scientists and Asian and other cultures have this much in common (though I'm not sure they would both see things this way): they both see the world as complex, rather than complicated.

We however, are stuck with an older view of things: the Newtonian model, the perfect classical physics. It is perhaps hard to believe that one dyspeptic 17th-century mathematician, astronomer and logician, Sir Isaac Newton, could have enslaved our minds so much and for so long. Newton saw the world as a giant machine (!) and sought to extrapolate the mechanisms of the world he saw from observation and experiment. His 'laws' have worked well enough to fill the world with all kinds of good things – my electrical juicer and my iPod – but they are only approximate extrapolations of what he observed. You may remember the kind of examples that your physics teacher used to demonstrate Newtonian laws: perfectly spherical billiard balls on perfectly friction-free surfaces.

It was the Polish-born mathematician, Benoit Mandelbrot, who provided the first real challenge to the Newtonian approach. All very well, he observed, if you're considering a certain level of abstraction, but not good enough for the real world. No billiard ball is perfectly spherical, no billiard table surface friction-free. The real world is much rougher than this. Much dirtier. 'It's very hard to spot the tune', as a character in Tom Stoppard's *Arcadia* puts it.

Instead, Mandelbrot developed what he called fractal mathematics – simple algorithms which generate complexity of great beauty. And which seemed to fit real-world data much better than the complicated approaches of the so-called experts. He variously examined stock prices (winning a post in Harvard's economics faculty in the process), water, coastlines and even landforms such as mountains.

Similarly, you will remember from the last chapter that people who grow up in Asian cultures tend to see the world (and understand human behaviour) in terms of complexity – they see it as the result of interactions. Whether or not this leads them to compute algorithms, as Mandelbrot or his successors in the scientific fields are able to, is irrelevant to my argument here (I'm not sure they do, which is why they underestimate their ability to spot causal connections).

The point is that given the core mechanic of mass behaviour is interaction, we are always going to find it hard to understand the phenomenon and make sense of it if we cling to the Newtonian approach. In its place, I suggest that when we find it hard to 'find the tune', we just say, 'It's difficult to understand' rather than say, 'It's "complicated".' And then go back to the interactions, the real mechanics.

Interactive animals

Now that we all seem to have computing power beyond our wildest dreams (the power in the chip in my phone was sufficient to get three American astronauts to the moon and back), we are able to take Schelling's insight into human behaviour and perfect the application. And show 'human herding' in the same way that we can show animal herding.

In 1988, an animation-obsessed computer scientist, Craig Reynolds, created a simulation called 'boids' – an attempt to model group behaviour based entirely on local interactions between members of a flock of birds. While this is only a theoretical simulation rather than a retrofit model of a particular flock at a particular time and place (and therefore represents at any one time you run the programme a particular instance of flocking behaviour), it provides all of us an insight into one of nature's most beautiful visual sights.

Boids[3] is based on an algorithm with three simple constraints (or rules of interaction).

Rule 1.   *Separation*: steer to avoid crowding local flock mates.
Rule 2.   *Alignment*: steer towards the average heading of local flock mates.
Rule 3.   *Cohesion*: steer to move toward the average position of local flock mates.

The result is convincing and, for most people, mesmerizing, in the same way that watching fish in an aquarium is. Or indeed watching flocks of birds in the wild is. It is hard to spot the mechanisms at play but that is because we expect to see them in the surface behaviour – the tune, if you like.

Interactive humans

What's curious about the boids simulation is that no one bird is in control. There is no flight plan, nor a pre-flight briefing. This is distributed intelligence: each individual interacting with the others on the basis of some very simple, instinctive rules.

I learned to scuba dive a few years ago, and at a depth of 20 metres the same patterns are to be observed, in the beautifully coloured fish, interacting in and around the coral reefs. This – probably more than the Zen-like trance that comes from breath control, or the excitement of seeing an unusual species of fish or swimming with turtles or sharks – is the real pleasure I get from training as an aquatic ape.

I see the same patterns with the human beings I have watched from my eyrie above Cabot Square in London's Docklands. Or the pedestrians I watch on Oxford Street or the newly traffic-free Trafalgar Square in the heart of London. A while back, I was discussing the idea of a book on open-air markets with my friend Peter in Sydney. The next day I found myself at an open-air market and watched how these shoppers just interact, intuitively and instinctively and in doing so create the beautiful patterns that are at heart complex.

You might think about these patterns of mass behaviour as random, but beware: I think this overstates the challenge of making sense of them. There is an old story told about an architect who had built a square lawn at the heart of a university. Where shall we put the paths? he was asked. Where people make them, he replied, enigmatically. The point being that these patterns made by distributed intelligence seem random but they tend to produce – over time – a strong sense of stability. Complexity can produce very stable patterns over time as well as sudden change. And the mess that appears 'random'.

Back to the football

The football World Cup in 1986 was memorable for a number of reasons: Maradonna's shameful 'hand of god' goal is probably the one that most English football fans remember. But the greatest gift to the world of sport was probably the suitably named, 'Mexican wave'[4] (or la Ola, as the Spanish has it). If you've been to a major sporting event anywhere in the world in the last 20 years, you will have seen one take place – if not taken part yourself.

This strange example of mass behaviour involves a lot of standing up with hands in the air and then sitting down. One small group of individuals stands up and is copied by their neighbours, their neighbours follow suit so that the 'wave' rolls around the stadium. One section of the crowd follows another in taking their part in the wave. Analysis of the wave suggests that at any one time only a small portion of the crowd are involved (chunks of only 15 seats wide are frequently observed). And moreover that waves tend to roll clockwise round the stadium. Speeds of about 12 metres (or 20 seats) per second are common.

The team led by Dirk Helbing of the Technical University of Dresden has managed – through careful study and clever modelling techniques derived from (curiously) the study of forest fires and wave propagation in heart tissue – to produce a convincing quantitative description and simulation[5] of *la Ola*. Each individual is considered excitable (by others!) depending on the *proximity* and *density* of neighbours, as well as the direction of influence (those on the right tend to have a stronger influence).

What is so clever about the maths behind this is that they have found a way to quantify these factors and test them against real examples to provide not only an entertaining visual simulation (visit www.helbing.org to download) but also a means of understanding this ever popular form of crowd behaviour.

Learning from the Mexican wave

What Helbing's work provides us with is a workable example of modelling mass human behaviour through understanding the key mechanic – *interaction*. As such it is a really important first step in putting our herd approach to work.

Helbing himself has used similar techniques to model both pedestrian traffic flow and that of vehicles; he is after all holder of the professorial Chair for Traffic Modelling and Econometrics. In one really practical project he and his team have submitted a plan for a self-managing traffic-light control system, based on their work on pedestrian behaviour at bottlenecks.

As he puts it,

> The operation of the traffic lights is based on local information, local processing, and local interaction. The emergent collective behaviour of neighbouring traffic lights leads to synchronization patterns such as green waves (i.e. clean runs). The underlying traffic model allows for the estimation of all traffic streams with only a few sensors installed at the nodes of the road network.[6]

In other words, it creates a great deal of self-organization, which is responsive to traffic flows both immediate and in the locale, from sensor inputs in just a handful of locations. In addition, the system is flexible and robust. It is distributed – and thus doesn't require pre-calculated signal plans or some super brain centre that might be subject to human error.

Helbing has high hopes for the approach. He notes its potential to improve business processes generally and product and service delivery specifically. Imagine if online production and distribution, scheduling and coordination of organization processes could be self-organizing! How much more efficient could we be? In a world in which we all struggle to keep up with our customers, what IBM have called 'the on-demand world', what a boon this would be.

At the office

But you don't need Helbing's clever maths to apply the learning to your business. Bill Hillier of University College, London, has pioneered the application of this kind of approach to public spaces and architecture, from the small scale (individual rooms) to the macro (entire cities); from shopping centres and malls to hospitals and art galleries; from airports to offices.

It should not surprise you to learn that Hillier has focussed on the rules of interaction in these spaces. His approach is to use that metaphor of language: he talks of the 'syntax' in this context. Also, the 'visual language of space'; Hillier's contention is that line of sight plays an important role in the way we interact with each other in space. This allows him to explain how we often feel lost in new housing developments – we don't 'get' the language of the space. By contrast, Hillier points out, traditional urban environments are easy to navigate because we understand how the space should be used.

Hillier believes that the problems with our urban spaces goes back much further than the brutalist architecture of the 1950s and 1960s – tower blocks and aerial walkways which dehumanize the inhabitants and reduce them to tiny ants. Indeed, he sees the problem arising 200 years ago with the replanning of our great cities along geometrical lines.

So what does Hillier do in practical terms? The first thing is to understand how people 'naturally' use a space. This involves both new observations and learning from previous analyses to understand the space. Second, Hillier and his team suggest 'interventions' into the sightlines in order to bring about changes in the behaviour of those who use the space. For a long time this approach to urban planning and architecture was seen as something of a cul-de-sac; a marginal interest which was interesting but not very practical. Hillier himself had a loyal but minority following among architectural students. But more and more practitioners are finding this approach has real practical applications (even without the expensive quantitative data collection the academics use).

Meanwhile, somewhere in Aberdeen

Barr Gazetas[7] are a small architectural practice from London who use the principles of this way of thinking to inform their larger architectural projects such as the Millennium Plaza outside the refurbished Millennium Dome in London's Docklands as well as for their smaller-scale office refit work. One of their projects for Enterprise Oil in Aberdeen was awarded a British Council for Offices award for improving profitability by nearly £1 m in the first year after the refit. Rather than approaching office design on the basis of making things look good, of concentrating on who sits where, they try to work out how to generate the kind of interaction between teams and functions that neat seating plans ignore. First they observed how teams currently interacted and what their paths or trails through the office were. Only when they felt they had a grasp of these natural behaviours within the space did they start to think about the changes they might make to get informal interaction happening between teams.

By judicious introduction of facilities (for coffee and so on) they sought to make the different functional teams interact more often. This rather than the beauty of the finishes (although these are perfectly fine) or the use of the materials (ditto) is what made the difference to the productivity of the business. It also did a great deal for corporate spirit, which has a rather longer-term benefit in terms of business performance but is nonetheless important. Happy staff do better stuff. Enough said.

Here's a personal plea to all office managers contemplating office refits or reorganizations everywhere. Don't worry about where people sit (this is not a filing exercise); but think instead about how people will naturally interact in the space. Maybe it's just me, maybe it's just my experience of certain advertising agencies, but almost every office refit I have ever had to suffer has made things worse.

Summary so far

Mass behaviour is not a different kind of thing from individual behaviour – many since Le Bon (Chapter 3) have suggested that mass behaviour is some kind of collective madness. Mass behaviour – in the urinals, in the lecture theatre, in public spaces, in cars and in football stadiums – is strictly speaking a complex phenomenon. That is, it is the result of individuals interacting with each other and is as such understandable through modelling their rule-based interaction.

The teenagers on the canalside in Camden are gathered there, all dressed the same because others are. The BMW drivers all think they are individuals because they interact most often with people who don't drive BMWs – vanilla car owners as they see them – and respond to the cues of individuality that BMW designers and marketers have highlighted.

Every day, every day, in every way . . .

We live very crowded lives. Human beings interact with each other every day in lots of different ways; some have suggested that if you added up all of the interactions with other humans that the average urban dweller has in the course of a day (passing on the street, sharing a tube train, being in the elevator, sitting in a cinema, standing in the queue at the coffee shop, etc.) you end up with something like 10,000 contacts with other individuals every day.

Compared to our relatives, the chimpanzees and bonobos, this is an extraordinarily large number of interactions; chimps live in groups of up to 50 individuals and these groups rarely interact with each other. It is therefore all the more curious – and striking in comparison – that our lives are so peaceful. Only very rarely does human–human interaction lead to physical violence. Indeed, one estimate suggests that we are 10,000 times less likely to be the victim of violence than our cousins, the chimps, are.

We have developed all kinds of means to avoid conflict with each other: the ability that mirror neurons give us to intuit other people's behaviour has already been discussed in Chapter 2 but it is an essential mechanism for avoiding trouble.

So too is our culture, which provides us all with a set of accepted rules of thumb for this purpose. So long as you follow certain rules, you are safe in these high-volume interactions. This is the stuff – strictly speaking – of the anthropology department, and is becoming more useful to business in applied forms. How does it work? Once again, by examining the interactions and behaviours that a particular group of people has, it is possible to identify the underlying rules that drive it.

One of the best and most tangible examples is to be found on the tables of Indian restaurants. We in Britain have certain rules about how food is presented: protein at centre of plate, carbohydrate and vegetable to the side. Yet if you ever eat in Indian homes, the same food on the same plate would be laid out in an entirely different way.

While you might think that such rules are insufficient to explain individual behaviour (and try and sneak that pesky 'I' back in), rule-based anthropological understandings of mass behaviour are often full of insight into how we come to behave as we do. One of the most readable examples of popular anthropology is the work of Kate Fox,[8] a brave but diminutive experimenter. She describes her fieldwork, not just in terms of observation (although there does seem to be quite a lot of that); she also tests her theories by 'doing the wrong thing': that is, by breaking rules she believes shape and modulate our frequent interaction with each other.

One example is what she calls 'reflexive-apology' rules (the automatic subservience which kicks in on contact with others):

> I spent several amusing afternoons in busy, crowded public spaces (train stations, tube stations, bus stations, shopping centres, street corners etc) accidentally-on purpose bumping into people to see if they say 'sorry' . . . My bumping got off to a rather poor start. The first few bumps were technically successful in that I managed to make them seem convincingly accidental, but I kept messing up the experiment by blurting out an apology before the other person had a chance to speak . . . Having perfected the technique, I tried to make my experiments as scientific as possible by bumping into a representative cross section of the English population, in a representative sample of locations. Somewhat to my surprise, the English lived up to their reputation: about 80% of my victims said 'sorry' when I lurched into them, even though the collisions were clearly my fault.

So culture provides yet another means for us to avoid human-on-human violence in our busy and crowded worlds. But that doesn't mean that crime (and violent crime) is not a reality of our modern lives. Curiously, that too can be explained and managed as a function of human interaction.

Crime and punishment

All across the Western world, governments have struggled with the crime statistics; very often the way the numbers are calculated is changed, apparently to conceal what we really believe is going on – our fear of crime is much greater than the probability that we will be the victim of crime.

Governments have also tried a number of solutions. Left-wing governments have traditionally blamed crime on poverty and social disadvantage and have therefore looked to reduce crime by reducing poverty and disadvantage. Right-wing governments tend to be keen on punishment – thus have spent much of their time on stiffer penalties and more law-enforcement resources. Even the New Labour project with its 'third way' (a bit of both) has not varied from these two views – 'tough on crime and tough on the causes of crime' was the cry of one A. Blair before he swept to victory in the 1997 landslide election.

But is either (or both) of these approaches based on anything more than ideology and gut feel? What can the first principle of herd theory – interaction – tell us about how crime levels have come to be what they are, and how we might go about changing that level through policy plans?

New York, New York

In his best selling book, *The Tipping Point*, the Canadian writer Malcolm Gladwell[9] makes much of the epidemic of crime that raged in the New York of the early 1990s – many parts of the city were virtually no-go areas for public and police alike after nightfall. Crime, drugs, prostitution and murder were all at record levels. Taking the subway was a dangerous option. Homelessness and public squalor snuggled up closely to the glamour and riches of Wall Street and Madison Avenue. In fact, you could say that New York was more crime town than anything else – some 2,000 murders a year and 600,000 serious felonies were committed within the five boroughs.

Gladwell's explanation of how New York stopped and reversed the inexorable rise in crime rates is interesting. He uses the broken windows theory of Wilson and Kelling to suggest that crime is – in the words of the cliché – an epidemiological phenomenon. Crime literally and metaphorically spreads through a population like a disease and is best controlled by means suggested by the medical metaphor. If a broken window remains unrepaired, the message this can send to an entire community is that nobody cares; that nobody else is interested in proper behaviour. He cites Wilson and Kelling to make his point:

> Muggers and robbers, whether opportunistic or professional, believe they reduce their chances of being caught or even identified if they operate on streets where potential victims are already intimidated by prevailing conditions. If the neighbourhood cannot keep a bothersome panhandler from annoying passersby, the thief may reason it is even less likely to call the police to identify a potential mugger or to interfere if the mugging actually takes place.

Gladwell goes on to describe enormous public policy changes which were put in place to implement the 'broken windows' philosophy. Kelling himself was hired by the NY transit authority as a consultant. At the same time, David Gunn was brought in to oversee a multibillion-dollar rebuilding of the subway system. While the accepted wisdom was to worry about reliability and law enforcement, Gunn focussed on the 'broken windows' of the system.

> The graffiti was symbolic of the collapse of the system . . . when you looked at the process of rebuilding the organisation and morale you had to win the battle against graffiti. Without winning that battle all the management reforms and physical changes just weren't going to happen.[10]

As the transit system was cleaned up, so the Transit Authority (under its new head of transport police, William Bratton, also a Kelling fan) then moved on to the next kind of broken window – fare-dodgers (or 'fare-beaters' as the Americans have it). At this time, Bratton estimated that some 170,000 individuals were free-riding on the system every day. Once a handful of people start to be seen to do it and get away with it, then others who might tend to be more law-abiding also start to follow their lead. And so the crime spreads; and other crimes become more likely.

Recovering an individual $1.25 fare had not seemed worth the effort or the money involved – just the paperwork involved was a disincentive to the Transit Police. However, to Bratton, showing that these things are important was worth much more than the immediate return. So through various means – including a mobile police station – Bratton introduced a major clampdown on fare-dodgers. Very quickly, fare-dodging dropped but more importantly, the real hard core who were responsible for other crimes that reduced the safety of the system were identified and weeded out. The police were surprised to learn that of those arrested for fare-dodging one in seven had an outstanding warrant for a previous crime and one in 20 was carrying a weapon of some sort. A clean-up on something really simple – fare-dodging – was able to reduce the overall level of much more serious crimes (and the perception of it) rapidly.

Following his success in applying Kelling's ideas to the transit system, Bratton was appointed chief of the NYPD. His 'broken glass' this time was the kind of antisocial behaviour which has the same effect above ground as graffiti and fare-dodging do below ground: squeegee merchants, public drunkenness and urination, and three-card tricksters. Seemingly minor offences were addressed with verve and energy. Soon, as the crime figures on the street followed the same downward path that those underground had some years before, Bratton and his boss, Mayor Giuliani, were able to celebrate the success of their zero-tolerance policing policy publically.

The physics of crime

Of course, Gladwell is trying to make a point to illustrate his epidemiology metaphor – that is, behaviour spreads through a population like diseases do. The point that the case raises for me is this: how does the epidemic of crime work *except through the interaction of individuals in a given context?* If we understood this underlying mechanism for the patterns that *The Tipping Point* traces, it would allow us to see the truth behind the metaphor of disease, and the tactics to combat crime that follow from it.

In a wonderful book,[11] which describes the many attempts over the years to apply the notions current in the world of physics to social issues, the science journalist Phillip Ball describes his own experience as a researcher into phase transitions: those points on temperature and pressure scales at which say steam converts to water and water to ice.

For those of you who have forgotten your school physics, the first thing to remember here is that different levels of temperature are not the only factors influencing these changes in a substance's state. For example, under greater atmospheric pressure, water evaporates at a different temperature. At sea level, it is 100°C but on the top of a mountain slightly less. These are known as the equilibrium states for the system under a given set of conditions.

But this is not the end of the story: it is possible for a gas to remain in that state way beyond the normal phase transition, due to alteration of the

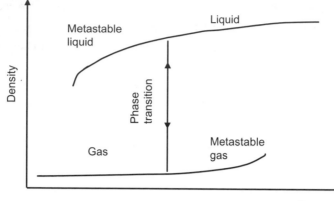

Figure 4.4 *Metastable states*
Reproduced from Ball (2004) by permission.
Note: The first-order phase transition between a liquid and a gas (evaporation and condensation) can be induced suddenly by only a slight change in pressure. Each state can persist metastably beyond the transition point, until the branch ends at a spinodal point.

conditions. It is not permanently stable (physicists call this 'metastable'); but will remain so until something causes it to change to the equilibrium state (which it will do rapidly). Figure 4.4 shows how this might work.

In particular, what can change the state from metastable to the equilibrium is this: nucleation. Just as when a liquid freezes below freezing point, a tiny crystal of solid will suddenly grow to transform the majority of the mass concerned. In other words, 'If a sufficiently large region of the more stable state happens to form by chance in the metastable state, it can expand rapidly to engulf the whole system.'[12]

More crime, less physics

Ball uses this to add new light to theories of the influential economists Campbell and Ormerod on crime. He suggests that this is why we see sudden changes in crime levels when small changes are made to the context and the experience of interaction between individuals. And why – after all – some socially disadvantaged neighbourhoods have high crime levels and some low crime levels.

These two heavyweight economists – themselves heavily influenced by Schelling – believe that it is the interaction with others that determines how likely any of us is to commit criminal acts. They see individuals – like molecules of gas – as interactive agents subject to the influence of others, who exist within a context which consists of physical conditions and – most important of all – other agents like themselves.

Crims, saints and floaters

Essentially, the model suggests that (demographics aside) each of us belongs to one of three groups: 'crims', 'saints' and 'floating voters'. Some people are always going to be strongly inclined to crime – the ability to dehumanize victims seems to be an important but not necessary characteristic of a criminal lifestyle. Whatever the truth of this, most of us would agree that there is always going to be a small hard core of bad sorts in any group of society. Equally, saints are a relatively small group but common in every society. They are consistently law-abiding and tend to be (as Campbell and Ormerod suggest) female and/or pensioners. That said, female criminal masterminds are not unknown to readers of the tabloid newspapers; also, the *Godfather* movies and the real history of organized crime in the USA suggest that the leaders of the US Mafia have more often than not been elderly gentlemen. However, these are exceptions to the rule and not reflective of the overall pattern of demographics. Women and pensioners rarely feature as perpetrators of crime.

The majority of any social group are likely to be floating voters in lots of ways and so it is with regards to criminal behaviour. They are individuals who are neither criminal nor saintly by nature; rather they are open to the influence of others around them. While the crime figures will show that young men tend to be responsible for the majority of crime of all sorts, it is precisely because they are so subject to the influence of others that this turns out to be correct.

Campbell and Ormerod suggest that this is why neither of the kind of levers commonly pulled by public policy makers (changing social disadvantage or bringing in heavier punishments) have a straight-line impact on crime figures (Figure 4.5).

The chart on the left presents the effect of changes in social disadvantage on crime levels; the one on the right shows the impact of heavy punishment. What strikes me is the similarity to that of phase transitions. Can there be an equilibrium state and a metastable state for crime levels in a given population, given certain social and law enforcement conditions? If so this would

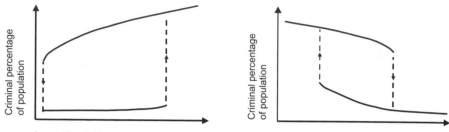

Figure 4.5 *Relationships between crime levels and social deprivation (L) and between crime level and severity of punishment*
Reproduced from Ball (2004) by permission.
Note: The incidence of criminality in a society can depend on social factors in ways that are not obvious or easy to predict. Ormerod and Cambell's model shows sudden jumps between 'high-crime' and 'low-crime' states that can be triggered by only small changes in social conditions. Changes in criminality are shown in relation to (a) the degree of social deprivation and (b) the severity of punishment. In both cases there are abrupt phase transitions between two different states, which must happen at the end of each brand (if they don't do so before then).

explain, says Ball, why the sudden changes happen when very small changes happen. And why two strong drivers of criminality have anything but a straight-line relationship with crime levels themselves.

My point is this: criminality is the result of interactions between individuals and the conditions. Not just the latter. It is what we see around us – in the behaviour of our peers and those we know – that determines what we do in terms of criminal behaviour. As Gladwell puts it,

> Far from being someone who acts for fundamental, intrinsic reasons and who lives in his own world [i.e. The 'I' view], [the criminal] is actually someone acutely sensitive to his environment, who is alert to all kinds of cues and who is prompted to commit crimes based on his perception of the world around him.[13]

This is also why the broken window theory and its resulting strategies seem to work. Why little things can make a big difference. And why good can go bad and bad good.

Fighting on the beaches (and in the suburbs)

Armed with this understanding, it is now worth considering a real case, to understand the mechanics of mass behaviour using the tools we've just explored. And to begin to suggest some answers.

Riots and mob rule have long been seen – as Chapter 2 highlights – as emblematic of all that is mad, bad and dangerous about human mass behaviour. How can these things arise, we ask ourselves. How can normally decent people find themselves doing such bad things? From here, it is all too easy to find ourselves descending into stereotypes of the criminal mind – to demonize rioters – or to blame outside forces (or individuals) which have 'made people do bad things'. Let's try to approach these two events with an open mind and with the basic idea of interaction and the physics of crime we have, and see if this can provide a better model for understanding the nature of the outbursts and how to handle them. How will you do?

The facts

On Sunday 11 December 2005, approximately 5,000 people gather in a purposeful protest near the beachfront at Cronulla, a southern coastal suburb of Australia's largest city. SMS text messages have encouraged the crowd to assemble there 'to reclaim the beach' in the face of recent assaults and aggressive behaviour of non-locals (reported in the local media as Lebanese Muslim youths from the western suburbs). Most salient in these reports is an incident from the previous weekend: two surf lifesavers on Cronulla were allegedly victims of an unprovoked attack by a group of men of Middle Eastern appearance.

While the crowd initially appears good-natured, drinking and bantering in the December sunshine, there are some unpleasant elements to it. Racist material is handed out by members of such groups as the Australia First Party, the Patriotic Youth League and the Newcastle-based Blood and Honour group. A number of hard-core racists are carrying banners with such messages as 'We grew here, you flew here' or 'Aussie pride' or even the disturbing 'Fuck Allah – save Nulla'.

As ABC news subsequently notes, the festive atmosphere suddenly turns nasty.

> Earlier in the day the atmosphere had been party-like, despite the large crowd . . . that changed when a man of Middle Eastern appearance was chased into a hotel bistro. Within a minute the hotel was surrounded by several thousand people screaming and chanting. About a half an hour later a fight broke out across the road and police led away a man with a shirt over his head as the crowd lobbed beer cans at him[14]

During the course of the day, a number of other individuals of 'leb' appearance are assaulted, including a Jewish teenager and a Greek girl. In all 25 people are injured and some 12 arrests are made by police in full riot gear.

That evening, reports come in that a number of people are travelling in convoys towards the suburbs, intent on retaliation. As several of these groups approach the beachside suburbs at around 10.45 p.m., police decide not to intervene but instead to record number plates. However, what happens next is just as shocking as the events of the daytime. Cars and windows are smashed in Maroubra and Rockdale. Property is damaged at Rockdale railway station. One man is stabbed by a gang of ten men of Middle Eastern appearance. The violence spreads through Sydney's suburbs: Brighton Le Sands, Ashfield, Bankstown and Punchbowl. Sixteen people are arrested and charged with offences including malicious damage, resisting, hindering and assaulting police, behaving in an offensive manner, threatening violence, affray and possessing a knife in a public place.

Monday 12 December. Political and community leaders meet and condemn the violence. Police blame the 'un-Australian thuggery' and the president of the Islamic Friendship Association of Australia says the violence was 'bound to happen' and blames racist rhetoric in the media the previous week. A police strike force is established to track down the evildoers. And the New South Wales parliament is recalled for the next day, with the intention of increasing police powers (to include the closing of alcohol outlets and confiscation of motor vehicles).

That evening SMS text messages calling for more protests and retaliation start to circulate again. One thousand people gather outside the Lakemba mosque – Sydney's biggest – to protect it from white reprisals. At 9.30 p.m., when no reprisals have occurred, the crowd get into their cars and head off for the southern suburbs again. It is reported that cars and property in Bexley are vandalized on the way. Cronulla and Maroubra are reached and the local shopping centre is vandalized – some 100 cars are damaged by the outsiders. Local inhabitants barricade themselves in their homes but those who face down the mob are attacked with baseball bats and other weapons. Police find a stockpile of 30 Molotov cocktails and crates of rocks stockpiled on rooftops as hundreds of local surfers gather. Other weapons such as iron bars, baseball bats, knives and even firearms are found and confiscated.

The violence continues sporadically through the course of the week, despite the introduction of 'lockdown' powers for the police, which enable them to close down whole suburbs. SMS text messages circulate to mobile users in places as far away as Victoria and Queensland, from both Anglo-Saxon and Middle Eastern individuals, both calling for the revenge attacks to continue.

However, within a few days, the outbreaks of violence disappeared as quickly as they arose. While visitor numbers to Sydney's beaches were at an all-time low over the Christmas period, violent crime returned to a fairly stable and secure low level. The same as it had been before the riots. Few if any large gatherings occurred on either side of the community.

Analysis

This is where you get to do the work. Hope you have your thinking cap on.

Step 1

The first thing to do is to be clear about the traditional ways of thinking and discard them.

For example, bad people made the crowd do it. Alternatively, social forces such as poverty and social deprivation (true for both sides) are to blame. But neither of these explains the suddenness of the outburst. Racism is common and this must have made the riot happen and the revenge attacks were prompted by the same thing.

Alternatively, the hanger and flogger approach: the penalties for rioting were clearly not strong enough. Thugs thought they could get away with it. Or alternatively, drink is the cause. The first riot was caused by 'intoxication' (literally poisoning of good individuals).

Step 2

Think about the nature of the first Cronulla crowd. Were they all bad? Who were the crims, saints and floating voters? Is violence their natural state? Or is it a temporary and transitory state?

Step 3

Think hard about the nature and frequency of the interaction that started the first riot. Was this an organized or self-organizing protest? What does the use of SMS texting both here and in subsequent violence tell you about changes in interaction from normal conditions? What does alcohol and hot sunshine do to that interaction?

Step 4

Think about the first revenge convoys. What was the nature and frequency of the interaction between the Middle Eastern youths that made up this group? What had changed?

Carry on until you feel confident that you have a clear understanding of the mechanisms behind this. Because without understanding the mechanisms, any solutions might address only the surface problems.

What to do about such riots

In many ways the police response was traditional: separate warring groups, lock down suburbs, arrest perpetrators of crimes, take away their weapons, and so on.

All of this makes good sense but an understanding of the physics of mass behaviour is really helpful in deciding what to do.

In my mind, the first thing to do is to change the nature and frequency of the interaction: to stop the crowds gathering together. Key to this is intercepting the SMS recruitment messages and tracking down those sending them. Equally when crowds gather, disperse them rapidly. When convoys appear, break them up.

Second, following the broken window theory, arrest and charge the perpetrators of any minor offences on either side. If the NY Transit Authority experience is anything to go by, this will reveal the hard core on both sides and also serve to discourage the floating voters from following their example.

Third, and in the longer term, address the underlying long-term issues and rules of interaction which make for such a combustible situation. Are the issues of social disadvantage addressable? Are they the same in both communities? What constitutes an acceptable base level or 'equilibrium' given the social conditions and the legal framework? How do, for example, the separation of communities (that follow the principles of physics) help create the conditions for such 'us and them' thinking?

What would you do?

Markets and interaction

Many of us of a progressive mindset will see markets as somehow an evil or dehumanized phenomenon. This may well be partly due to the pronouncements of the gurus of neo-liberalism during the 1980s: the 'market demands' or 'market forces cannot be resisted' and so on. But stock markets – as understood by economists – are just another sphere in which human beings have formalized their interaction with each other, and thus are subject to many of the same insights as we have already observed.

Markets can be stable for long periods of time (with a slight upward trend driven by inflation and the desire of those involved in buying and selling to make a margin) but we tend to think about the extremes of market performance – when we won or lost; when a bubble occurs or when collective confidence is lost and the whole thing crashes. Perhaps the best explanation of why we remember the downs and ups more than the steady state is to be found in evolutionary psychology again. Our cognitive faculties seem to be particularly good at spotting change in the environment around us (in people or in things). Remember the driving example from Chapter 2? So it is that we remember the outliers in any data plot. Also, perhaps because we – and people we know – have suffered great losses as a result of market crashes or bubbles bursting. So it is a good thing to keep these to the front of mind as we scan the world.

This may also explain the curious phenomenon from the world of prospect psychology (how we think about the future) that we are biased towards protecting what we've already got rather than thinking about what we might have if only we tried a bit harder. In fact, we tend to make twice the effort to protect what we've got than we do to find new or more things. Well, most of us anyway. The ever-upward curve of investment and stock markets (at least until the crash) seems to promise us never-ending growth of our investments. So we get caught up in interacting with others hoping not to be the sucker caught with the worthless stock.

Behavioural markets

The term 'market' is also applied more loosely to for example the European automotive market or the British computer market or the British music market – that is the market in which all of the manufacturers compete for consumers' hard-earned cash. It is this use of the term 'market' which I think could do with some rethinking.

We tend to count the size and the value of the market in terms of either total individual sales (volume or value) or of the total number of individuals who are buying within that market in a given period. Or indeed to some combination of the two. And then we measure our success in terms of our share of the total. Sometimes our share is up on the past and sometimes it is down.

Where I think we go wrong is in the way we try to understand the initial conditions: the state of affairs that we want to change. By this, I don't mean just that we take one point in time (normally last year or last period) and assume that this is the equilibrium, the natural state if you like of the market, although this basic error is committed far too often in business and in the City. Our retail businesses, for example, are constantly bullied by the financial analysts comparing the performance of like-for-like stores versus the same period last year. Every manager in a publicly quoted company is all too familiar with the need to manage the business and report on a quarterly (or monthly) basis of improvements. As if the comparison point was in anyway typical of the equilibrium of that business's performance. While over the long term, many markets are stable, many also shift suddenly and surprisingly.

Rather, I mean that what lies behind this misunderstanding is our failure to see markets and our performance in them as somehow something other than *the product of mass behaviour.*

We tend to see this kind of market as somehow reducible to individual behaviour and decision-making. Sure, we count the individual transactions and their value (to the manufacturer this means cash money). But this is all we have to count.

What if we were to see market size as the result, not primarily of the supply side (increasingly every market is oversupplied with equally good products); but instead of the interaction of the demand-side individuals? What if we were to recognize that market size and market share are predominantly determined by consumer-to-consumer interaction? This would force us to be more careful in the way we compare new data points with historical data points. We would be able to accept the short-term volatility of any markets or business performance that we consider. We would also be able to begin to find more useful ways to change the outcome by focussing on the interaction between those individuals on the demand side and discovering new and better ways to intervene in it, so that the outcome (the mass behaviour) would be more what we want it to be.

The challenge for market research

The next chapter will deal with some issues that this raises for the one-to-one marketing community (it seems the theory misses the key mechanic of mass entirely) but their data from which we work in all marketing disciplines isn't helping us.

Interaction drives mass behaviour but we know very little about it and how it works in marketing terms. This is where market research professionals really have to do some heavy lifting. All our traditional means of measuring and calculating market size are essentially means to aggregate individual behaviour, claimed (and Chapter 2 reminds of the dangers of believing what they tell you) or observed. Very little effort has been put into understanding and modelling the interaction which gives rise to mass behaviour, the normal human interaction that makes up the majority of our lives (and as Chapter 1 suggests is the main focus of our existence and the reason for us being the creatures we are).

Yet again, the interaction between individuals is what really matters but very little has been done to understand or find ways to really get to grips with the key mechanic of mass behaviour. When I've challenged my colleagues and other research practitioners and users, what comes back is a general defeatism and pointing towards focus groups as the answer (which give the illusion of real-life consumer-to-consumer interaction from the false context and group format – very rarely do the respondents become anything more than temporary allies in an illusory community unless you specifically recruit them as such).

Issues arising

This changes both what we worry about and what we do; the questions we ask, the things we measure and the goals we set. It also changes how we think about the tools we use to bring about changes in mass behaviour. And that's next.

There are some people working out new ways to think about this and new things to do. These are the subjects of the next few chapters. In each, I highlight the new tools and underline the weaknesses of the existing models. Strap yourself in: much of what we take for granted is going to have to go – most of it is built on the old models for mass behaviour.

Implications and questions for marketing and business

1. All mass behaviour is the result of interacting individuals within a specific context. We do what we do largely because of other people and our interaction with them. It is *not* because we decide on our own. Nor because huge external forces are acting on us and somehow mesmerize us. We do what we do largely because of other people. How does this impact on the way you think about mass behaviour?

2. This applies to all kinds of mass behaviour – from which brands we buy, to criminality, to which urinal we use. It also applies to businesses and organizations; these are, whether we like it or not in the boardroom, complex adaptive systems driven by the interaction of individuals and the rules that govern that interaction. Organizations are not machines (as the Newtonian worldview would have it and the business schools teach us). Organizations are built on the interaction of individuals – truly and way beyond the truth in the cliché of 'our people are our most important asset' – and not on functions, value chains, reporting lines or asset values.

   This means that if you are going to study mass behaviour with a view to changing it, you have to understand the interactions between individuals (as well as the other contextual issues). You have to go beyond describing individual experiences of a particular behaviour (such as delivered by opinion polls and the other traditional tools of market and social research) and see the interactions in a given population. What forms of human–human interaction do you observe and record in your work place and in your markets?

3. You have to understand the rules of interaction – the accepted behaviours and rules of thumb of the individuals whose interactions generate the complexity of behaviour that you are studying – because these will

shape the outcome of interactions. This is the real work of market research, and many of the tools we have inherited from an earlier age are clearly lacking. Much work needs doing here, because market research is dominated by asking individuals and then aggregating the scores up. How and where can you look at interaction?

4. Equally, the obsession with one-to-one communications about individuals (and those ready to buy now) may be fine for the short term, but this should not be your long-term focus if you want to change mass behaviour in any substantial and sustainable way. Is your use of one-to-one marketing recognizing this truth?

5. Within competitive strategy thinking, we need to see markets not as separate phenomena but also as examples of mass behaviour: each individual agent is interacting with others on a set of rules of thumb. For a long time these can be stable – this is why many of yesterday's brand leaders are still brand leaders today. But they can also suddenly change, given slight variations in the context or the rules of interaction or indeed in the volume or nature of the interaction between participants. How stable are your markets?

5

Key Principle No. 2: Influence

What this chapter will cover

Why influence is important. The extent to which we influence each other (and how little we are aware of it). Evidence from conformity research. How influence lies behind so much of mass behaviour in the form of peer-to-peer or consumer-to-consumer influence. Why 'persuasion' is a much less useful idea. How this calls into question the traditional approach to targeting and the fashion for customer-relationship marketing. Some alternative approaches to defining your audience are also described.

Most people are other people. Their thoughts are someone else's opinions, their lives a mimicry, their passions a quotation.

Oscar Wilde

Saturday night's all right

On Saturday night, my band played a gig for our friend Jude's 40th birthday, out of town at the gloriously bland Ramada Resort in Newbury. Well, it's not exactly 'my' band, but I'm the singer and we often get called Marky Mark and the Big Shorts, so it's an easy bit of egomania to slip into (and an enjoyable fantasy for me, too). And egomania is what most people assume a 40-something ska punk band leader needs in order to win the audience over. Even if the audience is friendly and most of them familiar faces who have seen us play more times than anyone should have to. But perhaps a big ego – not unlike that of most companies and their managers when faced with their sea of customers – is not what is needed in this game after all.

As we were playing that night, it struck me very forcibly that winning an audience over and getting them going (largely my job as the front man, I thought) is very much about using their influence on each other, rather than just about playing the right music (although that is important) or playing the music well (we are none of us professional musicians and as a singer I would never survive the audition for *The X Factor* or any other talent show). But we play with gusto, rehearse hard, have a lot of fun and only mess up one or two songs each gig, so we do better than we might hope, I guess. No, the trick to people really enjoying a gig like Saturday's is this: to get the audience interacting with each other and enjoying doing so. In other words, using the power of influence that each audience member has over the other.

Faces in the crowd

British crowds are notoriously diffident – from the cool set to the kind of people who are my friends – we are a little embarrassed and inhibited about enjoying ourselves (hence I suspect our huge thirst for alcohol). We stand at the sides of the room; we glance around; we don't want to let ourselves look foolish by doing anything as terrible as enjoying ourselves and dancing. Unless, that is, all of this social reserve is overridden by what other people are doing. I've seen it before at 'proper gigs' by talented and exciting young musicians that my sister has uncovered (she's rarely wrong). Cool people hang around, bottle of Red Stripe in one hand, cigarette in other, while betraying only the slightest hint of excitement by tapping their feet or nodding along. And then suddenly, the crowd seems to change and everybody's leaping up and down.

If you watch closely, the change in the crowd's behaviour comes from something within the crowd (just like the physics example from the previous chapter) and less so from a substantial change in the band or what it's playing. It is what other audience members are doing that changes what you as an individual member of the audience do and feel. Although I'm not sure that you or I would ever be really aware that this is what's going on (as we'll see, the academic literature on influence suggests that it is largely unnoticed), particularly as starting to dance is not one of those hugely rational decisions; you just find yourself dancing and singing along as others around you are.

Of course, some people are more likely to start than others. In the case of our audiences, these are mostly our 'WAGs' (wives and girlfriends) but also to be found among these early adopters are people who are just less inhibited than the rest of us (naturally or through liquor). If you get enough people like this going early on, then their enjoyment seems to encourage the others, who in turn encourage others by example (rather than by any obvious persuasion). This – rather than the brilliance of my Joey Ramone impersonation – is the real key to unlocking a brilliant evening for all. And as any performer will tell you, if the audience responds well, then the performer responds back with more energy and fun and the energy of the whole room goes up.

Actors, musicians and comedians all talk about 'having a good crowd/ house in' and equally bemoan the opposite. If you consider your own experience of meetings, presenting to groups of people who respond to what you are saying (not just back to you but also and more importantly to each other), good meetings are full of peer-to-peer energy and bad meetings are not.

I will never forget pitching for the Goodyear Tyre advertising account in Akron, Ohio (famous only for tyres and the 1970s electronic popsters, Devo). The room was huge and around the horseshoe table were some 30-odd tyre executives (yes, there are such people and they describe themselves as such), all clad in the same blue suits, the same white shirts and the same blue ties and with just the one haircut between them. My creative partner and I did our very best to engage and encourage interaction in this crowd but try as we might, the room remained Brooks Brothers silent. For two hours! Needless to say we didn't win the business but it is a meeting that I will never forget (in fact, I use it to remind myself that no meeting could ever be quite as bad).

1-2-3-4 . . .

This chapter will explore this core insight – that peer-to-peer or consumer-to-consumer (C2C) influence is the key factor in shaping mass behaviour; how it can be harnessed and why it is so much more important than what we normally worry about; how we in organizations try to do things to individual customers or citizens to 'persuade' them to do what we want them to do.

In the end, what matters is what they do to each other. Once we've established this we'll show how this changes the traditional idea of targeting (and how we apply this change in practical terms).

As Newy, our drummer, would say, 1-2-3-4 . . .

Brainwashing

Shortly after the Allies brought Nazi Germany down, the Cold War broke out. Having combined to defeat the evil of the Third Reich, the two most powerful players in geopolitics fell out with each other and their allies fell in line. Distrust and fear both took up residence in the hearts of the two great superpowers of the time, the USA and the Soviet Union. And not just at the top, in the ranks of the leaders and policy-makers, but also throughout the cultures of these two countries. The McCarthyite witchhunts for 'reds under the bed' on the one hand; the purges and suppression of dissent in postwar Hungary and Czechoslovakia is its corollary on the other.

Think of the great movies that this has made – the *Harry Palmer* series that made Michael Caine the superstar he was born to be and the original *Manchurian Candidate* (which won Frank Sinatra his only Oscar and is reputed to be the original source for the plotline in the first *Godfather* movie, which ends with the horse's head in a Hollywood producer's bed).

Both of these deal with a deep, abiding fear of the time – *brainwashing*. That is, the ability to manipulate and change the way individuals think and behave, to bring them to do things against their instincts, a task largely accomplished through sinister means. In *The Ipcress File*, Harry (Caine) resists the brainwashing which is designed to make him betray his boss (Ross) and his country, with the help of a handy nail driven into the palm of his hand; in *The Manchurian Candidate*, Angela Lansbury facilitates the brain-washing of a whole team of all-American heroes with the intention of turning them into trained killers.

Brainwashing and conformity

But the fear of brainwashing also seemed to drive academic and clinical research (sometimes funded by the respective Cold Warrior governments). In the 1920s and 1930s, a number of respected psychologists had started to concern themselves with related subjects (Freud's *Mass Psychology*[1] is in many ways an attempt to make sense of the rise of the Nazis in Germany and Austria and at the same time to pick the bones from the Russian Revolutions of 1917).

During the Cold War, academic researchers were considering the power of others to influence an individual in lots of ways. The name given to this field of study is social conformity (or just conformity) research. Mustafer Sherif's classic book[2] on normative behaviour features a number of his experiments on the theme which all add fuel to our suspicion that we are very easily influenced by what other people say. But perhaps the best known of these conformity research projects made the reputation of the pioneering social psychologist Solomon Asch.

Asch was an extraordinary man. He was born in Warsaw in September 1907. He arrived in the USA at the age of 13 and soon demonstrated his academic brilliance, earning a PhD from Columbia at the early age of 25. Asch embraced the influence of his mentor there, Max Wertheimer, and brought the very European gestalt, relation-orientated approach (which was very alien to the then predominantly positivist culture of psychology in the United States) to the study of such phenomena as perception and metaphor.

He was one of those rare individuals who shapes the future development of his whole discipline (his protégé, Stanley Milgram, took his work to new and often notorious heights in his exploration of obedience and the terrible things that people will do if told to, as we'll see later in the chapter). In particular, Asch negotiated a middle way between the rival camps of psychoanalysts (who saw the contents and layout of our mental cupboards as being all important in understanding human behaviour) and the behaviourists (who saw that as entirely irrelevant to the task in hand). Asch also insisted on a basic truth about perception that is still widely accepted in many circles; namely, that how we perceive a situation is more important in determining how we respond to it than how it 'really' (i.e. objectively) is.

Parallel lines

But his greatest work and biggest influence lies in the area of conformity.[3] Let's see how you do, looking at Figure 5.1.

The question that subjects were asked is this: Which of the three lines on the left is the same length as the one on the right? Easy, huh? Which did you choose? A, B, or C? Put a tick against the line you chose.

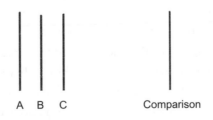

Figure 5.1 *Asch's conformity study*
Source: http://www.dushkin.com/connectext/psy/ch15/asch.mhtmln. Reproduced by permission of The McGraw Hill Companies.

The clincher to this experiment shows the genius of Asch. He and his team then gave the subject a second go, commenting that the majority of respondents had chosen C. Your go again. Which will you choose this time? The same as before or a different one?

Asch found *that more than one third of respondents* who initially chose something other than line C were happy to change their minds and follow what they perceived to be the majority point of view. Just as you see on *Who Wants to Be a Millionaire?* or *Blind Date*, most people will happily accept that their initial cognitions are erroneous and that others have the correct answer! Just by telling individuals that there is a normative or majority view, we can get many of them to change or adjust their point of view.

Fear and needles

Using this simple and rather basic experimental approach, Asch established that influence is key to shaping how we see things and how we behave. Brainwashing, if you like, is not such a fiendish dark art as *The Manchurian Candidate* and other Cold War propaganda would suggest. We are influenced in all kinds of ways by the others that surround us and often unwittingly (it's only after the experiment that you realize you have changed your mind about such a simple objective fact as the length of a line).

The unwitting nature of this influence is something subsequently explored by – among others – Schachter and Singer.[4] Their most famous experiment utilized a trick now popular in such reality wind-up shows as MTV's *Punkd*, 'the stooge'. That is, somebody who pretends to be a subject just like the real subject but is in fact working for the researchers.

Here's what happens in their best-known experiment. Imagine you have volunteered to take part in an experiment. You are given a shot in the arm (you don't know it but this is in fact just a fairly harmless and ineffective adrenaline injection) and then led away to a waiting room before the experiment starts, apparently to give the shot time to take effect. In that room, you meet another subject (actually the stooge). This other subject is (depending on the instructions of the experimenters) either acting really angrily and violently or really sadly and morosely. You watch and wait for the experiment to start. You may feel slightly uncomfortable but you wait.

Subsequently, you are put through a number of tests (which are in fact of no interest to the experimenters and completely irrelevant, but you don't know this) and then, almost as an afterthought, you are asked about your experiences in the waiting room and how you felt after the injection. Here's the interesting bit (both for the experimenter and for my point here): you are very likely to describe yourself as having felt angry or distressed, in line with or in reaction to the stooge's behaviour. Moreover, you will be very likely to ascribe the cause of this to the (harmless) injection you were given and not to the stooge's behaviour.

In other words, you have absorbed and internalized what someone else seemed to be feeling, without ever realizing that this was happening. Indeed, you falsely ascribe the cause of the feeling you were influenced to have to the (pointless) injection. Other people can make you feel emotions that you have no objective reason for feeling, without you realizing how this effect is achieved.

Hands together, please

The illusionist Derren Brown has shown how just such a mechanism can create the experience of a séance. In one of his TV shows, he takes a group of students down the darkened dusty corridors of an abandoned hospital – conditioning their expectations as they plod on to the basement with their sensory experience and the things he says.

It's curious, he observes, that in this very place 30 years ago a bunch of students, very much like the group with him, gathered to conduct a séance, which changed their lives and led to the premature death of the most brilliant of them all. Tonight (dramatic pause) the group is to reenact the séance as an experiment into paranormal phenomena. Nervous giggles ripple around the group. Some individuals brazen it out (they must feel they are immune to such things, clearly). But Derren has done his work: they are overstimulated and nervous or oversensitive about what is to come. Cortisol must be pumping round their bodies; their hearts beating faster than usual; their breathing shallower than it should be. But they dismiss these symptoms without thinking; the séance is about to start.

Deep in the darkened basement, with special night-effect cameras, the students sit around the table. Derren has already got them to hold hands (more nervous laughter among this now physically connected group) and to focus on something else – a voice or a sign that there might be some ghostly presence emerging. And then having distracted them, he does something very simple to the over-excited group. It is very, very simple: he very gently squeezes the two hands he holds, one on either side. And suddenly the group erupts in anxiety, squeals and whoops, rapid breathing and other signs of panic. Like the master illusionist he is, he has got them aroused but focussed on something other than what he is doing. What they think is happening is not what's really happening (he has distracted them with talk of ghosts, mysteries and the setting); what is really happening is that he is getting them to give panic signals to each other via the circle of hands. He has got them to influence each other without realizing that they are doing this to themselves. To get them to feel an entirely inappropriate emotion because of how they are touching each other. A masterful application of conformity research.

The placebo effect

This phenomenon also seems to have its roots in conformity effects – our tendency to be influenced by others. Essentially, whenever a drug is tested, some subjects are given a non-active treatment (the placebo) and others the active treatment. There is always a proportion of the non-active subjects who claim that their symptoms are much improved (often showing as much improvement as those taking the trial drug). After all, the doctors gave me the pills . . .

This makes it important to design the tests properly so that the trial drug results are clearly distinguishable from the placebo influence. In the West we are dismissive of placebo effects but in the East it is different. When Western companies first started using Asian subjects for drug tests, they found that many Asian doctors see placebo as 'good medicine' (rather than the fraudulent type). 'Good' in the sense that it involves no significant intervention in the patient's body chemistry but it still works . . . another interesting cultural difference.

What do you do to me?

So far, we've seen how 'other people' can influence what we think, how we see the world, and how we feel. Of course, other people can also make us *do* what we wouldn't otherwise do.

When pressed by your host, you take a second helping of dinner, even though you are determined to watch your weight. You may have too much to drink on a night out – more than you planned, anyway – because your friends are encouraging you.

You may go to a movie that you dislike because everyone else and the reviews recommend it. You wear the same clothes as others – partly because of the way the clothing industry copies itself, but largely because we choose to wear what other people wear. We look around – at people like us, at magazines, at films and TV – and develop a feel for what is socially acceptable and how we might put that look together. Magazines have now cottoned on to this – many now feature the 'cash-strapped' comparison of designer vs. high street takes on the latest looks.

Years ago, I was involved in a research project to understand whether and how middle-of-the-road men bought shoes. The client was convinced that such men were concerned only with function (fit, materials and manufacturing quality); after all, this is what research groups told him again and again.

We disagreed. We had a hunch that even the most unfashionable British male chose what he chose because of the influence of others. And indeed, with a more anthropological approach to research design than the usual focus group format we unearthed the strange phenomenon of 'checking out' among the mass market. When we got close enough to the participants in the study, they were happy to admit that they *checked out* what other men in their social circle were wearing and followed what they saw around them. Many women are happy to discuss the same behaviour in themselves – the curious thing was to find men doing so.

Stupid boy

Fashion and clothing is just one example of the influence of others on our behaviour but it is all too easily dismissed by those who feel uncomfortable with the herd picture of who we are as 'superficial' or 'stupid' people. Kids, it is admitted, don't know any better. They suffer and succumb to peer pressure but now I am grown, I don't.

Wrong. The influence of others is in every aspect of our lives, in the big and the small things we do. We cannot escape it; even if we pretend we are superior and highly principled and self-determining, we all do it all of the time. We mimic each other from the moment we are born (as Chapter 1 showed).

Think back to the cellotaph story in the introduction to this book. How do the piles of bouquets and notes grow at any one spot? With one gesture which is then copied, which is then copied again. And so from spot to spot. Think back to the gig I mentioned at the beginning of this chapter. How do we get people to dance? By getting them to get each other out on the floor, *not* by persuading each individual to step out on their own . . .

Marky Mark and his influence

When we in organizations think about affecting mass behaviour in customers or staff, we tend to think as the egotistical lead singer of the Big Shorts did: that it is what we do that affects the way that our audience (curious word, that, isn't it?) behaves. We could represent this diagrammatically as in Figure 5.2.

Note the size of the arrow here. This echoes Marky Mark's inflated view of his own importance. He is powerful and talented and each member of the audience is putty in his hands. It's what he does to them that counts. That's certainly how it seems to both parties, but this is misleading.

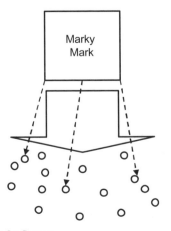

Figure 5.2 *Current model of influence*

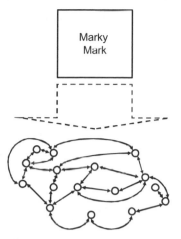

Figure 5.3 *How it really works*

How it really seems to work is shown in Figure 5.3.

What really matters is what each of the individuals in the mass does to the others. Note the smaller size of the arrow from Marky Mark to the audience.

This is something that management and particularly marketing theory finds difficult to grasp. We like the idea that what we do on behalf of the business is important and potent. We *don't* like the idea that what our customers or staff do to each other is more important than what we do to them. We constantly strive to show what we have done to customers – the actions we have taken – to justify our positions. It's hard to say to your boss or to your shareholders, 'we've done all we can now in getting the product and service right; it's up to the customers to tell each other about what we do and to get each other to the store.'

Why one-to-one is wrong

As I explained in a previous book,[5] it's not surprising that we think like this given that most of our current ideas about business and marketing come from the positivist 20th-century USA. Even when new technology comes along – computer processing power and database software, for example – we adapt it only to work within this frame of reference. That's why we have fallen in love with customer relationship marketing and database marketing. These allow us to further the illusion that what we do to customers is what matters;

they allow us to more precisely target individual customers and offer them differential propositions (normally with an incentive to ease the pain).

Of course, it can be effective and it certainly is easier to measure than other marketing approaches. But it is only a short-term and marginal activity to harvest low-hanging fruit; the easy wins if you like. Unless it is properly and sensitively managed, one-to-one marketing approaches will tend to ignore the mechanic behind individual sales (that is, other people). Mortgaging the long term for short-term bonusable objectives is a nice way of putting it; money-grabbing less nice.

Charidee, my friends

The charity sector is I think a great example of this. My mother is typical of the heavy charity donor, not because she is some dignified lady who organizes charity balls and the like, but because she was brought up to support charities and people that do good work. She has a range of causes that she supports – mostly around issues and diseases that have affected people in her life, such as cancer, diabetes, heart disease and so on. She also supports a family friend who works with streetkids in Latin America. However, she is now plagued by direct communication from charities armed with database technology – by post, by phone and now by email. Of course, they are just looking for the low-hanging fruit; all the indications must be that she is what they're after but most of these calls and mail-shots just serve to make her resentful and thus less likely to give to them at all.

I know for certain that she has cancelled direct debits to certain charities that have become too greedy and pushy. Being largely housebound, she counts the mail-shots and comments to me on the wastefulness of most of them. While the approach may be efficient in harvesting short-term opportunities, it is all too clearly working against the long-term opportunities as well as failing to harness the customer-to-customer mechanic that sustains mass behaviour.

Relation-canoes

The egotism that lies behind this approach has a number of other big problems.

First, it is described in terms of 'relationship' building – its proponents justify what they do in terms of building closer one-to-one relationships with individual customers. Now this is plain nonsense in most cases. Organizations struggle to build relationships with each other, let alone with an individual customer. The balance of power is too one-sided for that to be the case.

If anything it reminds me of what my late friend, Andrew (a self-declared relationship avoider) used to call relation-*canoes*. That is, something shorter and more easily steered by one person, to go where they want to.

Relationships

What kind of 'relationship' is it anyway? Very one-sided, for sure because it's only ever really about the money the customer spends with the company. Or rather, to reflect the egotism and selfishness involved on the company's part that it's only about the money the company gets from the customer.

It's not about what the customer might really find valuable in the rest of his or her life. And it's not about loyalty in any sense that a human–human relationship might be.

I know from working in this area that no sooner does a customer stop spending whatever is required to keep them in the top box than they get dumped. As the patterns of my business travel have changed so I've been moved up and down in the hierarchy of airline loyalty cards. BA have now started to inform each of their Executive Club members how many miles we have to fly to keep our privileges. They value me only so long as I generate vast amounts of cash for them. Even the application of Pareto's law (the old 80:20 rule whereby the majority of income comes from a small number of customers) is mistaken.

First, the top box (most valuable customer) is not a fixed group – customers come and go from this for a range of reasons. Second, the other customers (some of whom may not be profitable in themselves) are often economically essential to the functioning of the business. Without them, the overheads are not covered. Third – and probably most interesting for our view of mass behaviour – Pareto's law is just a feature of the world which we see everywhere; it certainly isn't anything particularly magical or insightful. It is a *mathematical power law*: that is, a statistical feature that suggests the behaviours being studied are far from being *stable and granular* (i.e. made up of individual self-determining agents) but *complex and interdependent* (just as herd theory of mass behaviour would suggest). And thus subject to rapid change. At heart, the ease with which we deploy Pareto's law in one-to-one business tells us that the world is exactly the opposite from how we assume; that mass behaviour is complex and interactive. And thus potentially un-stable. So whatever we do to our customers within the one-to-one frame, we are ignoring the real underlying mechanic: what our customers or staff do to influence each other. This affects all aspects of what we do.

Channel tunnel vision

Of course, this is all made worse by what I call *channel tunnel vision:* we in marketing, business and indeed in government are fixated on channels and sending messages or extracting money rather than in understanding the dynamics and mechanisms of mass behaviour.

This affects all aspects of what we do. Advertising people tend to think about advertising affecting lots of individual people through their broadcast channels (we count how many eyeballs are out there and worry about the things we are sending out, how many individuals receive or remember and how many claim to be persuaded by what we put into the channel and so on).

This is the fertile ground on which the seeds of 'one-to-one revolution' were sown. In highlighting the weakness of advertising channels (declining audiences for the mainstream channels in all Western countries, rising costs of TV airtime and the difficulties in linking short-term advertising actions of the company to sales), one-to-one has offered more precise targeting, less wastage on more measurability (you can track, learn and improve both response rate and your targeting over time). But this doesn't deal with the mechanism of mass behaviour – person-to-person influence. It's just another example of the egotism of business and marketing folk. And our unwilling-ness to do the hard yards and think things through.

From me to you

Even when the one-to-one world has embraced newer technology, such as the Internet or mobile phone technology, it's the same story. When you ask marketers about how they see the Internet, they see it first and foremost as a channel – a means to send messages and extract money from customers. New media gurus such as Seth Godin have made a fortune trashing other channels for their inefficiencies, just as the one-to-one pioneers did to TV, rather than making sense of the new opportunities for influencing the peer-to-peer mechanism that drives mass behaviour.

In fact, the Internet is a means for peer-to-peer, C2C interaction and influence. This is how it has grown – eBay being the best-known example of a business built on C2C interaction over the net. Mobile phones are primarily used for person-to-person communication. SMS is not another channel to abuse; it is a cheap and easy way for real people to communicate with each other (and only occasionally with business). Whatever the tech-heads tell you, the real growth in these new technologies is in this area and this is what is challenging the traditional marketing approaches. According to Cambridge firm Cachelogic,[6] peer-to-peer networking traffic now exceeds business-to-consumer traffic or information-searching by a factor of ten to one, depending on the time of day. Networking sites like Friendsreunited were just the beginning. Friendster.com, Bebo.com and Facebook.com are all – for their different audiences – highly valued networking sites. Flickr.com enables individuals to upload and share their photographs with the world, each with its own unique URL or address. Youtube does the same with video technology. More than 100,000 downloads are made from this site alone, everyday.

Recently Rupert Murdoch's News Corporation spent the equivalent of sizeable country's annual GDP on buying MySpace. Everyday 220,000 new members join. They create their own pages with pictures of themselves, their families and their pets, with diaries and mini-blogs of their thoughts and feelings, their successes and their challenges. They upload paintings they have made, music or films they have made and chat and interact with both real-world and newer virtual friends. Many of the users are younger adults, but not all. Indeed such is the broad appeal of MySpace that it is claimed that it now gets more hits than the traditional internet giants such as eBay and Google combined. Peer-to-peer sites, for example, cover every romantic networking need from adultery (www.philanderers.com offers 'discreet extramarital personal ads exclusively for discriminating men and women seeking an extramarital affair') to the ultimate female fantasy (www.SingleFireFighters.com is 'the *only* place to meet firefighters without call 911'). And the Rolling Stones have their own MySpace site (not sure what this tells us but it's true). And guerrilla gardeners, dating sites and academic communities (the original participants) are all flourishing.

All of this passes marketing people by as they struggle with their channel tunnel vision. Even politicians are blinded by it – they worry more about what is said on what channel, rather than the mechanic of citizen-to-citizen interaction. So long as their story is on *News at Ten* and positively covered by journalists, they are happy.

Getting beyond egotism

If we want to affect mass behaviour, we need to acknowledge and dismantle our own egotism. Peer-to-peer or C2C communication is what matters, not what we in business do to those individuals. As far as mass behaviour is concerned, it's they that influence each other, not us who *persuade* or *incentivize* them out of their hard-earned cash. The important relationships are the ones our customers and employees have with each other, not those we claim to have with them. Our job is to encourage what they are already doing to each other, which we can do through our actions and our openness, our generosity and our creativity. Oh, and our humility.

While we like to describe our customers as consumers (that is in terms of the money we get from their consuming), they are really people with lives to lead in which they influence and are influenced by each other all of the time.

There are three things that I have found really useful in doing this.

1. Throw the channels away. Don't think about what you're going to do or say or communicate until you've got a grip on how your customers influence each other.
2. Second, throw away the differential marketing notion of targeting the 20%. The 'most valuable customer' may not be the one who spends most money with you; indeed your real MVC is going to be the one who influences more sales than others do.
3. Be useful. Don't just go on acting on your own interest with a thin veneer of customer-orientation but instead really work out what would be useful and interesting for customers in their real lives with their real relationships with other people.

More influence?

It's only when you understand the degree to which human beings can be influenced to do things that they might otherwise resist that the penny drops and you start to see the herd mechanic in its rightful place. But just what can other people make us do? How extreme can the behaviour be?

More conformity

Perhaps the most famous example of this is to be found in the work of the late and infamous social psychologist, Stanley Milgram. He was born in New York in 1933 and graduated at 17 from James Monroe High School, alongside the man who was to become just as notorious a psychological researcher, Phil Zimbardo (famous for his prison experiment).

Milgram's inner-city upbringing shaped his thinking and his work – he was interested in the things he saw around him, in the behaviours and processes that govern our everyday lives, in how we affect each other in many ways. He completed a PhD at Harvard under Gordon Allport on the degree to which conformity was a culturally dependent phenomenon (this took him to Norway and France). But it wasn't until he came under the direct influence of Solomon Asch at the Institute for Advanced Study in Princeton that his true work began. Asch, you will remember, was interested in the degree to which an individual's simple judgements about objective reality can be influenced by other people. Milgram took this premise and – using a creativity which still inspires today – turned it into one of the most important experiments in the history of behavioural science. And in doing so revealed just how readily individuals can be influenced by others to do the most dreadful things.

The Milgram experiment

In the summer of 1961, just 12 months after the trial of Adolf Eichmann in Jerusalem, Milgram's experiments started in the basement of Linsley-Chittendon Hall on the old campus of Yale University. In these genteel ivy-league surroundings it is hard to believe that the kind of extreme cruelty that Eichmann was charged with would be shown to be not just possible, but the norm in most of us.

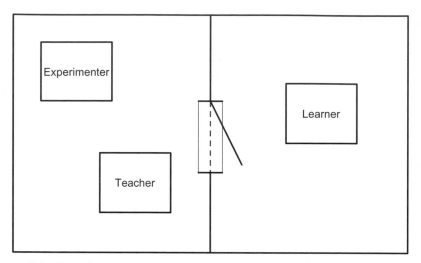

Figure 5.4 *Floor plan of Milgram experiment*

Subjects from a range of educational backgrounds were recruited in a very old-fashioned manner – local newspaper ads and direct mail – and told that the experiment would last one hour, for which they would be paid the princely sum of $4.50.

Here's what you would have experienced if you had been one of the volunteers. You turn up at the allotted time and, together with another subject (actually an actor pretending to be a subject), you are met by the experimenter. You are both told that the experiment is about the effects of punishment on learning. One of you is to play the 'teacher' and the other the 'learner' and you are asked to pick one of two slips of paper to determine who plays which role (in fact, both said 'teacher' but the actor-stooge was briefed to claim he had got the learner role). With a really cute touch, the learner happens to mention his heart condition (a lie) before he is led off into a separate room, which is linked by audio even though you cannot see him. The layout of the two rooms look something like what is shown in Figure 5.4, with experimenter and teacher in one room and into the next, separate from the first two, the learner is banished.

Let the tapes roll

As the teacher, you are now shown the equipment used in the experiment and your role is explained to you. You are to read out a list of paired words first and then just the first item of each pair with four alternatives. The learner is told to press one of four buttons in front of him to select his answer from the four options you give him.

If the learner gets an answer wrong, you are told that the learner is to be given a small electric shock. The experimenter gives you a 45-volt one just to show you what it feels like, but tells you that each time an incorrect answer is given this will increase by 15 volts. Oh yes, and you have to do the punishing.

So, the experiment starts and things go well for a little while. Some correct answers and the occasional wrong one. When this happens you press the punishment controls and hear what sounds like the immediate cry of pain from the other room (in fact this is the output of a tape recorder which is cleverly integrated with the level of shock you administer to the learner, but you're not to know this).

On and on the experiment goes and when you reach a certain level of voltage, the actor next door starts to bang on the wall that divides him from you. He mentions his heart condition again, but the experimenter keeps encouraging you to continue. It's only when the banging stops (at 135 volts) that things get a bit weird. It's likely that you – as so many of the respondents – ask to check on the well-being of the learner at this point but the experimenter urges you on. Either with a simple 'Please continue' or with reference to the needs of the experiment or, indeed, just telling you that you have no choice.

If you still insist on stopping after four successive verbal prods from the experimenter things are wound up. If not, the punishment continues to escalate up and up until you give the learner the maximum 450-volt shock three times.

How good people do bad things

Milgram's genius in the design of this experiment was to show how easily normal, well-adjusted individuals of all ages and classes can be made to do bad things. In his first experiment, 65% of subjects administered the full 450-volt shock (although many did express concerns at doing so and every single respondent stopped at some point and questioned the nature of the experiment). Not one of the initial subjects quit before the 300 volts, despite the screams, the banging on the wall and the knowledge of the learner's heart condition.

Milgram's biographer (Thomas Blass of the University of Maryland, Baltimore County) has shown in a meta-analysis of all the versions of the experiment conducted by Milgram and his associates around the world that there is little variation in the scores – between 61% and 66% of all respondents, no matter what class, culture, gender or age, will all go to the max. That said, when the experimenter is not in the room with the teacher, compliance goes down. Equally, when the learner is right in front of the teacher (and the teacher actually has to put the learner's arm onto a shock plate), a full third of teacher-subjects still complied to the limit.

As Milgram puts it in his own words[7], what was learned about who we are was shocking and proved timely (in the wake of the Eichmann trial):

> With numbing regularity good people were seen to knuckle under the demands of authority and perform actions that were callous and severe. Men who are in everyday life responsible and decent were seduced by the trappings of authority, by the control of their perceptions, and by the uncritical acceptance of the experimenter's definition of the situation, into performing harsh acts. A substantial proportion of people do what they are told to do, irrespective of the content of the act and without limitations of conscience, so long as they perceive that the command comes from a legitimate authority.[7]

Someone we see as an authority can influence us to the extent of committing acts of extreme cruelty and, in anybody's way of thinking, downright evil. Milgram later tried to draw some sense out of the behaviour of American forces' terrible My Lai massacre by referring to the power of military training to harness this capability. The basic thrust of military training, he suggested, was to break down an individual's sense of separateness and make him – through isolation – subject to the influence of authority figures. Subsequent studies by the Pentagon's own psychologists have revealed the truth of this; it is one of the prime objectives of military training to turn the majority of combatants who would not normally be violent into those who will instinctively and without thinking obey the orders of their superiors.

All of which curiously prefigures Desmond Tutu's compassionate musings on the inability of white South Africans to challenge the apartheid system prior to 1994 and the ease with which violent and cruel punishments and attacks were handed out by black insurgents who remained otherwise moral individuals. 'We are all dehumanized and victimized by the system of apartheid,' he writes. 'All of us have suffered.'

Targeting rethought

Choosing your target audience is one of the key building blocks to a marketing strategy. Peter Doyle, the London advertising scene's favourite academic, used to describe it trenchantly as the first of three key steps to building a marketing strategy: who, what, how . . .

In my experience, the choosing rarely happens (except for new product or business launches and even then . . . quite sketchily). What marketers seem to have been taught is to go hell for leather for 'insight' – whatever they mean by that – and not worry about the audience that much. So it is worth spending a few moments thinking quite clearly about targeting, particularly in the light of what we have learned about influence.

Whenever you come to define your target audience, it pays to bear in mind that there are a number of dimensions to this definition.

1. Who your audience actually is (including where they are, etc.).
2. Who they think they are.
3. Who they'd like other people (including you) to think they are.
4. Who influences their decisions.
5. Who *they* think they are, and so on.

Most of the time, we struggle with the first couple and rarely get down to the important stuff in 3, 4, 5 and beyond. Just in the same way that our egotism blinds us to the peer-to-peer influence that shapes individual purchasing behaviour and everything else (i.e. the important stuff in people's lives), so we rarely worry about the influencers, except as an afterthought.

Born unequal?

Each of us is different from every other person who has ever lived in small but important ways. Every man is more like all other men than like his sister or other close female relative. Each of us has a slightly different gene set and each of us has developed through interaction with our environment in different ways. Even identical twins (i.e. those from the very same egg) are different from each other in important ways: in bodies, in minds and in responses to different situations. Given this complexity, it would seem entirely plausible to imagine that some people are going to influence the behaviour of others more than the rest of us. Some people are going to be more influential than you or I. The tricky questions to answer are *Why?* and *How do you identify them?* At the moment there is much debate around this issue and many different views about what to do, so it is worth taking a rounded view on the debate thus far.

Many businesses still cling to the notion that the most influential consumers in any given market are the so-called 'early-adopters' – those who pick up and try new things. It is reassuring in a way, for a business to feel that the most important people share the same degree of arcane knowledge and passion for the product as the product designers at corporate HQ; much better than the ill-informed and frankly only slightly interested mass market.

Sadly, a lot of marketing money has been wasted trying to target these people in specialist magazines and the like. Wasted? Yes, w-a-s-t-e-d. I say this because the studies that we have done with the current hot technologies (mobile telephony, computing, GPS traffic systems, cars and so on) would suggest that early-adopter types are too busy playing with their devices (or with themselves, as my colleague Mark Oldridge suggests) to be able to be much influence on those with a less passionate interest in the products and their technical background. And, of course, the thrill of the latest thing in their hands.

It's a bit like collectors of white-label vinyl; an interesting thing but unless they get to share the contents of the record library with you and me, it is a bit of a dead end (certainly as far as the music is concerned).

One recent study[8] suggests that there is a strong biological basis for our susceptibility to novelty – something to do with variations in the gene for monoamine oxidase A. Also we know that, for most of us, age is negatively correlated with neophilia (the love of new things); the older you get, the less excited you are about new things. Douglas Adams had a very good line about this: technology that appears in your life between birth and your 15th birthday is not technology at all, but just 'natural'; technology that appears between your 15th and 35th birthday is wow-technology; and anything that appears after your 35th birthday is 'unnatural'.

It riles me that our obsession with the leading edge (at the expense of the real influencers in mass populations) continues even among those behavioural scientists studying the subject. Sociologist Colin Campbell[9] identifies three types: *pristinians* (who have an almost hip-hop pathological desire for things that are pristine and fresh); *trailblazing consumers* (largely young men into leading-edge gadgetry); and finally, the third and most common type are 'victims of fashion . . . fickle consumers who succumb to the lure of advertising' (i.e. me and you).

At the soap bar

Another curious idea has its roots in Hollywood. If a famous person wears a certain designer's clothes or uses a particular face cream or drives a certain car then – it is believed – the average individual consumer will follow the celebrity's behaviour because they want to be or look like that celebrity. This has become a cliché of marketing to women (and one which is largely rejected as Polly Eveliegh's study for Ogilvy[10] shows, as the pipe-smoking David Ogilvy suggested nearly 40 years ago, the women in your life aren't that stupid; they know what marketers are trying to do). Most children who grow up in our modern consumerist world learn that celebrities get paid to wear certain labels and drive certain cars. This doesn't stop designers and sneaker companies paying a fortune for the services of a Beckham or a 50 Cent. Celebrities may not be the influential figures that their agents would have us believe but their use does get the product or your marketing activity some much-needed attention (Kevin Kelly, co-founder of *Wired* magazine observed 10 years ago that attention is becoming the scarcest and thus most valuable commodity).

However, there does seem to be something in the generally related heuristic, 'It's what people I admire/respect buy'; this and its broader corollary, 'It's what people like me do/buy/wear/drive.' Hence the repeated use of what an old boss of mine used to call, 'Eat s***, 500 million flies can't be wrong' or some variant of this strategy. But beyond some general insight into how others influence our choices, this doesn't get us very far.

Naturally influential?

Another line of thinking is that some people just have natural influence because of the kind of people that they are. In an important book, *The Influentials*, Ed Keller[11] describes the 10% as naturally influential. Despite the fact that they are neither the most affluent nor the most educated Americans, they are highly influential for lots of people around them because they are well informed and their opinion is trusted. These folk are sought out for their

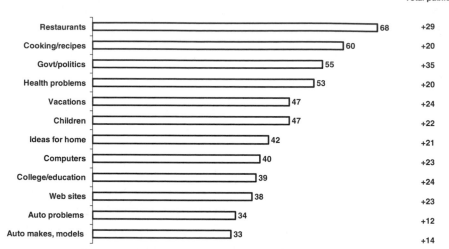

% of Influential Americans ® regularly asked for advice/opinion on topic   Point diff.
Total public

Topic	Value	Point diff. Total public
Restaurants	68	+29
Cooking/recipes	60	+20
Govt/politics	55	+35
Health problems	53	+20
Vacations	47	+24
Children	47	+22
Ideas for home	42	+21
Computers	40	+23
College/education	39	+24
Web sites	38	+23
Auto problems	34	+12
Auto makes, models	33	+14

Figure 5.5 *Keller's influentials*
Also: participatory sports (32% (+20), careers (31%, +10), how to invest (30%, +16)
Roper Reports 2005
Source: 'Influentials Training' presentation by Ed Keller and Jon Berry to the Word of Mouth Basic
Training Conference, Orlando, FL, January 20 2006. Reproduced by permission.

advice on many subjects including products and services: Keller claims[12] that they are twice as likely to be asked for their advice and opinion as the average citizen but this varies over a wide range of subjects (see Figure 5.5).

Certainly, given the unusual social structure of American society (unusual to us Europeans, anyway) with the strong role for church and children's sport and other hobbies, it might well be the case that there are some individuals who are more community-minded and thus influential (the type to teach Sunday school, organize church picnics and also coach Little League teams). But if I understand Keller correctly, these influential types are influential by nature, rather than activity.

Social influencers

A similar line of thinking has led the UK research agency, Opinion Leader Research (OLR) to recognize that the old 'opinion leader' model of the rich and powerful in business, politics and the arts influencing the views and behaviour of the rest of us is not as powerful as might be thought (even though the media constantly utilize both experts and the professionally opinionated to extremes).

Instead, they have developed the notion of 'social influencer' consumers; that is, individuals who shape the opinions and behaviour of their peers.

In every social network or community, there are trusted people others turn to for advice. Opinion Leader Research calls these new trusted figures 'social influencers'. The power of a social influencer lies in their natural ability to persuade others in their peer group or network of their views.

In contrast to the perceived 'spin' of much institutional communication, social influencers are trusted by their peers due to their authenticity and lack of 'agenda'. OLR's Viki Cooke suggested to me that this is more personality- or disposition-based, than anything else:

> It is not about gender or age, occupation or level of education. They are everywhere – you find them in the office, on the building site, in the playground, and in the cafe. We estimate that one in 15 people in the UK are social influencers . . . [in]contrast to their specific peers, social influencers are more articulate, charismatic, and engaged. They tend to be involved in a range of different pursuits and activities, and act as 'connectors' between different social networks. They communicate stances, positions and recommendations through their networks with passion and vigour.

As we will see in Chapter 9 (on co-creativity), OLR have developed a panel of UK social influencers, which they use in a startling 'open source' research methodology for some major British institutions such as the Government, the BBC, and so on.

Anne Stephens of Yellowwood Consulting in South Africa has developed a very similar notion and conducted large-scale surveys to refine her definition; her work is also very usable (certainly a number of large corporations there have deployed it).

Connectedness

In the last few of these approaches, the degree to which an individual crosses social and interest groups seems very important. In other words, the degree to which they are 'connected' seems both a result of their personality and a source of their influence itself.

Malcolm Gladwell's first bestseller, *The Tipping Point*,[13] uses the work of network theorists to show how his core thesis – that behaviour spreads like disease through populations by network connections – impacts on a whole range of mass behavioural phenomena. In particular his work is rooted on the pioneering work of one Stanley Milgram (yes, him again).

One of the subjects that fascinated Milgram is how our connections with each other affect the way we live, not just in urban environments but across the country and beyond; how we connect with each other through webs of influence. In this area of study, just as before, Milgram's creativity in experimental design shed a whole new light on the subject.

In his first pilot study (which is documented in an undated paper 'Results of Communication Project') Milgram sent 60 letters to various members of the public (rather than psychology undergrads, which is the universe on which too many psychology studies are based) in Wichita, Kansas. Each subject was asked to forward a letter by hand to personal acquaintances who the subject felt might be able to reach the target (the wife of a divinity student) either directly or indirectly better than the subject him- or herself. In this first study, only 50 subjects took the first step and of these only three reached completion. However, after some further experimental adjustment (e.g. the perceived value of the parcel was an important factor in motivating the senders), a number of useful findings emerged from further studies.

First, for chains that reached completion, the mean number of hands that the parcel passed through was six. Hence the notion of six degrees of separation – we are connected to each other much more closely than we think: the academic mathematical world's 'Erdos' number (which uses shared published papers as steps to the great Paul Erdos) and the entertainment world's 'six steps from Kevin Bacon' (where those who have acted with KB count as a step).

Second, what Milgram called 'the funnelling effect' – that is most completed trails tended to pass through the same few hands at some point. Some people seem to act as 'super-connectors'; that is, they are people who connect different social groups and networks together.

Meet Lois

Gladwell's original *New Yorker* article[14] (on which his later book was based) introduces us to Lois Weisberg, Chicago grandmother and super-connector. Whoever tells their tale about first meeting her, describes the same high-energy experience:

Lois (everyone calls her Lois) is invariably smoking a cigarette and drinking one of her dozen or so daily cups of coffee. She will have been up until two or three the previous morning and up again at seven or seven-thirty, because she hardly seems to sleep. In some accounts – particularly if the meeting took place in winter – she'll be wearing her white, fur-topped Dr Zhivago boots with gold tights; but she may have on her platform tennis shoes, or the leather jacket with the little studs on it, or maybe an outrageous piece of costume jewellery, and, always, those huge rhinestone-studded glasses that make her big eyes look positively enormous.

But her dress sense isn't the thing that really characterizes Lois; it's her constant connecting of people and worlds. She has the amazing ability to connect with anyone and everyone.

Her little black book includes doctors, writers, lawyers, park-lovers (she helped save a park), train buffs (ditto the railways), politicians, flea-market fans, musicians, visual artists (she was the driving force behind the Block 37 gallery project which involves young people and the arts in an unusual way), architects, hospitality-industry people, and so the list goes on. As Gladwell puts it, 'Lois is to Chicago what Burgess Meredith is to the movies.'

We all know people like this. At the school gates, in the workplace, in our interest groups and clubs and in our churches. My late friend Andrew was just one such – from Formula 1 drivers to nuclear scientists, from art-directors to actuaries. In fact, all of the members of the band I play in were brought together by Andrew. Not in any calculating way, but just because – as with Lois – this is what he did in life.

Targeting rethought (2)

So you could take from Gladwell and co. the simple conclusion that all we have to do is find these new super-connectors and target them. Certainly, this is the business proposition of Keller, OLR and the like.

But is it true that these are the only people who have influence on individual behaviour? This seems a bit far-fetched, particularly when you look how actual behaviour is influenced. Perhaps looking at things from this bird's-eye perspective – in terms of networks and society at large – loses some of the practical application that those of us need who want to influence mass behaviour of a particular sort, or in a particular area. In other words, is looking so high the end of the matter, or does the idiosyncratic behaviour of an individual reveal additional insight?

This was precisely the task that Fiona Blades,[15] of the direct marketing agency Claydon Heeley Jones Mason, and Stephen Phillips of Spring Research set for themselves: to examine who influenced specific purchases for identified individuals. For the initial study, cars, golf clubs and mortgages were chosen as suitable areas for study. The approach focussed on a specific behaviour – a purchase of a named item – and then tracked back through all of the influences (media, personal and other) which seemed to have been in play in this particular purchase.

The qualitative research methodology chosen was iterative. First, a purchaser was interviewed for an hour about the purchase, tracking back from the purchase event to the initial purchase thought. Any named influences that emerged were tracked down – be they media or personal influences. In other words, all of the people who were identified as an influence on the purchase were also interviewed. And their influences also. Here's one example.

Alison's new Mercedes[16]

One day, Alison found herself the proud new owner of a Mercedes A class. But a bit surprised at the same time; she had bought a Ford Fiesta only some seven months previously. What's more, she was very pleased with the Fiesta but somehow found herself buying a new Mercedes. She certainly didn't need a new car, but she bought one. How did this happen? How could someone be influenced to do this? (see Figure 5.6.)

The research revealed that the primary influence on this was Alison's husband Nick (and through him Nick's ex-boss, Gary). Nick is a car fanatic – he spends weekends with his autoporn both on- and offline, 'dream-building' as Alison puts it. One rainy Saturday, Nick suggested that they visit a Merc showroom. There, Alison took a test-drive and within two weeks the car was sitting outside their house.

Nick – it turns out – had spent some time with Gary in the weeks before that rainy Saturday. Gary already owned a Mercedes CLK and had just bought his wife an A-class as a surprise present. Nick readily admitted the hidden influence of Gary's advocacy of the Mercedes brand on his direct influence of Alison.

But another line of influence was also clear but also negative: Alison's sister-in-law had just bought a Renault Scenic. This prompted Alison to think about a bigger car – like an MPV – but she felt it would be antagonistic

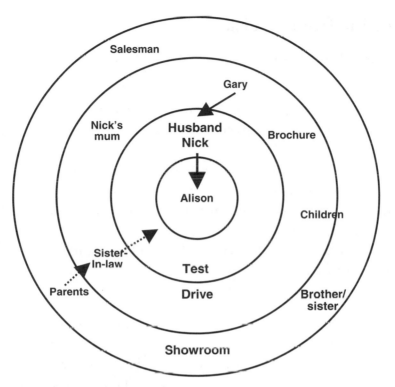

Figure 5.6 *Alison's new Mercedes influence map*
Source: 'Decision Watch UK' , Winner, Best New Paper, MRS Awards 2005
Fiona Blades, Claydon Heeley Jones Mason, & Stephen Phillips, Spring Research

to copy. However, this did make it possible to consider something of the A-class's style and size.

When the team interviewed Gary, it became clear that he too was subject to influence both of other people and things (such as media messages). His path to purchase was curiously long (almost two years) but marked by what Blades calls 'the littered wrecks of other brands'.

Gary had been considering a Toyota Rav4: he liked the styling, the look and the price. But a chance meeting with an acquaintance that was driving a Rav4 put him off, not just this model but also any car purchase. A throw-away comment about gear problems sufficed, even though Gary could not know what his acquaintance's automotive knowledge was. It was enough.

Some months later, Gary was considering the A-class. The actual purchase was fast-tracked by two influences: first, a price-ad in a magazine and second, positive comments on the A-class by two friends. Gary went from considera-tion to purchase in two weeks, just as Alison did subsequently.

Learning from Decision Watch

This approach gives us a profound and powerful set of insights.

1. It shows us how approaching individual purchases from the point of view of influence allows us to place what consumers do alongside what we do to them.
2. It shows us how influence is a game of 'snakes and ladders' as Blades puts it – influence can be both positive and negative (this undermines the traditional step-by-step customer journey model that most marketers prefer to deploy still).
3. And perhaps most of all, there are different kinds of influencers on purchase decisions.

Blades and Phillips identify seven types of influencers, including: *the researcher* who enjoys gathering information regardless of category. He or she enables the purchaser to access relevant info easily. And *the reassurer* who reinforces the purchase decision because they are seen to know what's right for the purchaser. This means that the purchaser can check if their choice is right. Of course, any one individual (like Gary to Alison) can play a number of influence roles (which ones would you say he plays?). And these headings are in some way arbitrary and conceptual – the important thing is to understand the nature of influence on any one purchase decision.

Blades and Phillips go on to describe how this has led them to recut database information to create separate influence-audiences and to develop marketing communications programmes which take the herd influence as its starting point rather than something nice to have. (why *do* all automotive manufacturers want to talk to motor sport fans? Come on, please try harder than that!)

But the profound truth that Blades and Phillips have unearthed is this: understanding purchase from the point of view of the herd is the place to start in defining your target. Who influences the purchase and in what way? Once you have this down pat, you can begin to make interesting and powerful change programmes. And you can begin to put word of mouth – the most interesting and tangible form of C2C influence – to work for you. But that is the subject of the next chapter.

What this chapter has shown

'Influence' – peer-to-peer, consumer-to-consumer – is much more important than 'persuasion' (business-to-consumer or -to-employee). However self-contained and self-determining you might feel, you and I and the rest of the human race are designed in such a way that what other people do, say and think has a profound and continuous effect up our own actions, thoughts and feelings. This challenges many of our underlying assumptions about how to bring about changes in mass behaviour. About who to target and the importance of the businesses actions.

The next chapter explores what is known about the most tangible (and frankly the most trendy) form of influential behaviour: word of mouth. At the heart of this lies a fundamental misunderstanding about its nature.

Highly recommended (this might make more sense later).

Some questions for marketing

1. How does it feel to learn that – like Marky Mark – your role in bringing about changes in mass behaviour is much less important than that of the members of your audience on each other?
2. How does this change your definition of your job in marketing, communications or government? For example, if marketing used to be understood as the identification and satisfaction of consumer needs, what should it be now? How would you rephrase it?
3. How does it change the things you measure to monitor the success of your business and its attempts to change mass behaviour? For example, currently we tend to measure at the interface between B (business) and C (customer). In research, we look at things such as reach, persuasion, recall and so on. In reporting we focus on the effect our activities have had on individual sales. What might you add to/replace in this list?
4. Maybe I've been a bit harsh on one-to-one marketing. To what extent does it affect the mechanic behind mass behaviour (i.e. C2C influence)? How can you shape what you do to do so more often and more profoundly?
5. Which is the most useful of the 'influence' targeting models for you? Do you think influence is a fixed characteristic of an individual or does it change over time? Does it vary by category?

6

Key Principle No. 3:
Us-Talk

What this chapter will cover

Word of Mouth (WoM) is an increasingly important influence on individual behaviour and purchase decisions. However, current fashionable interest in WoM hides a fundamental misunderstanding: it is neither new, nor limited to responses to the faddish WoM marketing techniques being increasingly deployed. No, WoM is merely the most tangible and observable form of herd influence behaviour, which lies behind mass behaviour. It is – and always has been – as natural as breathing to we super-social apes. 'Exogenous' (marketing-stimulated) WoM is important but much less so than 'endogenous' (naturally-arising or system-generated) WoM. Why WoM metrics provide a good indication of general business health.

*The mass do not now take their opinions from dignitaries
in Church or State, from ostensible leaders, or from books.
Their thinking is done for them by men much like themselves,
addressing or speaking in their name, on the spur of
the moment . . .*

John Stuart Mill

Don't believe the hype

The music industry is no stranger to hype and spin, to packaging and plugging individual artists to appeal to certain audiences, to extracting as much money as possible from its chosen consumers (in terms of record sales, concert tickets, merchandise and so on). However, in the last 12 months it has had a major wake-up call – a challenge, if you like, to its basic business model. And all of this generated by four unlikely lads from one of Britain's less salubrious Northern cities.

The Arctic Monkeys got famous themselves, rather than pay for the financial might of a major record label to browbeat consumers into buying their records. Or rather they got their fans to do it for them. In the space of six months, t'Arctics went from nowhere to cooler than cool. They managed two British number ones, a number one album which also just happens to be the fastest-selling ever debut, six major awards (Best New Act 2005 Muso awards, Best British Breakthrough Act 2006 Brit awards, Best New Band, Best British Band and Best track 2006 NME awards and, hotly tipped, they won the Mercury Music prize). But to paraphrase the *Sun* newspaper headline – it was the fans what done it.

The band started in the time-honoured fashion, local boys discovering guitars and girls and building a strong local following in the pubs and clubs of their home town. Alex Turner (lead guitar, vocals and lyrical genius) met drummer Matt Helders at Barnsley College in 2002 and both decided to ask Santa for instruments that Christmas. They started rehearsing early in 2003 in a warehouse in Neepsend on the outskirts of Sheffield and their first public appearance was in June of that year at The Grapes in Sheffield City Centre. They continued gigging and rehearsing nearby for the next two months, managing to build up a considerable following in the area.

However, what changed things for the band was their practice of giving away demos (rough recordings) of their music at gigs. They made their music freely available and allowed if not actually encouraging fans to share it with each other. Many fan sites on myplace.com etc. started to upload the music and make it available for free for download, and these made their way on to mainstream radio stations – the like of Radio 1 and XFM. In particular their first official EP, released on their own label, 'Five minutes with Arctic Monkeys', was limited to 1,000 CDs and 500 seven-inch vinyl copies but was available to download from iTunes and from a number of fan webpages and sites.

In taking this route, the band studiously avoided the interests of the major record labels (until recently, record company scouts were banned from their gigs. As Alex put it, 'We've got this far without them – why should we let them in?'). The band also shunned traditional publicity (little is still known about the private lives of the four band members, apart from their ages and the fact that they still live with their parents. How is it then that Alex could have been voted coolest male on the planet by *NME* readers?).

Children of the revolution

By the summer of 2005, the word had spread and the band was in demand for appearances on festival stages – talked up by the specialist music press and the *NME* in particular. Their performances were received by enthusiastic crowds and press alike, but what characterized them was the fact that the crowds of many thousands sang along to songs that had hardly had any exposure: they had only been available either on one limited edition EP or on the Internet as downloadable demos. The same thing occurred in October 2005 when the band sold out the London Astoria in minutes (this is a venue which more established acts struggle to fill) and the 2,000 or more fans squeezed inside sang along to all of the songs.

Eventually, the band signed to a small label, Domino Records, rather than to one of the majors. This proved a sound base camp for their assault on the UK charts. Their first single after signing, 'I bet you look good on the dance-floor', was released on 17 October 2005 and sold 38,962 copies, beating Robbie Williams and McFly, two of the dominant chart acts of recent years, to the number one slot. Their second single, 'When the sun goes down' (originally called 'Scummy man') was released on 16 January 2006 and repeated the trick, selling 38,922 copies. Their album, *Whatever People Say I am, That's What I'm Not*, was released on 23 January to a similar enthusiastic response. On the first day, the album sold 118,501 physical copies and 363,735 in the first week, making it the fastest-selling debut rock album. While the US response was weaker (only 24 in the Billboard charts) this still repres-ented the best ever debut from a British indie act. And the US debut live performance at the South By South West festival in Texas in March 2006 was sold out several times over. Official wristbands for entry were exchanging hands for over $1,000 a go, so hefty was the demand from the music industry's brightest and best to witness Alex and the Boys, the coolest band on the planet at the moment, for the first time on American soil.

So why is the record industry so scared?

The music industry, like so many of the so-called creative industries, may be populated by very creative individuals, but it operates in an extremely con-servative way – thanks largely to the consolidation of ownership in recent years and the application of traditional marketing and business thinking to satisfy the shareholders and minimize the risks in what is – like any business – an unpredictable environment. Familiar?

Rather than risk novelty, Artists and Relations (A&R) executives seek to buy the next big thing (rather than develop it – this is the role of the inde-pendent labels) and all of them at the moment are seeking to find copies of the James Blunt phenomenon (last year's big thing). They enslave individual acts into contracts with huge advances (which means basically a loan – the artist pays for their own recordings and the label acts as bank). They cosset and infantilize them with the promise of fame and riches and various other sweeteners (as Bill Nighy recommends in Richard Curtis's sentimentality fest,

Love Actually, 'Don't buy drugs; become a popstar and they give you them'!).
In effect, labels are little more than mortgage companies but they feel they
'own' the artists and their work given the investment they make in them.
No wonder a number of high-profile stars such as Prince and George Michael
have taken legal action against their labels in the last decade. Then, if the
music fails to sell sufficiently to recoup the investment, the labels drop the
artists suddenly and with little empathy for the misery or in particular the
dependency that they have created.

Just as conservative as this is their approach to product format and distribution. Products come only in regular formats (either you pay a premium
to get a single – the equivalent of the old seven inch vinyl – or you have
to buy the whole album). Very few labels have experimented with other
product formats as yet. As you'd expect, they've pursued the blockbuster
marketing campaign and price promotion to keep their volumes up in the
face of new retail distribution and pressures from the grocery retailers
(supermarkets).

Moreover, the mainstream of the industry has been very slow to wake up
to the reality of downloading[1] and this has cost many of them dear. On 12
January 2006, Alan Giles[2], the CEO of HMV, one of the UK's biggest music
retailers was tipped to resign following a poor Christmas performance by the
company's stores. Among his many mistakes was a myopia around physical
distribution.

'A year ago I was saying the Internet would plateau at about 10% of this
market . . . Now I say that I was wrong. I just don't know now how far it will
go. This is a brave new world for retailers'.

Scary Mary

The rise of the Arctic Monkeys has scared the industry for simple and understandable reasons: The band developed their own national fan base without
industry help; the band used its own 'product' (as the industry calls
music . . . ugh!) as a means to get its fan base to spread the word and gave it
away for free (shock horror!); or, rather, the band did not prevent its fans
doing what they wanted to do – share their favourite stuff with their friends
for free and rant and rave about their passions. Indeed, most of the downloads
are from fansites which are driven by chat and discussion rooms rather than
any commercial purpose (and the downloads are a happy addendum).

As Jarvis Cocker[3], another one of Sheffield's favourite son's puts it, what scares the industry is that the band's success is:

> real . . . I think it's very important because they [the Monkeys] have done it without trying . . . the only reason people have got into it is because they've listened to it and they like it, so it's something real. I guess all the music industry will probably think 'how can we emulate that or what can we do?' I think there's nothing that they can do about it because it's something that has happened naturally, there's no way to apply spin doctorism to it.

'Something that has happened naturally', exactly. As opposed to something engineered and manipulated by the labels. The excitement and commitment of the fans to share their passion is what has made the Arctics so big – of course, the music is top-notch and the live performances memorable – but the biggest driver of fandom (and therefore of the sales byproduct) is the fans' own word of mouth to each other. And this is crucial – selling records seems to be of secondary importance. The Arctic Monkey's phenomenon is really all about the fans and not about records at all. And as if to prove the point the fansites keep growing – my current favourite is one[4] which produces remixes of the band's tracks with other current indie 'choons', all of which are free to download.

Not only is the record label (and all its machinery for garnering airplay and physical distribution) made largely unnecessary by the Monkeys and their fans but also the selfish and exploitative view of fans as mere purchasers has blinded the industry to the real possibilities for a band such as the Monkeys. Privately, I also suspect that for the cool hunters that populate the darker corners of the music industry, the DIY nature of this phenomenon is the scariest thing. What are all these execs for, if not to create such successes?

What can we learn from the Arctic Monkeys' success?

The central lesson of the rise of the Arctic Monkeys is this: at a time when those deploying the traditional marketing toolkit are struggling, word-of-mouth (WoM) recommendation is capable of driving enormous and rapid changes in mass behaviour. As such, it scares those organisations (and the folk who toil for them and their financial stakeholders) who rely on the traditional toolkit to create a sense of certainty and predictability – organizations like the big beasts of the music industry.

The question is what to do about this? They – and you – may simply see the Arctic Monkey word-of-mouth phenomenon as something that's *there for the copying*, as Jarvis Cocker suggests. Something to be ripped off and emulated in a cynical manner (even the Rolling Stones now have a myspace site!). If this is how you feel, then take a deep breath: *you have missed the point entirely.*

Boom time for WoM

Word of mouth is undoubtedly the groovy thing in marketing right now; there's a whole lot of buzz around buzz-marketing (as it is also called). As *Advertising Age* puts it:

> buzz, or word of mouth is on the tip of the tongue of every marketer that's sceptical about just how effective its ad dollars are, particularly now that the age of interruption marketing has come and gone. The new era of consumer control is well suited to take advantage of ordinary conversation, the kind of discourse that's actually heard above the din of competing marketing messages[5]

Ed Keller (Mr Influential) and Simon Chadwick cite[6] Jonah Bloom[7], Executive Editor of *Advertising Age*, when they say that word of mouth is not the next big thing, but 'a big thing right now'.

It is not difficult to see why WoM is suddenly so hot. As every market becomes more and more competitive so traditional media costs spiral upwards; at the same time the media landscape is fragmenting. The major broadcast options are crumbling: US networks lost 25% of their audience and in the UK the main commercial TV channel, ITV, continues to haemorrhage its viewer base. Demographic changes, the explosion of new channels and media and last but not least the rise of the EPG devices (like TiVo and Sky+) have all in their own way contributed to this trend. As if to make things tougher, marketers are being put under more and more pressure to justify their budgets to their colleagues. So while a procession of 'silver bullet' solutions has been paraded in front of marketers in recent years, each and every one has failed to deliver the promises made for it. No wonder marketers are becoming more and more sceptical of any traditional approach.

Word-of-mouth marketing seems to offer something completely different – a media- (and cost-) free medium. Moreover, a medium that suffers from none of the scepticism that others exhibit. A clean, cheaper, more powerful and – to use the vocabulary of the old model – persuasive channel to generating sales.

And of course, at heart we all instinctively recognise the truth of the fact that if people are talking about you, then you must be famous (more than one creative colleague of mine still uses the 'pub-test' to evaluate proposed work, the key question being, 'will they talk about it down the pub?'). So the WoM-ers may be onto something. But have they got things down right?

What do we (*really*) know about WoM?

Unlike other marketing fads, the early pioneers of WoM marketing and market research are making the effort to share their knowledge and insight. They have been joined by latecomers in official bodies like WOMMA[8] (the Word of Mouth Marketing Association, founded in late 2004). For once a trade body is being useful – their website has a number of really useful studies and how-to guides available for free download. Their membership is not limited to the enlightened few either: major fast-moving consumer-goods (FMCG) players such as Kimberly Clark, S.C. Johnson, Kraft, Nestlé and other marketing giants such as Microsoft, GM and Discovery are mixed in with major ad agency and PR networks. The UK branch is similarly cosmopolitan – with academics, on- and offline marketers and their agencies – all meeting to share and debate the key themes and issues around word of mouth.

Academics and practitioners are still staking out the ground: a number of disputes about key principles have not yet been resolved (e.g. are some people more prone to generate word of mouth than others? Ed Keller,[9] AKA (Mr Influential), says yes; others such as the authors of 'Where's Debbie?' disagree and suggest that most adults are generators/transmitters in at least one category). However, in the last two years, a wealth of basic data has been collected which allow us to establish some basic facts about marketing-led word of mouth.

---

4 Big word-of-mouth facts to tell your friends

Fact 1. WoM is more important than other purchase influences
Fact 2. WoM is getting more and more important over time
Fact 3. WoM operates in both B2B and B2C
Fact 4. WoM is a global – not just a US – phenomenon

WoM Fact 1. Word of mouth is more important than other influences on individual purchases

A number of studies over the years have shown that individuals claim that what other people say is more influential on their purchasing behaviour than more direct means deployed by firms trying to change that behaviour (such as advertising). A lot of the early work was done in the USA and reveals that *even at the time we think of as the peak of mass media marketing*, the USA was actually a word-of-mouth market. For example back in 1955, Columbia sociologists Lazarsfeld and Katz[10] estimated that word of mouth was seven (!) times more powerful than newspaper or magazine ads in motivating brand-switching. Two decades later, the Roper Organization showed that word of mouth was mentioned as the best source of information about new products and services (67%) compared to advertising (53%) or editorial content (47%). A Cap Gemini study[11] into the influences on automotive purchasing showed that 71% of the 700 respondents pointed towards WoM (compared to only 15% for TV advertising).

More recently in Europe, the same point has been made again and again – Mediaedge CIA's data suggests the influence is acknowledged by UK consumers to be of the same order.

Even if we take into account the self-reporting effect (which self-respecting consumer will admit to dropping £20,000 on a car as a result of seeing a TV commercial? What would that say about them to the researcher?), the absolute power of word of mouth as the most immediate influence on purchase is difficult to argue with. The great and the good of the business world certainly think so: McKinsey have estimated that word of mouth drives two thirds of the US economy.

WoM Fact 2. Word of mouth is getting more and more important over time

Some WoM-ers talk as if word of mouth is some new phenomenon; as if it had spontaneously emerged as a result of the efforts of genius; as if human nature had suddenly changed in response to the wiles and guile of modern commerce. Which is of course nonsense (see below for why) and tells us more about the narrow and self-serving mindset of marketers today than it does about human nature in general.

However, public opinion survey findings (for what they are worth) do seem to be suggesting that word of mouth is now more and more important than ever before[12]. The Roper Organization has shown that over the last 30 years, word of mouth has increased dramatically in its perceived value as a source of information and ideas about new products, as far as US consumers are concerned (from 67% of respondents to 91%). Over the same time period, advertising and editorial are steady or slightly down in consumers' eyes. Roper themselves point to the 1990s as the period in which this change happened (they measure this kind of thing regularly) – it was in this decade that trust in traditional sources (government, politics and business) started to slip.

It's almost as if consumers have 'looked behind the curtain' and seen the pathetic truth of those they previously respected and feared. Most of us involved in communicating to mass markets will recognize the truth of this. When I used to conduct a lot of focus groups, it was still just about possible to pretend that respondents were naïve and guileless; cynical respondents were the exception rather than the rule (we simply ignored them).

The same explanation is echoed elsewhere – in their fifth Annual report on trust among the world's opinion leaders, the communications company Edelman say this:

> People are replacing their trust in traditional authorities with trust in each other. They create personalized 'webs of trust', cherry-picking information from sources and people they relate to – colleagues, friends, family. And they now require multiple exposures to a message from a variety of sources before they will accept it.[13]

In other words, word-of-mouth has always been a filter on information that enters a social group from a third party (particularly via paid-for communications) but as we trust authority less and less, the filter has greater and greater power.

This challenges our traditional view of communications as being some kind of *transmission of data* or argument (company–consumer, company–shareholder, company–employee and government–citizen) in which all that matters is reach, impact, recall and persuasiveness of the data-transmission vehicle. Russell Davies has a marvellous visual example of this way of thinking about mass communication from his time working with Microsoft at Wieden & Kennedy. In the top left corner is a circle representing the all-powerful company; in the bottom right corner is a stick man representing the helpless and grateful consumer. An arrow flows from the company to the consumer, an arrow that is labelled 'data-streaming'. Now, clearly communication doesn't work that way – it isn't 'data', it isn't 'streamed' and the important interface is not company–consumer but we, like the folk at Microsoft, mostly would prefer to think that it does work like that. It's easier, neater and it gives us the sense that we are in control of communication.

Edelman[14] underlines this with the notion of the 'democratisation of influence':

> The credibility of 'a person like yourself' continues to increase both in the US (from 22% in '02 to 56% in '05) and in Europe (33% in '03 to 53% in '05) and along with independent experts such as 'doctors or healthcare specialists' are considered the most credible experts.

WoM Fact 3. Word of mouth operates in both B2B and B2C

Business-to-business (B2B) practitioners have long suffered the patronizing attitude of those working in consumer markets – somehow marketing and communication are supposed to be purer in the latter world. Maybe this arrogance is rooted in the undeniable fact that much marketing theory and practice originated in FMCG (and that it is much harder to do anything but communications management in B2B marketing, given the complexity and economics of B2B businesses). But maybe the differences aren't as great as B2B specialists in their attempts at self-justification would aver – certainly, the axiom that TV is irrelevant to B2B marketing has been debunked by the success of IBM's e-business and on-demand work with Ogilvy. On the other hand, while the idea of relationship marketing emerged from the B2B space as a way of building long-term sustainable sales growth through an intimate relationship between supplier companies and their customers, it has proved very difficult to make the economics work in mass markets like most consumer goods.

All of this said, it is clear that word of mouth is just as important in B2B as in the consumer markets examined by the likes of Keller and MediaEdge CIA.[15] Just consider the rise of word of mouth as marketing discipline – it's only because other people are using it and talking about it that we really bother with it at all. Equally as IBM and Ogilvy know all too well, reputation is not just a matter of persuading lots of individuals (who in any case won't be able to make the decision for a multimillion dollar computing contract) but is a group and word-of-mouth phenomenon. What your colleagues, peers and friends say about your providers is key both to getting consideration from B2B buyers but also in making purchase decisions. That's why IBM use TV. Doh!

As Jeremy Bullmore put it in his seminal pamphlet, Posh Spice and Persil[16], for someone or something to be 'famous' requires more than lots of individuals knowing about it; it entails each individual knowing that other people think and feel the same (and one of the ways we learn about something is through what other people say). In the business services sector, trade publications, the Internet and water-cooler interactions all fuel the conversations around suppliers and build or break the reputations of individuals and businesses.

Moreover, just as consumers are now much more exposed to business-to-business information (one thinks of the employee relationship struggles of Walmart and the management trials at Marks and Spencer in this context), so business decisions are often influenced by consumer-orientated word-of-mouth. My own experience in studying the effectiveness of Royal Mail marketing activity revealed a significant effect on business's use of mail deriving from consumer-focussed communication.

WoM Fact 4. Word of mouth is a global – and not just a North American – phenomenon

While the US marketing community have led the world in establishing the power of word of mouth on behaviour, there is ample evidence of the power of word of mouth in other countries.

'Where's Debbie?' provides a useful set of data to demonstrate that the UK is just as prone to the word-of-mouth effect as the USA and that it is also growing in importance (Figure 6.1).

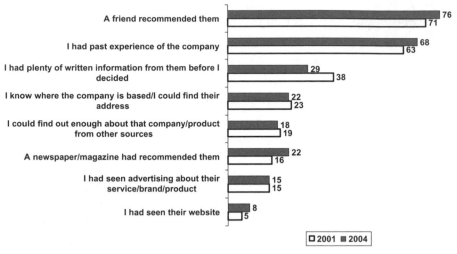

Figure 6.1   *Where's Debbie? WoM in the UK*
Source: Where's Debbie? (2004). Reproduced by permission of Mediaedge:cia UK

Keller and Chadwick[17] also cite the work of Integration® IMC – an international consultancy which provides business customers with the means to compare the clout and the cost-effectiveness of the different communication channels: mass media, one to one (i.e., word of mouth), point of sale, point of consumption, sponsorship, etc. Over 6500 brands have been studied in 54 countries.

> Across a variety of consumer products and services, and across geographies, Integration confirms the importance of word of mouth. Word of mouth is globally reported among the most influential contacts audited through Integration's MCA methodology. It scores 1.5 times more influence than the average contact across all categories and markets

In UK travel services, word of mouth from friends, family and colleagues ranked third out of 27 different contacts. In French personal hygiene products, recommendations from friends ranked seventh in importance out of 35 consumer contact points. And in a German luxury personal care product, Integration found that recommendations from friends/relatives were the sixth most important form of consumer contact out of 35 items.

The film industry has long known this and sought to generate word of mouth by big opening weekends and good reviews. Of course, the Internet has thrown up any number of intermediary sites that comment and review films at test screenings; specific tactics have evolved to deal with these.

As we look around the world, it becomes clear that word of mouth is more and more important; both more than we realized (because we've never really looked at things this way before) and also than it used to be. It is as much a part of the political world (both democratic and extreme – terrorism works in this way, not just in terms of recruitment but in the way it achieves its effect). Which should not be a surprise to you if you have been paying attention to what I have been saying in this book – word of mouth is as natural as breathing. It is what we humans do. So wherever there are humans, we can expect word of mouth. For good or ill.

New opportunity, traditional thinking?

Sadly, the way the marketing community has embraced this new opportunity is predictably conservative – as conservative as the music industry's response, in fact. It tends to see WoM as a new 'channel' (that is, a means to send messages or extract money from punters), rather than an aspect of the underlying mechanic of mass behaviour. It sees it as something separate and discrete from other marketing activities (or in some cases as a top-up to existing activities).

Building on this, a number of entrepreneurial types have launched bespoke WoM marketing companies to help the uninitiated through this scary new world. As previously with TV advertising, Direct Marketing and web-based communication, all you need is this particular silver bullet (fired by an expert hand, of course) – nothing else matters, nothing else is of any value, nothing else is 'up-to-date'.

Which would be fair enough, if only WoM was a separate kind of thing, requiring specialist tools and skills. But it is far from new (human beings have always relied on each other's recommendations and censures). And it is far from specialist. WoM is merely the most observable and tangible form of the underlying mechanic of mass behaviour: peer-to-peer influence. And, as such it underpins all marketing activity – and all attempts to change mass behaviour.

How did everything get viral?

'Viral' marketing seems to be the communications industries' response of choice to increased awareness of the power of word of mouth. The major advertising festivals such as Cannes, Clio and D&AD all seem to be awash with 'viral' creative work (by which I mean cool and often funny adverts or film clips that we can send on to our friends) and the executives who sit in darkened rooms judging the quality of work of their peers seem particularly taken by 'viral' work. Some of it is indeed very striking and seems to be associated with strong sales success – Crispin Porter Bogusky's very funny 'subservient chicken' work for KFC is one much heralded example. But is this because of some industry-wide conversion to the power of C2C marketing? Do they really believe that what matters is the extent that creative communications can encourage customers to market to each other? Or does something else lie behind this newfound passion?

Put simply – as client professionalism becomes greater and greater, as procurement and measurement procedures limit the scope for the real creativity that attracts new clients, as the government and consumer lobbyists seek ever greater controls over marketing communications content, *creative agencies see the viral space as a rule-free environment in which to do the shocking, talk-worthy work which makes or breaks their own reputations*; a place in which the wild and crazy and weird stuff that will attract attention to the business and its principles can be done. A place where the newer technologies – the Internet and mobile telephony – can really be exploited. To create word of mouth for its creators?

Of course, the viral game is being seen through by the public. Many of us just delete emails from our viral-obsessed acquaintances without opening them. So the WoM-ers are trying other means to generate their buzz. 'We now want to seed social networks like chatrooms, offer a good bit of content and use it to get people to register on a site to download it voluntarily', says Rana Reeves of Jackie Cooper PR[18]. Another approach is to recruit communities of semi-professional consumer advocates yourself, such as FMCG giant Procter & Gamble have done. 'Tremor' is a teen consumer advocate site – teenagers are encouraged to trial and spread the word of new products among their peers; 'Vocalpoint' is the 'mom'-targeted equivalent. While in both these cases, the branding and intent are clear and transparent, this is not always the case. Some of the WoM-er tricks are less than tasteful.

A wolf in sheep's clothing

So what happens when our attempts to generate word of mouth get revealed as artificial and company-generated? One such example was highlighted in spring 2006 around the Johnson & Johnson skin product 'Holiday Skin' – essentially a moisturiser with a tiny amount of fake tan. According to two British newspapers (*Mail on Sunday*[19] and *The Scotsman*), the National Consumer Council has identified concerted efforts by agents of J&J and a key competitor St Tropez to infiltrate chat rooms in disguise and 'plug' their products (in contravention of other marketing regulations to underage consumers in the UK).

One posting, for example, on girland.com (from the dubiously named 'anonymous') asks out of the blue:

'Hiya, I was wondering if anyone has seen the advert for Johnson's holiday skin moisturiser on TV. It is meant to be good for the skin and leads to a natural looking tan . . . thanks!

Not to be outdone, in the middle of a discussion about tanning, Dokta posted the following:

'Try St Tropez, the Number 1 brand in alternative tanning products'

The Mail on Sunday points the finger at the Girls Intelligence Agency[20] (the GIA, geddit?), based in California. This research and consulting business uses all the language of the secret service to find ways of understanding and influencing teen and preteen girls. It claims to have some 40,000 youngsters ('agents') on its books who will not only reveal their interests, behaviours and lifestyles to businesses who pay but also work together to seed new products and services in 'slumber parties'. No mention is made of the chatroom infiltration on their website but this kind of behaviour is not unknown in other sectors.

Equally, it is worth noting that by the time the Arctic Monkeys made their first few live appearances in the US (for example on the *Saturday Night Live* showcase), the US audience were spotting the spin – postings after the show were much more cynical and negative than the band might have expected from their UK experience. Now, I suspect that this is nothing to do with differing musical tastes but with the US audience being more aware of the Arctic Monkeys Phenomenon than their UK counterparts could possibly be (few US consumers were exposed to the buzz around the Arctics directly; most had only indirect, second-hand reports of the spin). Marketing's attempts to generate word of mouth were clearly distinguishable from the 'naturally' arising version. Whether in skincare or rock music, the truth is the same: even if 'real' and 'marketing' word of mouth look similar at first, as soon as the latter is revealed for what it is, it suffers by comparison.

The wrong end of the stick?

The way the industry is discussing word of mouth is largely confined to the result of what the industry itself does ('exogenous' WoM) and not what arises, flourishes and spreads without it ('endogenous' WoM). This is why it seems to many that WoM is a new phenomenon; why WoM has been invented only recently; why it was created by those clever marketing, advertising and (yes, I'm sorry) IT boys and girls.

So now is the time to get things into perspective if you are to work successfully with word of mouth, if you want to harness the real power of the talking herd, if you want to avoid the risks of being caught doing so, if you want to be rather more than this year's thing. You've got to grasp this important distinction: between 'exogenous' WoM (the result of external stimulus like Marketing trickery) and 'endogenous' WoM (that naturally arising from the system itself).

The whole cake (not just the icing)

WoM is not an additive phenomenon or the result of additive activity – some funky icing on the marketing cake. The Artic Monkeys represent the kind of 'natural' word-of-mouth success that is the whole cake, the icing, the filling, the sponge and even the hundreds and thousands scattered as sugary decoration on top of the cake. Word of mouth is an expression of how (well/badly) the mechanism of mass behaviour – peer-to-peer interaction and influence – is working.

Sometimes this will be in your favour and sometimes not. The key to taking advantage of it really lies in being able to stand back from your own (selfish?) perspective and see the system which gives rise to 'endogenous' mass behaviour as something independent of yourself and your concerns – *the system, its participants and their real interests.*

How bad science changed the mind of a nation[21]

In 1998[22] the authoritative medical journal the *Lancet* published a paper by a team led by a little known medical researcher from the Royal Free hospital in North London. Little notice was paid to the paper – essentially a report on a work-in-progress small-scale study – but within a few years the views articulated in it became accepted wisdom, despite the debatable science involved (so debatable that almost all of the co-authors of this original paper have since disowned the paper's conclusions).

Dr Andrew Wakefield is a paediatric surgeon who specializes in the gut. He has long believed – quite plausibly, given that we absorb all kinds of things into the bloodstream from the stomach – that gut conditions can affect the brain and in particular its development in children. Prior to the *Lancet* paper in question he suggested that Crohn's disease was caused by viral conditions of the gut but he failed to substantiate this claim with the kind of evidence that the scientific community expects if such a hypothesis is to be taken seriously.

The *Lancet* paper dealt with the much more emotive condition, *autism*. Despite the fact that it was based on a very small sample (12 children) it still made a significant claim that subsequently resonated around the world – that the condition itself (see Chapter 1 for more details) is *actually caused by* the widely used MMR (combined measles, mumps and rubella) infant vaccination.

'In eight children, the onset of behavioural problems (i.e. autism) had been linked, either by the parents or by the child's physician, with measles, mumps and rubella vaccination.'

This remains an astonishing observation[23] to make – that a vaccination in widespread use could have such a devastating effect on even a small number of children. If it were true then government and health professionals would have to seriously rethink vaccination procedures and the programmes which are intended to protect our children from terrible childhood illnesses; illnesses which can cause blindness, deafness, infertility, brain damage and death. No, if Wakefield and co. were correct, a whole plank of health provision would have to be rethought. And quickly, because there is nothing less damaging to politicians' interests than threats to voters' children.

Very few of those who subsequently advocated Wakefield's position bothered to read the highly specialist paper itself – the parent groups which grow around such conditions tend not to, but prefer to listen to the headline claims at their many jamborees and on their websites. If they had read the original paper with any degree of scientific training they would have noted first that the authors could do no better than report '*association*' (the two phenomena – vaccination and onset of the condition were seen to be connected, more specifically, seen to be linked chronologically). Indeed, the original paper specifically states that it 'did not [even] prove an association between measles, mumps, and rubella vaccine and the syndrome described' (my parentheses). It merely notes the parents' and doctors' belief in an association in eight of the 12 cases and then points to the need for more 'virological studies . . . [to] help resolve this issue'.

Observing an association is one thing (and reporting that someone else has observed an association something else again), but in science what is required is a causal explanation and evidence for it. Wakefield's explanation was this: the measles virus causes (in some manner) a stomach condition (the hyperplasia of the paper's title) which then itself causes the brain damage which leads to the condition of autism. Which could of course be true.

Unfortunately, neither at the time nor since have Wakefield or his associates been able to consistently identify traces of the measles virus in children with autism or do so in a way which is verifiable by his peers (one Dublin-based associate Professor John O'Leary rejected Wakefield's claims that his work supports the MMR thesis thus: 'It in no way establishes any link between the MMR vaccine and autism'); neither is there any evidence of the measles virus doing so when given on its own (the so-called single-shot vaccination); nor has Wakefield and his team managed to explain why the combined vaccination should have this effect. Unfortunately, this didn't stop Wakefield from calling for the combined vaccination to be 'suspended' at a press conference.

As it turned out, the science was also flawed in another, more important way. Rather than being randomized, the sample had allegedly been partly recruited specifically to support a legal case that made the same claim against the Government. At least four of the study's cases in which the association had been observed were part of a £15 m legal aid case already underway when the data was collected by Wakefield and his team. It is alleged that Wakefield and his team received some £55,000 to fund their work from the legal team. But none of these things were noticed at the time, certainly not by the media or the special interest groups. Nor was the fact that Wakefield and the Royal Free were themselves preparing patent applications for MMR alternatives – alternatives to the vaccination that they were themselves questioning.

Instead, the simple claim that 'MMR causes autism' – subsequently re-published by Wakefield in a second review paper in 2001 (in a relatively obscure journal with no new data) – fuelled a feeding frenzy from journalists and parents' groups who wanted to believe that the causal link was there, who wanted to believe that we were being misled, who wanted someone to blame. One analysis by the ESCR[24] suggests that in the first 9 months of 2001 10% of all science stories in the mainstream British press were about the MMR 'scandal'. The topic was also most likely to generate readers' letters and the most likely science topic to have generalist 'op-ed' coverage, in depth.

The journalists involved were not stupid or obscure or easily manipulated sorts. All of them intelligent, well-read and decent-minded individuals. Lorraine Fraser of the *Daily Telegraph* wrote a dozen or more articles (including one admiring interview of the 'champion of patients who feel their fears have been ignored') and was subsequently awarded Health Writer of the Year at the 2002 British Press awards by her peers. Melanie Phillips of the *Daily Mail* is a widely respected and thoughtful columnist but she and others took up Wakefield's line and persisted in damning the medical establishment who she felt keep such dangerous truths from parents. Nigella Lawson, Libby Purves, Suzanne Moore and Lynda Lee-Potter all joined in on Wakefield's side. Justine Picardie even did a wholesome 'at home with the hero and his family' piece for the *Daily Telegraph* Saturday magazine.

As each new piece of counter-evidence emerged, top-class journalists like these turned the facts on their head[25]. One even claimed that the results of a systematic Cochrane review showed exactly the opposite of what it did. Claims that MMR were safe were 'a load of old baloney', it was suggested. Moreover, some defended the lack of evidence for the causal link in Wakefield's research by describing the tools of epidemiology as being insufficient to detect the measles virus (even though they are able to detect a much rarer skin condition which is caused by the virus in only 20 infants in the UK each year).

Real impacts

I know from my own friends and acquaintances that as each story about MMR appeared in the press, so parents' discussions turned the scary new view over and over, gave it a veneer of credibility through repetition, then passed it on as fact and fell into line: public opinion shifted rapidly against the vaccine as the coverage began to suggest that medical opinion was equally divided on whether MMR was safe. By the end of 2001, 53% of UK adults believed that both sides of the debate are on equal footing, as far as evidence is concerned. MMR had become a 'cause célèbre'.

Government health officials were surprised and overwhelmed by the sharp shift in public opinion and the behavioural and epidemiological implications of this shift. As they tried to prove the absence of a negative (When did you stop beating your wife?), MMR immunization rates dropped as low as 60% in some parts of the country and to 84% overall. The net result is that measles cases have almost trebled in the six years since Wakefield's original paper, putting tens of thousands of young children at risk of serious brain and other developmental damage which would blight their lives no less than the autism that Wakefield and his team were so keen to combat.

What can we learn from the MMR case?

You may think this a strange and even chilling example of the power of word of mouth to consider in a business book; you'd be right and that is why I have chosen it as a counterpoint to all those 'buzz'-obsessed business scribblers. Its real strangeness lies not so much in the subject matter but in the nature of the word of mouth behaviour described.

What the MMR case really tells us

The social system, its participants and their interactions matter most

Endogenous WoM is very powerful (and more so than what we can create through WoM marketing)

What the MMR story really tells us is that what matters first and foremost is the system, its participants and their need to interact around a subject. Op-ed journalists who fuel our belief in conspiracies – that 'we are not being told the truth by big business and government' (delete as inappropriate). Parents who want someone to blame for their troubles and the rest of us who just like a good yarn that supports our instinctive mistrust of authority. *Da Vinci Code*, anyone?

Second, that *endogenous* (or self-generating) word of mouth is far more powerful than the kind of superficial marketing-generated word of mouth that buzz-fiends regale us with. Indeed, the MMR case reveals the deep, abiding and fundamentally human trait of talking about a subject that fuels our interactions with others. The Arctic Monkeys' success is built on a similar social system-dynamic: namely, the uncontrollable urge that many of us have to share our grand passions and obsessions with others. But the truth is the same in both cases.

We'd all prefer to think that it is what we change-masters do to stimulate word of mouth that matters – this is why too many writers on the subject suffer an inoperable myopia. But as I've tried to remind you at each turn in this book, what matters is what people out there do to each other. And word of mouth is no different from any of the other human–human interactive behaviours already described.

So, before we consider specific applications of this phenomenon in business, it is worth spending a little time putting marketing- or business-led word of mouth (powerful as it is) into context. To remind ourselves why this is no new thing.

Grooming gossip and feeling good

We primates spend an awful lot of our time grooming each other. If you watch our close relatives in the wild or even in captivity, a huge amount of their waking hours is dedicated to mutual grooming. Picking nits from each other's fur; smoothing rough patches of skin and generally keeping each other clean and tidy. The pleasure each gets from being groomed is one side-benefit, but is also an indication to many evolutionary psychologists that this is important behaviour, in evolutionary terms at least.

As Desmond Morris and other primatologists point out, grooming serves a cluster of social functions – it not only calms the individual being groomed, but it also establishes and reinforces social bonds between individuals. It is not just that a subservient ape will groom his or her superior and vice versa or a peer his equal; or indeed a mother her offspring. Ape-on-ape grooming is common whatever the social relationship between individuals happens to be and it helps to build and reinforce social relations between individuals.

Without this the complex social structures of chimps, bonobos and other great apes would be at breaking point; alliances would become fragile and social confusion would reign. Which in itself would defeat the whole purpose of being a social animal – safety.

So it is worth considering how much of our human-to-human verbal communication is essentially 'grooming' behaviour. When we say hello to our neighbours, when we comment (in our English way) on the weather, when we enquire about each other's family and partners and their health – all of these are etiquette-shaped 'grooms'. More intimately, with our friends and family we touch, we hug, we kiss and we stroke. So much of our contact with other people is 'grooming' one way or another. And we do it without even thinking, all day and every day. It is as natural to us as breathing.

Talk and grooming

As Chapter 1 pointed out, our species' amazing language ability is derived from grooming. Both Robin Dunbar[26] and Stephen Pinker[27] suggest that the language skills we use to communicate complex and subtle thoughts in both the spoken and written word are built on and harness grooming behaviours. Language – and our ability and love of communicating verbally – is the ultimate extension of those interactions between a newborn infant and its mother. It is not separate or discrete but built on top of everything else about us.

In other primates, grooming is often accompanied by vocalizations (and the tone of these changes the experience of being groomed and the effect on the groomed individual); think how much of person-to-person communication depends on our tone of voice and our pitch rather than our words (as well as gesture and body language of course). Think how a person's vocal characteristics affect how we feel about them and how this changes as their tone or pitch changes. You could just try a little experiment: try reading this paragraph back to yourself in three different tones: first, angrily; second, submissively; and third, nonchalantly. Tone really matters for meaning, far more than we give it credit.

More grooming talk

The important thing about spoken person-to-person interaction is that it happens all the time in social groups – we talk a lot. And just as with our cousins, the chimps, it primarily serves to build and reinforce social relations (rather than being for data transmission). Moreover, much of the content – up to 50% in one estimate – is about social relations (who did what to whom or who is not to be trusted – this includes governments and medical authorities, by the way). In a recent experiment[28] on human subjects, Robin Dunbar and his colleagues have shown how we pay particular attention to this content – or rather how social content in human-to-human interaction is particularly memorable. In the experiment, individual subjects were asked to read a short piece of prose. They were then asked to pass the contents of this on to another subject. This was repeated twice more so that a chain of four subjects was set up. Curiously, when the researchers compared the original and the final versions of the prose text, the social content proved to be particularly well remembered to the detriment of the other content.

If you are honest with yourself, much of what you say to others during the course of any given day is similar – either directly or indirectly (in that it has social consequences). Many cultures downplay the value of gossip ('women's work') and rumour (not related to the 'manly' objective facts) and yet this is clearly essential to the functioning of our social groups. And an essential stimulus and precondition to other behaviour, both immediate and later.

The conversation has already started

People chatter to each other all of the time, about all kinds of things; they like doing it and they always have done so. The growth of peer-to-peer networking sites is just one example of what newer technologies are revealing about us.

As is the rise of SMS text messaging. In seven years, the UK went from zero to thousands of millions of text messages per year. This explosion in an apparently new behaviour is merely an indication of how readily individuals (particularly young socially mobile individuals) like to communicate with each other. The language of texting has evolved to make this behaviour even easier but it is thrilling and compulsive. Despite my advancing years, I am addicted too. I recently spent ten days without text messages or mobile phone calls and felt so isolated and unsure of myself, which is silly I know, given that I only started a few years ago.

So if you were sitting in the Policy Unit at the Department of Health during the MMR scandal and managed to maintain a clear head, what you were observing was endogenous word of mouth. The social system (including the Op-Ed journalists in the British press) were generating word of mouth around a subject that was admittedly important to the individuals within that system but served one of its bigger needs: to find an explanation for the condition and with it, someone that the system could blame. It wasn't about the science, or about Dr Wakefield himself. Or even 'about' autism.

If you were a member of the parents' groups, you would want to tell and hear about this new explanation of the cause of your child's (and your fellow parents' child's) condition – we all love to identify a 'cause' – some external factor which is to blame for our misfortune. If you were a journalist (or a parent) you'd want to hear and tell others about an example of how some third party had and was continuing to deceive you and your family (remember Edelman's trust barometer?) You'd want to pass on the story (even if you didn't know or understand the science behind it or the validity of that science) to fuel your interaction with others. And you'd transmute the base metal of fact into opinion that served these goals as you went (hence the description of Wakefield as a heroic defender of parents and autistic children against the wicked, deceitful, medical profession and government).

In many ways, poor Andrew Wakefield – whatever you think of his science and his motives – was a bit part actor in this drama and largely irrelevant to it. Anyone with a similar point of view could have been picked up and championed by the system's word of mouth. His opinions were seized upon by others (parents' groups, journalists and middle-class dinner parties) with other agendas.

What the authorities failed to grasp was this: the system was primed; Wakefield merely prompted the talking. And once the talk started it was difficult to silence (or even counter). Because the talk wasn't about the thing – the safety of MMR – at all. But about the participants in the system.

And the same could be said for those sitting in the A&R teams of the record labels as the Arctic Monkey phenomenon took off: the system was primed and generated its own word of mouth.

It's not all (or even mostly) about you!

This is true in every circumstance: the conversation out there in the real (or virtual) world is already underway. People are talking to each other about all manner of things. And finding new excuses to do so (like text, email and so on). You would do well to remember this, rather than assuming that those out there are hanging on the oracle's every word, waiting for the truth from the horse's mouth. They will talk whatever you do and sometimes it'll be about you and what matters to you but mostly it's not. Or, if it appears to be about you, it's likely to be a reflection of some deeper, hidden issue within or about the system itself.

Humans have always talked to each other and always will. A lot of what they say is both uncomfortable and irrelevant to business or those in authorities. The truth is that the modern age has just made it easier to do just this (and easier for we students of mass behaviour to observe). It remains profoundly difficult for business to embrace the truth of this – the truth that most conversations are not about you-the-business; even when you are paying people to have that conversation.

Paying for it

Really? *Even when you pay people to talk about you?* Take a look round the next meeting you sit in on. Imagine the other participants are not executives discussing the finer points of CRM implementation (or whatever it is that they are paid money to be discussing) but instead *apes in suits*. Watch them groom each other with words, tone of voice and gesture. Watch them closely – turn on your Babelfish (Douglas Adams' ingenious all-purpose translation device) and watch these hairless chimps go through their routines. This meeting – like all meetings – is not *about the subject* under discussion; it's *about* the social interactions *around the subject*. Watch and listen to the information that is shared about other players – those not in the room, those beyond the room; about customers and competitors. Listen carefully to see how 'information' is traded and twisted to serve the social needs of individuals in the group. How the notion of objective verifiable truth is undermined at every turn for social needs. Even the act of passing the plate of biscuits around is part of this bigger game.

Talk in the real world

So it is with the real world that most of us deal with. Real people have real lives to lead but we see them only as marketing or policy initiative *targets or audiences* – consumers or voters or employees. But their real lives are full of interactions with other people and relationships with other people and other people's relationships with each other and so on (to paraphrase Thomas Schelling – see Chapter 4).

Your organization's existence and its goals, objectives and sacred cows are largely peripheral to real people and serve only to help, hinder, enhance or diminish the interaction of real people with each other in their real lives. What we worry about in the boardroom barely registers as important, even for employees or fans of a particular band or a candy bar, except in so far as it affects social interaction and identity. We – the business, the management, the brand and the Government – really don't matter; the conversation is not about us; nor does it exist for our benefit. But it is this bigger conversation that remains all important.

The simple schematic in Figure 6.2 sums up the relative unimportance of what we think of as word of mouth in real lives.

So seen from the primatologists' perspective, the word-of-mouth behaviour that we worry about is really a small part of human behaviour, albeit a powerful one. I hope this serves as a bit of a cold shower to buzz-mania. Exogenous (marketing-stimulated) word of mouth is important but not as important as endogenous (or naturally arising) word of mouth. The stuff you get by trying to get word of mouth is important and powerful as an additional driver of mass behaviour; more powerful still is the stuff you get without trying. Be it good (i.e. in your favour) or bad (otherwise).

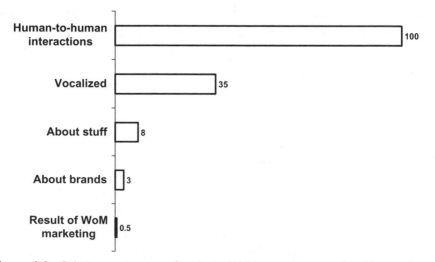

Figure 6.2   *Relative unimportance of marketing WoM as a percentage of total human–human interactions that are . . .*
Note: amounts are estimated

The truth is, as Oscar Wilde put it, that there is only one thing worse than being talked about: *not being talked about*. Sadly, most businesses, most products, most management initiatives and most government policies are just not going to get talked about without trickery of some sort, because they are just not that interesting (our ways of thinking about business have squeezed out the interesting stuff, by and large) but that doesn't have to be the case. Indeed the next few chapters will explore how to generate this kind of influential peer-to-peer behaviour by being, well . . . just a bit more *interesting* to start with. 'Interesting' in rather more profound way, in fact.

But before we get to the *hows* there's one more application of WoM to consider – how WoM metrics turn out to be particularly powerful indicators of business health.

One number to rule them all

Business likes numbers. Numbers make us feel safe. Numbers give us a sense of being in control and being on top of things, of being at the heart of things. Numbers give us the sense that the world is neat and tidy, understandable and tangible. That there are no difficult issues, no points of view or judgements to be made; that business doesn't have to really engage our own beliefs. Numbers give us the impression that there's only hard fact, even if (as Jeffrey Pfeffer[29] points out) if that 'fact' is irrelevant or part of a fallacious or ill-grounded theory of how things work. It's almost as if we believe that nothing exists or matters if it can't be measured. And because we can collect and analyse numbers like never before (thanks to the computing power available to us), we do it more and more. In fact we do it whenever we can. Business schools teach their graduates the mantra of measurement and off they go into the real world and chant it morning noon and night. And ignore the more important things.

Each tribe of vested interest in business promotes its own metrics – its own complicated measurement system. Loyalty monsters have theirs, persuasion monsters theirs, even corporate social responsibility (CSR) monsters theirs. The multi-faceted metric mania creates an intellectual tangle – like those wire coat-hangers you find at the bottom of every wardrobe, impossible to separate.

Every business meeting is full of measurement data – most meetings I've ever been in have a low hum of human data-processing units (that's the sound of the brains of the people in the room trying to make sense of the information being presented to them). And precious little thinking or debate about the problems or challenges in hand.

But there is one number that really matters; one really important metric for business. And this number is based on what customers are saying to each other (the same is true of what staff say to each other, if you are thinking about your employees).

Talk talk

Why should what your customers say to each other be so important?

- Why not what they tell you direct?
- Why not what money they give you?
- Or the share of their money?
- Or your share of the total money that the market spends?
- Or your profits?
- Or your share price?

Of course, if you want to discuss loans with your bank manager, it would be good to be on top of your books – to know how much your business is earning and how much it costs you to do so. So the financial measures are important. Equally, if you are talking to a prospective business partner or trying to make investment decisions it's good to know how you are doing relative to your competitors – are you a big brand or a small one? Are you selling to a small group of very loyal customers or a larger group?

But at heart, the central things that any business needs to worry about are simple: *how are we doing now with our customers and how well will we do in the future?* Without customers, the most finely tuned strategy is worth nothing. Without customers, the greatest technological advance is a pointless and expensive waste. As the great Kotler puts it, the purpose of business is to win and keep customers. All the other measures are either subordinate to this or the net result of doing it (i.e. sales figures or profits).

As we have seen throughout this book, business is a mass-behaviour activity. Individual customer behaviour is largely determined by what other customers do and, as this chapter has shown, by what other customers say. A sound measurement of customer–customer word of mouth should therefore be a really good proxy for this key mechanic of a business's impact on mass behaviour. If you do nothing else – if you measure nothing else – focussing on this measurement provides you with a clarity as to where you are now and where you seem headed as a business.

Talking about telly

One American academic interested in this area is David Godes[30] of Harvard Business School. Together with Dina Mayzlin of Yale, he showed how online word of mouth is highly predictive of the future ratings of a new TV show.

Every fall (like our British autumn but more dramatic), the major TV networks launch up to 70 major new shows in a programming head-to-head. Most of the new shows don't make it to Christmas and this constitutes a lot of money down the drain for the networks. What makes it harder for the TV executives to make decisions is the long tradition of sleepers; that is, programmes that start to build audiences only slowly and then garner mass support later in their (first or second) run. In the UK, BBC2 has long been the testing ground of such new shows – both in comedy and in drama – but the US networks have not had the ability to take this route. It's more of an all-or-nothing game there (and the way the economics of US programme-making goes, it is financially suicidal not to pull a poor performing show – new productions mostly make a loss, even the successful ones). So it should be no surprise that the US networks have long been on the hunt for the latest market research tools to help make better predictions about what will fly and what won't; and thus which shows to back, push and promote and which to cut.

Godes and Mayzlin analysed what was going on in Internet chatrooms and the like and found that however small the initial audience two aspects of word of mouth early in a show's run proved to be highly predictive of the eventual audience level.

First, the sheer volume of mentions of a particular show – *how much are people mentioning the show online?* And second, the distribution of the mentions – *how widely spread is the discussion?* While this may not have made either of the two academics rich yet (there are always strong vested interests within any industry or business to keep measuring things the way we have always measured them), the efforts of these two pioneers suggest that word of mouth is a powerful predictor of future success.

That one number again

Frederick Reichheld, Emeritus Fellow of Bain & Co. – the man the *Economist* magazine calls the 'high priest' of loyalty management – is probably one of those most responsible for the rise of loyalty-metrics. His first book, *Loyalty Rules*[31] set off a chain reaction of loyalty measurement and analysis of the type I referred to above.

Yet to his credit, just a few years later, Reichheld was able to acknowledge the error of his ways, and in particular, the lack of practicality that such measurement offers. In its place he offered 'one number'[32] derived from one simple survey question – which indicates not just the recent performance of a business (or one of its units) but also its likely future performance. Being so simple – and easy to collect, analyse and understand – this metric is of practical use in the boardroom, and in employee communications right down to the shop floor.

At its simplest, Reichheld's number is a measure of net word of mouth. Through trial and error, he and his team developed a simple 11-point scale – from 0 to 10 – where 10 is *very likely to recommend the company to a friend or colleague* and 0 is *not at all likely to do so*. Compared to other simple questions that Reichheld tested (e.g. How strongly do you agree that (company X) deserves your loyalty?') the recommendation scale proved to be the most powerful predictor of future growth and the easiest to understand.

Reichheld's genius is revealed in his simple, usable analysis frame: rather than take some mean score (deviations from a mean convey little to the average manager and are thus not very actionable), he proposed a simple way of analyzing the data, inspired by his contact with Enterprise Rent-a-car who look only at their most-satisfied-customer data. In Reichheld's scheme only those scoring 9 or 10 on the simple recommendation scale can be said to be truly satisfied; they are likely to be 'promoters' of the company's services. Anyone below 7 is clearly not satisfied and will not be singing the company's praises to anyone; in fact they are likely to do the opposite, spreading bad word of mouth to their friends and colleagues. The indifferents (scoring 7 to 8) he treats by ignoring them.

From this, he is able to derive his one number: the 'net recommendation score' (Figure 6.3). That is, the percentage of customers who score 9 or 10 on their likelihood of recommending the company minus the percentage of customers who score from 0 to 6 on the same measure. This he found – for

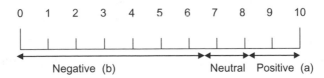

Figure 6.3 *How Reichheld calculates net recommendation*
Source: Adapted from Reichheld 'The One Number You Need' HBR

most industries – was the strongest indicator of financial growth in the immediate future in not just the 14 industries his initial study covered but in many, many more.

Of course, there are exceptions – a monopolistic market is unlikely to grow through the same means; alternatively, some markets are going to be driven more by economic factors affecting the whole market rather than individual companies. But again and again, the one number provides a very high correlation with growth and financial performance in most cases.

A number of challenges to Reichheld's work have surfaced in recent years but on closer examination none really hold water. First, there is the challenge that the USA has a culture of complaint – thus negative mentions are more likely to be prevalent and distort the net recommendation score. While the cultural assertion is debatable, there is little evidence to suggest its impact on the metric is important. Reichheld and his team have repeated their work outside the USA and Paul Marsden[33] of the London School of Economics has demonstrated that the same metric works just as well in the UK in particular.

Second, there is the challenge that one number cannot provide actionable data – many market researchers will find it too simplistic a measure to provide diagnostic help. Well, Reichheld is consistently clear on this point. It does not tell you what to do but it does tell you where to dig. He specifically mentions both in his original Harvard Business Review paper and in his subsequent book[34] on the one number theory that other diagnostic questions can be added on (but he warns against the off-putting length of most customer-satisfaction surveys and the self-serving nature of so much silo-driven data in business – we all know that marketing measures what it wants to, the call centres what they want to and HR what they want to. If you leave them to their own devices they will only generate more micro-metrics which don't add up to a shared understanding of how the business is doing and where it is going).

Reichheld is adamant on the usability of the data, both in the boardroom and in the frontline of business. On the one hand, the simple metric shows how all of your past efforts are impacting on the mechanism behind mass behaviour. On the other, saying to a car dealership principle that 'we need to create more promoters and fewer detractors' is much more easily understood than 'we need to shift the customer-sat scores by at least one standard deviation'.

One number in reality

The One Number is very important to those of us who believe in the herd theory of mass behaviour. It focuses on the key mechanic of mass behaviour (consumer–consumer interaction and influence) and helps us orientate our whole business and all our activities around this vital mechanism. Moreover it sees C2C recommendation as the result of all of a company's activities and not just the 'buzz' ones – though it can and should be used very effectively to measure the net recommendation changes which are the result of exogenous marketing activity – it gives us a good, usable and simple read on our overall success and future as a herd-business.

What this chapter has shown

Word of mouth is the most tangible and measurable form of peer-to-peer influence. As our trust in traditional sources of information and authority decline its relative importance as a source of influence has become much clearer. But that's not to say that it is a new phenomenon. No, WoM has always been very powerful. It's just that we haven't noticed. It is global – not just a US phenomenon. It works across categories and industries. And it turns out to be a really good metric for all and every business activity – simple, practical and actionable. But the trap for businesses waking up to the power of WoM is that most vendors and writers seem to focus on exogenous WoM; that is, WoM generated by specific discrete WoM activity. The real deal is endogenous WoM, the stuff that is generated by the functioning of the social system around your product, company or campaigning issue. This is hard to fake, but equally hard to avoid, if only you do things right.

What's next?

The next few chapters will lay out some of the key areas to examine in our attempts to do just this: to become successful herd businesses that generate endogenous word of mouth. What is it that you have to think about to generate a sustainable herd response? What do you have to do differently? How do you have to change the way you interact with customers and staff?

Ready now?

Questions for marketing

1. Word of mouth is really powerful – both as a positive and negative force. Do you think word of mouth is a new phenomenon (as WoM-ers suggest)? Or if it is not, why is it that we have ignored it for so long? Is it a cultural thing or is something else going on?
2. Why do people talk? What do they talk about? Try to monitor every talk-based interaction you have tomorrow (face to face, via phone and email) by making a note to yourself after every one. Review this and consider how little of it is of importance in the way we normally understand it. Try to persuade your friends and colleagues to do the same and compare notes. What does this tell you about us-talk?
3. Spend some time with your Babelfish translator to see the super-social ape at work. Sit in your next meeting or in the office just watching the SSAs at work. Listen not to what is said but watching the grooming and the stroking going on.
4. What metrics do you use to monitor the performance of your marketing or other attempts to change mass behaviour? List them. What doubts do you have about them? What world view do they embody? How much use would the one number be? How much more practical and usable?
5. When are you going to fire your 'word of mouth' agency?

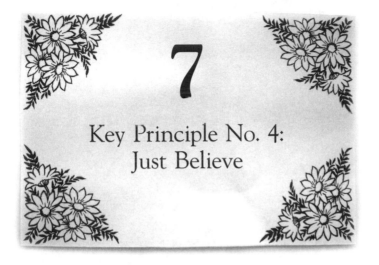

7

Key Principle No. 4: Just Believe

What this chapter will cover

How do you get the human herd talking and interacting and influencing each other around you? The annoyingly simple (but profoundly difficult) answer is this: *be interesting.*

There are no short-cut solutions to this. Really interesting businesses and products engage us because they are expressions of deeply held *beliefs* of the founders and employees, not some feigned or borrowed interest; expressions of personal commitment to something bigger than the business or products themselves. How and why this works for customers, employees and other stakeholders.

What you stand for is as – if not more – important than what you do
Simon Woodroffe, founder of Yo! Sushi restaurant chain

Disappointed of Desmoines (or Dunstable)?

Most business books oversimplify. They promise simplistic solutions, simple frames of analysis, lists of 10 things you can do to bring about the change you can seek, things to do and things not to do. They make internal sense and indeed some sense of what makes real businesses work. And the simplicity of such prescriptions is attractive and saleable – that's why business books deploy them so readily, in text boxes and cut-and-paste diagrammatical form. And we scan and photocopy the best of them and pass them round in the hope that they might change us and our business.

But the truth is that there is no simple, easy-to-use list of things that can get your business or product talked about or otherwise played with by the human herd; no one set of shapes can encompass the whole deal. And any list such as this would be either packed with platitudes or (God forbid!) mere WoM trickery. Which would soon be spotted, copied or otherwise devalued.

As Tessa Graham (the marketing brains behind Jamie Oliver and Stella McCartney) told me,

> The trouble with marketing theorists, with all their triangles and flow charts, is not that they are wrong. They just make sense of what good marketing does instinctively but after the fact.
>
> It's instinctive marketing – marketing which is based on your beliefs and your values – that makes the biggest impact. The impression that the

'after-the-fact marketing science' gives us is that in fact these things are unimportant, but at the end of the day this is what makes a brand distinct and gives it soul.[1]

I pondered this point of view as I worked on this chapter (if I were you, I'd cut Tessa's wise words out and stick them on your office wall). So I decided not to provide you with such a list or a set of geometric shapes.

Because I think things are a little more interesting than this kind of prescription would suggest. (So if you are disappointed not to have a list or a set of strategic shapes to play with, I apologize. But please read on, I *do* have some really important stuff to share with you.)

Meaning in a world of oversupply

The central issue that we all face in business today is this: the world in which we live is oversupplied. Oversupplied with equally good products and services (it is 10 years since JD Power revealed that there is no such thing as a bad car nowadays; they're all good). We have too much of everything – of information, of choice, of quality. Do I really need four decent choices of supermarket within 10 minutes' drive of my north London residence? Do I really need six liquor stores? Five gyms? Do I really need 12 coffee shops within 10 minutes' walk? Or three dozen places to buy trainers? Do I? No.

No wonder consumers and employees alike are both 'leaning back' in the face of much that business tries to offer them. Mostly they are listless and disinterested. They know that they are in control and that we are not. That we will do almost anything to get our hands on their cash or their time. Or first and foremost their attention.

How do we break through in a world of oversupply and disinterest? How do we get folk to lean forward to what we have to offer? How do we gain their attention? *How do we get them to influence each other* (the key mechanic of mass behaviour, remember) *on our behalf?*

Three principles explained

There is no simple analytic frame that explains what to do. Indeed, as you might suspect from Tessa's comments, an analytic frame is likely to work against the underlying principles of 'instinctive' belief-based businesses. Instead, what I am proposing is a way of thinking and running your business that is based on you. On what you believe. To be a bit more precise, consider these three key principles.

First, you must change your view of the outcome you seek; the trick is to create something of *social meaning* above and beyond the product or service.

As Douglas Atkin[2] writes in *The Culting of Brands*, brands such as Apple really appeal to the social identity and social needs of individuals. The many user groups and (inter)dependent communities that have grown up around Apple are strong communities whose own identity is sparked and underpinned by the abiding beliefs of those at Apple. Not that they give the corporation an easy ride; far from it. Whatever their particular technological or commercial gripes at any one time, Apple user groups reserve their strongest venom for the corporation when it truly challenges or threatens the core beliefs (witness the cacophony over the decision to switch to Intel processors in MacPro recently). But they are all Mac-fans, they all believe in the Apple commitment to personal and creative liberation. And believe that the rest of the world are doing it wrong; are limiting their own possibilities.

Second, the meaning must come from deep inside you. From your personal beliefs. From your beliefs about what's right and wrong in the world. In general or specifically in your industry. Or in the lives of your customers or employees. But it must be something that you are totally committed to. It must be personal. But it cannot come from your customers, because that just makes you seem like a nightclub hostess who is paid to be interested in her customers. So forget the usual customer- and staff-satisfaction surveys if you hope to find the answer. No, it must come from deep inside you.

Third, you must follow your beliefs and let them shape how your business works. You must turn your business from a vanilla one, a machine for making money, into a living, breathing embodiment of your beliefs; a vehicle for your personal convictions and not just another business. Hard decisions are inevitable but as we'll see a truly interesting and herd-able business is always guided by its beliefs. Indeed, it is when these businesses forget their driving beliefs that they tend to go astray.

I am not advocating the easy path here, just in case you thought this was where I am going. To build a belief business, you have to put yourself and your deepest convictions on the line. No amount of charts, fine words or mission statements will protect you. But you know what? Not only will you create something of worth in financial terms (as we shall see, belief businesses outperform vanilla ones by some margin), but you are also likely to build something that is of personal value to you and your colleagues. Something that means something to you. And this is what customers sense immediately and treasure. And share with each other.

Goodnight Vienna

All of the astounding businesses I describe in this chapter share this same approach. None of them has had an easy ride, but all of them are successful and have harnessed the personal beliefs of the founders and key employees to get the herd working for them.

But before we examine the individual examples, it is worth pondering for a moment why it is that belief businesses work so well.

Is it the novelty of belief in a world of oversupply? *Partly, I'm sure.*

Is it that belief is somehow more interesting than marketing trickery? *Certainly.*

Is it just that belief runs contrary to the prevailing cynicism of our modern world. *Absolutely* (remember Edelman's trust barometer from the previous chapter and the decline it traces in our trust of those cultural authorities which previously shaped meaning for each of us in our interactions?)

Or is it something more profound? Perhaps belief-led businesses touch something much deeper in us. Something powerful. A *deep need for meaning (shared or otherwise), perhaps?*

The Austrian psychotherapist Victor Frankl would certainly have agreed. His conception of what it is to be human suggests that we are all programmed to seek meaning and purpose and that this unites us in social groups. Frankl was a student of Freud and Adler, a Jewish psychoanalyst practising in Vienna before the annexation of Austria by Germany in 1938. But his own experience of the Nazi death camps – and observing how some people thrived in the random cruelty and others didn't – led him to believe that one of our central drives is this search for meaning.

> In contrast to the findings of Sigmund Freud, man is no longer sexually frustrated in the first place but rather 'existentially frustrated'. And in contrast to the findings of Alfred Adler, his main complaint is no longer a feeling of inferiority, but rather a feeling of futility, a feeling of meaninglessness and emptiness which I have termed the 'existential vacuum'. Its main symptom is boredom.[3]

Frankl observed that, in the camps, those who could create a sense of purpose for themselves were more likely to survive the terrible experience than those who didn't. And those who shared a sense of purpose . . .

I believe

This is my conviction: that businesses that are driven by beliefs, by a sense of purpose, do better than vanilla businesses because they touch something deep in the hearts of the individual employees and customers to give our lives the meaning we crave. As employees, they give us a reason to get up in the morning and go to work. They give us a sense of comradeship (a social benefit) both inside the firm and out; they serve our social needs. They transform our experiences, as employee or customer. They invite us in, rather than chasing after us desperately (as the marketing approach all too often encourages). They transform a pair of jeans into a social phenomenon; a computer operator into a tribe member in the crusade for personal liberation; a TV chef into a social reformer (and us into his fellow revolutionaries).

Such businesses are to be found in every sector. And in each and every case, they are built on the same principles I've outlined above. What the rest of this chapter will illustrate is how these same principles operate in all kinds of businesses. How social meaning, belief and living belief create a different kind of business from those that litter our high streets and malls. Let's see how they play out. First up, a company you probably don't know much about. A Welsh company. A Welsh clothing company!

Cardigan Bay's third biggest clothing company

If you like subtropical sunshine and/or urban grime, Cardigan Bay is not for you. Cardigan Bay is just about as Welsh as you can be and at the same time as west as you can be and still be in Wales (and let's just be clear, now: being in Wales is a good thing, a *very good* thing). The bay stretches from St David's head in the south to Anglesey in the north. It curves away along long empty beaches and rocky cliffs past ports that have seen better days (the family of the great architect Frank Lloyd Wright emigrated to the USA from Cardigan itself).

Being so far west and so far away from the majority of the population, Cardigan Bay is home to some of the most valuable natural marine habitats in the United Kingdom – its aquatic treasures include half of Europe's population of Atlantic grey seals and a population of several hundred bottlenose dolphins. Its coastal tracks are clear and steep, its beaches are wild and windy and its air as clean and sharp as any you might fill your bursting lungs with, as you race around: on bike, on board, or on other such device.

And it is home to howies (*sic*), one of the most interesting (and now not so little) companies I have come across in recent years. howies has grown from a tiny operation making t-shirts for a small number of bike enthusiasts to a major fashion brand that has out-cooled Nike twice in recent years (as far as the votes of the British population are concerned) and is sold around the world, from Tokyo to Turin.

Outdoor threads

David and Clare Hieatt have always enjoyed outdoor sports – mountain biking, kayaking and the like. So the fact that they have ended up making clothes for people who enjoy these activities is not surprising – the range now runs from t-shirts to simple but well-made denim jeans, from snug sweaters to hardworking really waterproof under layers, and shells that let you move and work your body up a muddy track but neither get wet nor stay sweaty. And people who enjoy these sports seem to like what they call 'howies gear' very much. And many people who are like the people who enjoy these outdoor sports also like howies gear very much.

'So howies make good clothes for today's outdoor types, so what?', you say, 'They are not the first to do so. They are not alone'.

No, they are not alone. There are lots of skate, bike, surf and boarding clothing brands out there. But howies do rather more than make good stuff for people who share their leisure interests. They do stuff differently. For example, quality is a given. As David puts it, they don't do it unless they can make it better than the next company. There's no point at all in a world of oversupply.

'So', you say, 'what makes howies different is just the quality of the product? Hardly earth-shattering that, is it?'

Well perhaps there's more to howies than quality. howies quality is there *for a reason*: because as the brand book puts it, '*the best thing we can do for the environment is to make things last longer.*'[4] Longer-lasting jeans mean less of the world's limited resources taken up on making, marketing and buying more of the same. In other words, at howies, quality is something much more than an attribute; instead, it serves as a clue to some other, higher purpose.

Nice to have?

David and Clare have learned to see the world in which they practise their hobbies as being fragile, exhaustible and in need of protection from business and society's worst excesses. They have thus pushed howies to pioneer the use of both eco materials (the cotton in my new jeans for example is organic and the dyes low-impact vegetable ones, rather than the high-impact chemical ones used by other manufacturers). In addition new tighter weaves and stronger stitching make a pair of jeans last twice as long, which means you don't buy a new pair for a while longer (in any case, don't we all prefer the feel of our old favourite jeans to the ones that have just come home from the shops?).

As David puts it,

> We knew exactly what we wanted to achieve with howies . . . to make high-quality clothing for our sports so that they last the test of time. We would make things stronger, use better materials and seek to make our clothing in a lower-impact way. We believed in a thing called quality because we believed a quality product would last longer. And that was what we were into. It made sense to us. It made sense to our customers. And from an environmental point of view, it made a whole bunch of sense too.

But howies is more than just green clothing for BMX-ers and mountain bikers: right-on threads for the outdoor fanatic, if you like. Fashion – even functional fashion – and ecological awareness are no longer unusual bedfellows. Indeed, if you had to brainstorm new brand concepts in this space, you would almost certainly come upon this fairly quickly.

No, what is different about howies is what drives the business. And what drives the business is precisely the thing that drives David and Clare. And Scania and the rest of the gang. Put simply it is this: *a passion to make people think differently about the world* – a passion that makes the business a vehicle for something more important than clothing or even an outdoor life. *A passion that makes the business personal.*

Think differently

Two unusual thoughts there: first, *passion* – this is a business in which people believe in what they are trying to do in the broader world. They see a world beyond their business; a world that concerns them. They are a bunch of people who love their day jobs, for sure (we all know that employees like this 'get things done'); but they get things done because they believe in what the company is doing to the world. The difference between success and failure in many businesses – large or small – is the degree to which the people make stuff happen. I'm sure that both the desire to get things done and the broader perspective are as elusive in your business as it is in mine. As David puts it, 'Belief is good fuel, it's different fuel, it's fuel that money can't buy.'

Second, making people think differently. This is the *content* of the company's driving passion, this is what drives the principals and the staff. *This* is what gets them out of bed in the morning. There's an old howies' proverb (!) which goes something like this: if you make a jacket just like everyone else's, you're just making a jacket; but if you make a jacket that is unique and better than what is out there you are making history. David and Clare have gone one step further; they've made a business which seeks to make history because it is a vehicle for their beliefs and convictions. The passion inside the company's driving force seems to affect customers, too. 'Customers are our best salespeople', says Clare. 'They believe just as strongly as we do and talk to each other.' Indeed, on a recent trip, they found a customer who'd spray painted the howies logo on to his van, because he felt it encapsulated who he felt he was and what he was passionate about.

Third, the passion is deep and personal and much more ambitious than it appears as you walk into the warehouse (like most clothing warehouses, it's just full of clothes). It's to do with changing the way that business works, by example. When I asked David and Clare what the root of this passion is, they explained that both of them originally came from industrial South Wales – the mines and the steelworks. They saw how companies exploited their workforce, taking 10 years off the life of their grandfathers – through overwork and lung diseases – and then making the sick sign indemnities to protect the company from lawsuits. 'We believed that there must be a better way to run companies . . . there just must', says David.

howies' passion is very serious; it is their key metric – the means by which they judge themselves ('Our success as a company should be judged by how much debate, talk and discussion we create'); it is the thing that gets them out of bed in the morning. It's the thing that gets them through the long, long, *long* nights and the stresses and the strains that any growing business faces. David used to rally the small team of the early days, as they packed t-shirts well into the night, by reminding them of the change that howies wanted to bring to the world. '[Just like the experimental rock band Radiohead] we don't want to be the biggest company in the world, but we are going to be the most important.'

And they have so many ways in which they can and do exercise this muscle: with slogans and t-shirt designs, with textile and manufacturing innovations, with packaging, distribution and point-of-sale materials, return slips, catalogues and sponsorships. And many things they haven't yet thought of.

The journey (home)

As I turned east and started to count the junctions down from 49 to one, I pondered what I had learned from meeting these two inspiring individuals. The power of belief, for sure. The importance of the personal, likewise. The way that passion and belief drive productivity inside the company. And how the same thing affects, engages and recruits customers to the cause.

But perhaps more important than this is the simple pleasure they take in the day-to-day of their business. The way they see the tricky challenges and dilemmas that are thrown up by the interaction between their beliefs and the realities of the industry. Others might see this as the hassle of a belief business, but for the howies gang, it is otherwise.

And it's not as if they started things the way they wanted things to be – that howies came ready-made. Both David and Clare readily acknowledge that they've still got a long road to travel to be the business they aspire to be, but their customers largely forgive them because at least they are trying to do things better. Because the journey is worth it.

As time goes on, they learn more and more that they want to change and in doing so face temptations to compromise their beliefs by falling in line with the rest of the industry. For example, they could use suppliers that don't quite live up to their ecological standards (for a few pence per garment), but they found ways round this and don't do it anymore. David's face changes when he says, 'nobody's thinking about what cheap really costs . . . all of the resources and all of the chemicals.' Clare is equally forthright on the subject.

They don't have all the answers – or even the questions – but each time they find something they don't like, they try to change it.

Given the small number of factories in the world that can weave organic cotton, they could have avoided the risk and the cost of using this raw material. After all, nobody was interested in organic t-shirts when David and Clare wanted to do them – particularly distributors (40% of the latter dropped the brand when howies tried this). But David and Clare did them anyway. Though no one asked for it, they pioneered the use of organic denim – from autumn 2006, all of their denim will be organic. And the manufacturing processes are now shaping the behaviours of bigger, scarier competitors – something of which they are enormously proud. The passion drives them on and on into the future: 'The more we learn about how the clothing industry works, the more things we want to change', says David.

It's not easy being howies in many ways; but it is easier for David and Clare than not being howies. Because given who they are and what they believe, this is the only road that they can take. Their road.

Jamie's dinners

The difference between Jamie Oliver and any of the host of TV chefs who have tried to tempt our appetite for food and cooking is this: Jamie believes. Jamie is driven by a very simple but powerful desire to change the way we buy, cook and eat our food. 'Better food for all' is the slogan version of it, but what it amounts to is this: change the way we eat, change the way we think about food, and change the lives of people by teaching them how to cook and enjoy real food.

Jamie was first discovered by the world as a gobby teenager in a documentary about Rose Gray and Ruth Rogers' River Café. He was an instant on-screen star. Soon he was showered by offers for TV work. Three series of *The Naked Chef* (a high octane celebration of fresh, tasty cooking) and a nationwide advertising campaign for Sainsbury's supermarket later, he was able to make his beliefs count.

First, at great personal and professional risk, he decided to launch a restaurant, 15, to provide employment and training for underprivileged kids in the catering business. Any restaurant opening is scary enough – most close in weeks at great cost to the owners – but this was made more difficult by not only training but also employing staff with no previous experience, and doing so in front of TV cameras would seem madness. Channel 4 TV screened an enthralling documentary series that covered the ups and downs of the development of new recruits – the heartbreak and the personal triumphs along the way. But what nobody knows is that Jamie put his own house on the line to make 15 happen. He believes. And so do I.

He also decided to use his own reputation to improve the food we serve our kids in the state sector. (For overseas readers, British school food has historically been as bad as they say the food in British restaurants used to be. Slop and deep-fried rubbish. Bland and greasy processed trash.)

Yet again he chose to do this in a high-risk manner; he signed up as a dinner lady in Kidbrooke School, Greenwich to prove that it is possible to produce healthy tasty food that finicky south London teenagers, raised on a diet of junk food, would actually eat. And all on a budget of just 37p per child. And again, all on camera; from the first episode of *Jamie's School Dinners*, broadcast on C4 on 23 February. Battling first against and then with the redoubtable Nora – a minor TV star in her own right now – dealing with the tears and tantrums of the kids, Jamie pulled it off for real, in front of the camera. But this was more than show; the story was always intended to provide the focus for a political campaign to actually change things, not just by example but by putting pressure on the Government.

'Feed Me Better' had hoped to garner 10,000 signatures on a petition to improve the standards of state school lunches; in fact, the petition Jamie Oliver took to 10 Downing Street contained 271,677 names. So successful had Jamie's TV-led campaign been that the Prime Minister had no choice but to order immediate action. The media were right behind him – not just the newspapers (in the UK and abroad) but the *Lancet*, the house journal of the British Medical Association also joined in. 'Jamie Oliver has done more for the public health of our children than a corduroy army of health promotion workers or a £100m Saatchi & Saatchi campaign.' (Sorry, Kate.)

School kitchens would be rebuilt, dinner ladies trained, parents would become involved, all overseen by an independent school food trust. All this would be supported with a pledge to spend £280 million ... to raise the average cost per child per meal from 37p to 50p for primary schools and 60p for secondary schools across the country.[5]

Of course, the Jamie Oliver 'brand' is now worth more than before either of these two initiatives. Jamie is not entirely altruistic and is happy to earn a decent wage for his efforts elsewhere, such as TV advertising (but only on the right kind of conditions and for the right companies). However, what he does represent is more than the ability to chop a few herbs or roast a chicken well or to show us how to do and enjoy these things.

He is true to himself and that is worth more than money. He risks himself again and again. Personally, commercially and financially. And – despite the crazy schedule he works to which now includes 15 restaurants and training schools in Cornwall, Melbourne and Amsterdam and product developments in partnership with a number of companies – he seems to enjoy himself more than most I have met in business. He loves what he does because he is passionate and about his personal beliefs. No bland 'brand values' statement for him. No 'Vision, Mission, Values' awayday. He lives what he believes. He knows what he wants to use his initial success for, and any of the businesses that suggest themselves subsequently. Boy, does he believe. And the more he lives his beliefs, the happier and more successful he is. And the greater his impact on our lives.

Being Naked

Naked[6] is one of the more successful media businesses in recent years. It has transformed the London marketplace, with a host of poor copies emerging (the first of which has just been folded). It has done the same in Sydney and is currently in the process of taking New York by storm. Wherever the Naked boys and girls go, it creates headlines for itself, through its new business wins, its recruitment coups and its co-creative collaborations with a range of partners. In the terms of this chapter, Naked is dead interesting.

So you won't be surprised to hear that Naked is a belief-based business, that its behaviours derive from a deeply felt personal view about what's wrong with the industry as far as clients are concerned. One of the co-founders, John Harlow, recalled the time when this belief first grabbed him.

> I was sitting in one of those 'all-agency' meetings with a major client. There must have been about nine different agency representatives there, all fighting their own corner, all arguing the toss about why they deserved the lions' share of the budget, all insisting that only their speciality could really solve the client's problem.

As he talks he becomes more passionate. Animated even.

> And then I saw the client's face – what he really needed was good advice about which communications tools and strategies to follow. And he wasn't getting that from any of the self-interested supplies present. I felt quite angry on his behalf. He wasn't getting what he needed and wanted and indeed paid vast sums of money for. Good sound advice. And no angle.

Co-founder Will Collin explains what this meant for the company:

> We were determined not to get involved in building a factory for making ads – that's what seems to stop these other smart people in advertising agencies or media agencies. They've got a huge advertising creative department and its support systems to feed. Or an army of media buyers that cost a lot of money that they need to provide work for. The factory has become what matters for these kind of companies and not what the client needs.

So from their anger at what their clients are not getting, John, Will and the third founding partner, Jon Wilkins, built an advice business with no factory to feed. One which works with anyone they need to – existing client partners or third parties that the job seems to require – anyone that the client suggests, although it does seem that their clients would be all too happy to have Naked's point of view on which suppliers to use.

As Will puts it, Naked 'bake fresh every day'. Or rather they get others to bake to order – or sauté or whatever it is they think the client really needs. They have no angle.

Which is of course where the name Naked comes from: transparency in all things, passionate and disruptive. Indeed one of the reasons why this name so appealed was the attention it draws to the vested interests which prevent clients getting what they need. And the fact that it reflects their very casual rejection of the pomposity of their peers.

This passion still fires them, and shapes the customer experience that the business almost alone among its peers delivers. Just doing the right thing is what comes across in all their client contacts. Naked people swarm a problem until they find the right solution, the right combinations of strategies and communications tools to solve the problem. And they do this with – rather than against – both the client and his existing partners. 'People often forget that marketing clients can have good ideas, too', says Harlow.

But it also serves as a management tool beyond compare. 'It makes it easy to make decisions about what to do with the business', suggests Wilkins. If a project needs best advice, they'll do it; if it doesn't they won't. If they need to build a team in another market because a client wants them there, that's easy too; talented people who share their passion for advising clients without an angle stand out from the crowd of would-be recruits. People like M.T. Carney or Paul Woolmington of the Media Kitchen.

But Collin's initial analysis is for now sacrosanct: they don't want to build a factory for anything – however much space their landlord has to offer them or clients want to pay them.

As you leave their offices in once-trendy Clerkenwell, and descend in the slow and grinding Parisian-style lift, it's hard not be impressed by the real and deep personal belief that these people have. Naked is much more than the latest groovy shop in the advertising world – all empty gloss. Naked is a business driven by a deep and shared passionate belief in what is wrong.

The empty office

There is another communications company that has shamed the great and the good of the London communications world by doing things differently. In 2005, *Campaign* magazine awarded their advertiser-of-the-year gong to an advertiser that doesn't (shock horror) use an advertising agency.

That advertiser is Channel 4 (or C4 as it is widely known). It has a similar take on the factory-feeding problem that Naked has addressed, but a different solution. As Richard Burdett, the chief of C4 Creative (their inhouse communications agency) puts it,

> The issue for advertisers is this – how do you get the most talented people, the people who do really groundbreaking work, to work on your business all the time? No agency in town has an exclusive on talent, even the best ones, so sooner or later you're going to look outside. This is wrong and unfair. Nobody wins.

(Note his anger here – righteous anger can be good if properly harnessed!)

The solution that Burdett and his colleagues at C4 Creative have come up with is this: a shell company who are as much commercials production- as idea-management people but they are armed with what Richard charmingly calls, 'the biggest black book in town'. That is, access to the brightest and the best freelance talent. This arrangement not only ensures that ideas people get paid to do what they do best and production people also, but the whole thing is much less painful to all concerned and quite a bit cheaper (no expensive salaries to keep on the books). The strike rate is good, the

Figure 7.1   *Shameless ad*
Reproduced by permission of Channel 4 and Peter Rad.

plaudits keep coming in and the work is consistently good (for my money the best UK campaign in the first part of 2006 has been for the second series of *Shameless*, the story of simple northern thieving folk. This involves members of the family stealing both the C4 logo, the lights and even the camera filming them – see Figure 7.1).

This organizational solution is not for all businesses (others have tried the freelance option before C4 Creative) but for this kind of advertiser it is a much better solution than adland would normally offer, both in terms of output and cost. It's all driven by strong personal belief. In Richard's case – as with the Naked boys – in what is wrong with existing supplier arrangements. And this shapes the everyday and the big decisions they make, as well as giving them a reason to get out of bed in the morning.

Enron and everything after

When I first suggested this thought about making things personal to one colleague, he interpreted what I had to say as being encouraging to the corporate cutthroats and ne'er-do-wells like those responsible for Enron, World. com and the like – devious and sly not-so-petty white-collar criminals.

Let me be clear: what I don't mean is 'take a business for all it is worth; help yourself and fill your boots with all the cash you can stash there'. Nor do I mean that you should be using the resources of a business to enhance your social standing (patrons of the arts and philanthropists everywhere look out) although I can see how that might be a byproduct of doing interesting stuff.

No, what I think the Naked boys, Jamie, Richard and the people at howies teach us is that truly interesting businesses derive a large part of their traction from the personal beliefs of those who founded, lead or otherwise are responsible for shaping them. This makes it possible for them to have some kind of authentic purpose about them; for them to be authentically *for* something and tangibly so; for them to be more interesting, in deed as much as in intention.

A challenge – *does belief pay?*

It's all very well, you might say, to cite a handful of cases; a handful of young and funky cases, even a handful of young and funky cases as successful as these. But is there more broadly based evidence – across industries and countries – that a business built on belief performs better than other breeds of business?

In their pioneering book, *Built to Last*,[7] Jerry Porras and Michael Collins demonstrate that – in the medium and longer term – purpose-driven businesses outperform businesses with similar asset bases, from similar locations, of similar age, etc. by a large margin. The study on which the book is based is longitudinal – that is it seeks to trace the long-term performance of such businesses; in fact, the study covers some 70 years and so doesn't suffer from the short-term distortions and noise that call into question some other studies which look over three or four years only.

Equally, the study uses pairs of companies from the same part of the world and the same industry to remove the short-term local variations that can hide significant differences between organizations (if two economies are at different parts of the cycle during the period studied then a company in one economy will perform differently from one in another, whatever other factors are involved). The pairs themselves are also of similar age (so the Disney Corporation is paired with Warner Brothers) and are cross-checked to ensure that they have a similar asset base (again to avoid this misleading interpretation of long-term performance).

If the company expresses its goals purely or largely in terms of financial performance then it does not qualify as a purpose-driven company. To do so, a company has to express what it is trying to achieve in broader or nobler terms.

To raise the bar further, the two companies are not just compared to each other (most of the other companies in each pair outperformed the stock market over both the medium and the longer term and would thus by any accounts be seen to be strong companies). Rather, the financial performance of both companies was compared to the stock market over the time period under consideration.

So what does the study show?

Put simply, the findings suggest that purpose-driven companies outperform what are already good businesses (i.e. ones which do better than the stock market) from the same part of the world, in the same industries and with similar asset bases. Put another way (in terms a punter might recognize): if you want to put your money with the best bet for higher growth over the medium and long term, choose a purpose- or belief-driven company over one with the same kind of skills or assets in the same industry, the vanilla choice. Purpose pays, almost always. By a margin of 7.5 : 1 over the long term.

A number of challenges have been put forward as to why this is. Why do Collins and Porras observe such a huge difference? Is it to do with the sample? No, such care was taken to reduce variation here. Is it to do with the length of time the study uses for observation? No, Collins and Porras are keen to make the point that while short-term variations may show a different picture (there is always a lot of noise in any dataset), the absolute level of difference in the performance of the two kinds of company is not their interest at all. The fact that purpose-driven companies deliver a superior performance at all is the point; not the scale of the difference.

You are not alone

You don't have to be 'right on' to be purposive; to use your business to be a vehicle for your beliefs (I have always felt uncomfortable at the hectoring tone of the Body Shop). You just have to care about something in this world beyond yourself and your bank account. And to care enough to live out your passions.

Ingvar Kamprad founded IKEA to bring 'a better everyday life to the many' – his underlying (very social democratic) belief is that our lives would all be better if we freed ourselves from the traditional ways of thinking and behaving which are transmitted and reinforced by the things we surround ourselves with. We should all 'chuck out the chintz' (as the early British advertising suggested) to create space for some nice, modern, value-free Swedish furniture. Every aspect of the business's behaviour is led by this underlying purpose:

big stores at cheap out-of-town sites, few staff and self-assembly all make it cheaper and more accessible to ordinary people (although an interior designer friend has taught me never to arrive at IKEA after 10.30 a.m. and never ever to visit a store on a bank holiday). Around the world, IKEA have experimented with other behaviours (such as a downtown showcase store in Manhattan a while back) but each time they do so they learn that the basic driving idea of a 'better everyday life for the many' is a good guide to what they should do.

Phil Knight founded Nike because of his great love of running and the track – Nike has grown and grown not because of its technical brilliance and ingenuity but simply because it believes that all of us should have the thrill and rewards that come with being an athlete. Whichever sport or type of apparel or technology Nike find themselves considering, it always has to be done from the inside, beckoning the rest of us to share the thrills and spills of the hard-core athlete. When Nike have forgotten this (when they start thinking of their trainers or clothing as fashion for example) they go awry. Nike never has been and never should be a fashion house like all the others. Nike has a unique signature (and I don't mean the swoosh here) because of the people who founded the business and the kind of people they instinctively drew to them; drew because of what they passionately believed. As Scott Bedbury[8] describes in his account of his time in Portland, Oregon, the usual tools of brand management [sic] such as brand books and brand positioning didn't seem to help him know what to do for the best – he found the lack of direction confusing at first – what was required was a 'feeling' for the company and in its beliefs and a total commitment to them, not an intellectual analysis of them.

Let everyone shine

Richard Tait and his wife have always loved Pictionary, the drawing game. 'Love' might be an understatement, in fact they excelled at it and regularly defeated all-comers, in fact anyone foolish enough to sit down long enough for a game of guessing what one person's scribbles might mean.

So when they found themselves on a wet weekend in the Hamptons being forced to play Scrabble – the classic word-based game – and feeling what it's like to be trounced by a couple who are as passionate about their chosen game as Tait is about his (he recalls that his friends were the kind of folk who keep their Scrabble scores on the refrigerator), Tait started to wonder what it might be like to play a game where everyone could enjoy a moment of victory. A game in which everyone could shine – at some point at least – and 'appear smart and funny in front of family and friends'.[9]

This was the beginning of the beginning of the phenomenon that is Cranium, Inc. The board games industry is highly competitive – 50% of games fail in their first year and of the rest, 50% fail in the second year. At one point, Cranium was growing at 35 times the rate of the rest of the indus-try and it won the industry's Game of the Year award three years on the bounce. In its first five years of existence, Cranium sold more than eight million boxes of shared fun (in an industry in which a few thousand sales is seen as a minor triumph). At the end of 2005, sales were 12 million in 50 countries.

Cranium games are different: not single-skill-based, not win or lose, not triumph or disaster (which encourages those family rows and endless sulking that populate everyone's holidays). Cranium games are built around multiple skills, giving each player a 'moment', as Tait[10] calls it, 'of glow, that moment of shine, where everybody celebrates them'. This might involve blind-drawing or plasticene-modelling or whistling a tune for your partner to identify ('hum-dingers') as well as the more verbal challenges like 'gnilleps' (spelling words backwards).

Not only does this make a Cranium game incredibly sociable for the young dating adults (the audience Tait and his partner Whit Alexander initially identified for their games), but also particularly suitable for young children. But this rethinking of what board games are for – their purpose, the skills involved and the competitive nature – in only part of the reason for Cra-nium's success. On its own this might well have created one, two or maybe three best-selling games. Cranium Inc. now has more than a dozen games in more than 50 countries, for all kinds of audiences (including one for execut-ives to play before a big meeting, now there's a thought . . .).

No, the secret of Cranium's abiding success lies in the way that Tait and Alexander have embedded their driving belief into the heart of their company, in the everyday lives of their employees and co-workers and suppliers and partners. Tait encourages each employee to be really clear what skills to bring to the party and to celebrate their personal successes in front of the rest of the company (by banging a gong to T Rex's 'Get it on'). The financial performance of each team is communicated via an animated visual (and normally, a party). The CFO himself (known as Professor Profit) signifies another million sales by skateboarding round the brightly coloured offices with a bizarre brain-hat on.

But more importantly perhaps than all of this is the clarity with which the business focusses on creating moments for every player to shine. In one children's game, Tait and co. spent ages trying to get a toy treasure chest to open suitably slowly so that the player who had achieved this would enjoy a really great moment in front of their fellow players.

Everything about Cranium, inside and out, is driven by this belief in the need to give everyone a moment to shine. To celebrate their abilities. And this belief, encapsulated in a unique vocabulary that embodies and shapes the behaviour of Craniacs large and small, allied with Tait and Alexander's experience in rapid prototyping from their time at Microsoft, is what encourages Craniacs inside and out to push games further and further to really – *really* – really deliver this. If a game isn't delivering this, it gets reworked or trashed.

And in new product and business development, it helps Cranium ignore the rules of a conservative industry again and again. Games for executives which aren't about crushing victory and defeat – sure. Games sold through coffee shops – why not? Adults playing with plasticene – let's see (Tait wasn't sure but an early play-test session confirmed the worth of the idea). Just check out the players' letters at the Cranium HQ website (http://www.cranium.com) and see what a difference this makes to Tait's consumers. Imagine making that kind of difference in the world . . . All you have to do is believe.

A is for . . .

Of course, probably the most high-profile belief company is that started in a garage by among others, that college drop-out, Steve Jobs. From the very beginning the Apple team instinctively understood that it wasn't computing that mattered but what it could help ordinary people do, how it could liberate and transform their lives by unlocking their creativity. From the way the box looked, the very first WP software, and even the name of the company – all of it was the antithesis of the military–industrial-complex computer that the industry was then obsessed with. As Steve Jobs[11] put it, in trying to lure John Sculley, then Pepsico's golden boy, from a corner office and big fat pension to join the garage full of geeks, 'Do you want to sell sugared water for the rest of your life or do you want a chance to change the world?'

And while Apple hasn't always been right – the Newton was a particularly bad attempt at getting hand-held technology to the market and the jury is still out (in the blogosphere at least) about the suitability of Intel chips to run Mac software – Apple continues to be driven by its beliefs. This – and not some great brand book or logo police operation – enable it to play the game it plays again and again.

Of course, more recently the genius of Jonathon Ives has set the standards for PC and mp3 design around the world through the example of his iMac and iPod but these products have only been able to come to market because of the company's commitment to its core beliefs, prime among which is the conviction that computing technology is valuable only in so far as it helps us unleash our creativity, not for its own sake.

Just as with howies, Jamie, Ikea and Cranium, Apple has gone wrong and will do so again. Having sound beliefs and a real commitment to them doesn't prevent any of these companies from doing the wrong thing at times. But at least they are able to admit it (if only to themselves, Appleheads!), which larger corporations struggle to do (take the Ford–Firestone debacle for example – despite the close ties between the two families at the top of each corporation, little was done to embrace the error and correct it, or not as fast as was needed).

Before we go

Thus far in this chapter, I have tried to show how building a belief business is the best way to get the herd working for you. How belief businesses touch something deep inside us and why that is so important in the post-marketing world. How it pays, big-time. How beliefs give us a reason to get up in the morning. How they shape our decisions inside the company. How they transform otherwise dull me-too businesses into things worth bothering with. How – each business being different – they behave differently (and find it easy to do so).

Before we conclude, I thought it might be useful to share some of my own practices and experience in wrestling with these issues: in trying to get business to work this way. It falls far short of the process that others might recommend, but I think that's only right. This is highly personal stuff and all I can offer you is a sense of how I have approached this kind of problem with clients and colleagues. I hope it helps. Please feel free to adapt and bastardize and share it with others. And tell me your experiences, *please.*

1. Be who you are

Be who you are. Don't be a suit or a drawing board or a laptop operative or another place at the boardroom table. Be who you really are and whatever else you do make sure that you don't give that away.

Ian Dury[12] had it down well:

Don't do nothing that is cut-price,

(BEWARE ANY COMPROMISE TO WHAT YOU BELIEVE IN)

you know what that'll make you be

(EVERY COMPROMISE TO YOUR BELIEFS DIMINISHES YOU)

They will try you – tricky device – tempt you with the ordinary

(EVERY DAY NEW TEMPTATIONS TO COMPROMISE WILL PRESENT THEMSELVES)

Doing stuff that isn't you just degrades you and your people and we can all see it a mile off. From inside the company and without.

But what '*is you*'? How do you know which of the myriad parts of you to build this on?

2. What do you believe in? Find it and live it!

What is it that you really believe? What do you believe with such passion that you just have to do something about it? Because it's what you do with your business that gives it meaning to you and your customers? And, for it to be authentic, you have to find something that you really deeply believe (and please don't just try on beliefs like off-the-peg suits – 'No, this one's a little tight around the shoulders', etc.).

Too many people – including some former clients and colleagues of mine – wrestling with this kind of problem, whether in a new or an existing business, start from an intellectual analysis. They spot 'gaps in the market' or they develop what they rather grandly call 'product and category *insights*' – they look for objective truths in the market rather than follow their own instincts and convictions. Which always reads very predictable and bland (as Adam Morgan[13] suggests in *Eating the Big Fish*, insights that get expressed as 'if you're the kind of person who . . .' are the tell-tale signs of pygmy thinking here – they also suggest that you are desperate to be accepted and will do anything to get alongside the customer and who likes girls or boys like that, eh?).

Instead, think about things the other way round. Start close at home – what gets your goat? What makes you mad? What really inspires you? – and grow from there. For example, ask yourself really personal stuff before you worry about business and market issues.

OK, let's try again: *what is wrong with the world for you and your family and friends* (surely these guys are important to you?)? Then and only then, for your colleagues, your customers and the rest of the world?

Unless you really believe in something – *really believe* – it won't be strong enough to shape your actions in the face of the everyday temptations for compromise that will present themselves to you and do so every day. Something you might agree or disagree with isn't strong enough. For my own part, there are lots of things that I agree with, plenty I disagree with and to be honest, quite a number that I both agree and disagree with – all at the same time. Things that I believe enough to act on are few and far between.

Beliefs can be embarrassing to express – they are highly personal – thus expressing them can make you feel vulnerable. In more European cultures (including the east coast of the USA) we are particularly resistant to the idea of expressing beliefs – not surprising given that many countries spent several hundred years fighting to make personal belief a legitimate private matter – and not something for the state or church to determine. Expressing our beliefs makes us feel uncomfortable because what we believe is a very large part of who we are; articulating this puts the 'who' (that's you) into play – leaves each of us open to criticism and possible rejection (and you'll remember how painful that can be for any primate . . .).

But that is precisely why what you believe is so powerful. Why what the key people in a business have to agree on is what they believe that their business or brand is going to exemplify – what belief is going to drive their business; what their business is going to be 'for'.

3. Act like you mean it (and don't act like you don't . . .)

The Ancient Greek philosophers puzzled over the problem of *akrasia* – that is, 'weakness of will'. How can a person be said to truly believe something and yet not act in accordance with that belief? How can I be said to believe that stealing is wrong, but get caught holding up a bank? Surely, if you don't act in accordance with your beliefs, doesn't that suggest that you don't actually believe them at all?

Looking back at my undergraduate philosophy classes I think I often took this for a question about belief in and of itself and what is required if you say you believe something. An attempt to define the idea behind the word 'believe', if you like. However, the more I think about it now, the clearer it becomes that the conundrum is as much about cognition – how can we know if anyone truly believes something except through their actions? If you think about it, all businesses find it easy to express their commitment to some standard of service, to some ideal or to some customer or other (two thirds of all FTSE 100 companies have an explicit commitment to customers' needs but few of them really deliver. They can't because otherwise they would feature in Reichheld and his associates' data on net recommendation . . . or indeed distort it.)

What differentiates a business which lives by its beliefs from one which just claims to do so is what that business does (or doesn't do). *Indeed, all that differentiates one business from another is what it does* (note to my advertising and PR friends, *not* what it says); particularly when we have taught the world to be suspicious of spin and news management.

Talk is cheap; actions can cost you. What you say is gone tomorrow but what you do (or fail to do) can stay for a long, long time. As the film school adage has it, all character is action.

Summary: taking a stand

I'm not recommending this just because it makes good copy. I believe it's great business sense. Businesses that are prepared to stand for something are businesses that justify the attention and interest of the broader public. They garner more of the employee's effort than the vanilla businesses. In the UK,

Waitrose's refusal to abandon its commitment to food quality and integrity in the face of the supermarket trench warfare around price has earned it a great deal of respect from its own and other shoppers and a sales performance to match. In the USA, Target has given the giants of the retail sector a good pasting as it pursues its flattery of the tastes of its price point buyers. Even Walmart have had to concede that their price-driven model has been challenged by Target's purposeful approach.

As the quote that started this chapter suggests, the big issue if you want to be interesting enough to get the herd interacting around you is this: *what do you stand for and what are you prepared to do to live that out?* To be true to your beliefs? What do you want to use your business *for? What change do you want to bring about in the world?*

And there are real personal rewards for doing this, beyond money and fame and power (the usual motivators that are supposed to drive us on, but that many of us are finding insufficient).

The business guru, Charles Handy, once calculated that each of us has only 100,000 hours of working life. Imagine if what remains for you was driven by your beliefs and convictions – was a vehicle for them. Imagine how that would feel. Imagine how that would change your experience of work. When you contemplate this, it's hard not to take the more difficult – but ultimately more rewarding – road. David Hieatt of howies has, as ever, just the thought for you: he asks simply, 'Do you want to respect yourself? Yes? Well, now seems a good time.' So why don't you try?

Some questions arising for marketing

1. Why is it that belief businesses create such a stir in mass populations? What is your explanation? Is it just about the founder? What would Nike be like without Phil Knight? Apple without Steve Jobs? What would Jamie Oliver's business be like without Jamie's beliefs? Would it make any difference if the people at the heart of a belief business remained anonymous to the outside world?

2. What are non-belief businesses missing? What are the disadvantages of non-belief businesses?

3. Where do non-belief businesses go wrong? Which are the crucial practices that pull them apart from belief businesses?

4. Why are 'Mission, Vision, Value' statements not the same as beliefs? Are they more like school mottos than live, essential beliefs? Why might the 'brand' be useful in making a belief business work? How might the 'brand' hinder a belief business?

5. What are the key challenges that a belief business faces? What new skills and capabilities might you need to be good at this kind of business? Which things do you need to drop?

8

Key Principle
No. 5: (Re-)Light
the Fire

What this chapter will cover

Most mature brands and businesses do not appear to be led by belief or purpose; some have forgotten their original driving ideas, some have had their beliefs quashed by brand-babble or money-mindedness, others never had belief or a sense of purpose. This chapter discusses the issues around lighting or relighting the fires of driving beliefs and the dangers and pitfalls around doing so. A number of high-profile examples are used to illustrate the key principles: the inevitable clash between belief- and marketing-led approaches; the behavioural imperative; making and keeping it personal; why consumer and media scepticism are not going to go away.

Leave those vain moralists, my friend, and return to the depth of your soul: that is where you will always rediscover the source of the sacred fire.

J.J. Rousseau

Keep the home fires burning

Throughout human history, fire has been important to our continued exist-ence. On the one hand, it is *fire-tamed* that warms us, protects us and enables us to transform the world around us, be it through cooking or smelting; on the other, *fire-untamed* destroys all that we hold dear; it smarts and it burns, it causes pain and it lays waste. It is no surprise that fire is one of the first and most powerful symbols in all human cultures, certainly all but a handful that we have so far discovered. And it plays a key role in the symbolic lan-guage of all the world's religions.

The Ancient Romans, for example, built their domestic theology around the hearth that each family shared. Daily religious practice honoured both the *Lares familiaris* (the spirits of each family), the *genius* of the *paterfamilias* or head of the family in the *Lararium* (home of the Lares) and then the *Penates* (the deities of the larder or stock cupboard) and last but not least the goddess Vesta whose job it was to protect the hearth – the fireplace and burning heart of the family. And Rome built its collective identity from such domestic parts. Just as the daughters of a Roman family were supposed to have been the guardians of the fire in the family hearth and thus particularly devoted to the goddess Vesta, so the daughters of the original Roman kings were encouraged to protect the nation's own hearth, as members of a unique religious college known as the vestal virgins.

If today you walk across the dusty ruins of the old Roman Forum, just across the way from the Regia – the original ceremonial home of the kings of Rome – stands what remains of a circular building, a round temple, the *aedes vestae*. Within this building, the sacred flame of the nation was maintained and protected by the six vestal virgins. Just as an individual family depended on its domestic hearth being maintained intact, so the nation came to believe that its fate was tied up with the maintenance of its own, symbolic royal hearth.

Service as a vestal was no simple matter of good deed, nor was it merely some honorary office for good-doers among the idle rich. Each vestal dedicated 30 years of their lives to the fire. The first 10 were spent as novices, the next 10 as active virgins and the final 10 was spent teaching the latest novices. Keeping the fire alive and safe became of such symbolic importance to the Roman State that strange superstitions and laws grew up around it and its keepers.[1]

The fire could be extinguished just once a year (at the end of February); if the vestals allowed this to happen at any other time, they could expect to be beaten by the *Pontifex Maximus* (the emperor from the first century onwards). If they surrendered their honour (as Cicero put it euphemistically), they could expect nothing less than the death sentence, albeit by novel means – deflowered vestals were immured deep below the ground. (An interesting thought to hold in your head as you read this chapter . . .)

The fire inside

The kind of brands and businesses that I discussed in the previous chapter seem to burn with some kind of fire – a fire of belief or purpose; a fire that drives and animates the organization behind the name, the people inside the company and the way they interact with each other; a fire that gets the founders and all the staff out of bed in the morning and bouncing into work; indeed, a fire that seems to animate and drive the way that employees, customers, partners and suppliers interact with each other around the brand or business.

But for every howies, there are dozens of other sports apparel businesses; for every Naked a host of communications consultants; for every Jamie, a myriad of TV chefs with books to sell; for every IKEA, there are dozens of

DFS, leather workshops and the like; for every Apple, there are hundreds of other IT equipment manufacturers. Most of these 'other' mature brands and businesses have no fire, no belief system, no reason to get out of bed in the morning. And as we saw in the last chapter, these non-belief companies underperform belief- and purpose-driven companies.

Perhaps that's a little unfair; many of these 'other' businesses have a belief system – a tacit set of descriptions of how we do things round here, a catalogue of 'whats' rather than 'whys' that is supposed to add up to a 'who' – as in 'who we are'. But more often this adds up to a 'what we don't do'. All too many have followed the advice of some business guru or other and written down some stodgy explicit version, in some 'brand values' statement, or even a 'Mission, Vision, Values' statement of the sort treasured by corporate communications teams. Most of these contain pointless bland motherhood thoughts, littered with phrases such as 'world-class', 'customer-orientation', 'benchmarked service excellence' and the like.

Many of these catalogues of 'whats' are driven by what you might call 'self-regarding' or 'inward' factory thinking – that is, concerns about what it is the company does and how efficiently it does it; rather than what it might aim to do in the world or the significance it aims to create through its actions. If such ambitions are included they are either expressed in unhelpfully vague terms (to deliver world-class solutions) or overly and selfishly precise (to be number one provider of . . .).

Worse still is the stuff influenced by brand-babble. Being such a vague and floppy idea,[2] 'brand' can be used to mean what you like. To justify what you want to do and to outlaw what you want to proscribe. To keep things the same as they always have been or to sidestep the tough decisions by wrapping everything in empty copy and glossy, beautifully designed, art direction that is sheer veneer. Brand this, brand that. Brand strategy, brand vision, brand personality, brand commitments, brand trousers (to be honest).

No wonder the fire burns low in most of these other businesses and sometimes seems to go out all together. Indeed it often seems easier to extinguish the fire of belief than it is to light it or fan the flames. Before we consider how to relight the fire and get it to energize and illuminate the behaviours of a given group of people, inside or outside the company, let's just see how easy it is to extinguish the fire of belief, how quickly this can happen and what it can mean to both customers and shareholders.

Easier to extinguish than light

There are many reasons why one company seeks to buy another. Sometimes it is to purchase production capabilities (but that is rare in the developed world); more often it is about gaining access to customers or markets that the acquirer cannot reach through any other means. The literature of mergers and acquisitions (M&A) suggests that two of the worst possible M&A motivations are rescue (too sentimental) or transplant (admits failure in change management in the acquiring company). Snapple – the soft-drinks company – is definitely one of the latter.

In 1972, in the small town of Valley Stream on Long Island, Hyman Golden, Arnold and Leonard Marsh – healthy idealists all – founded a small drinks company around a simple carbonated apple soda (hence the company's name). While 30 years on, this may not seem an unusual business idea, at the time it was a striking expression of belief. Today's mainstream is happy to rehearse interests in 'natural' foods, in health issues and in the quality of what we put in our bodies. This is hard to unimagine – the notion that *we are what we eat* has for most of the last three decades been seen as a kooky or extremist point of view. As you might expect from a business whose products have always claimed to be made from the 'best stuff on earth', Snapple were from the start a business driven by the fire of a profound belief. And a significant minority of believer-drinkers found their way to the product and the company; a crusading army of word-of-mouth marketers, if you like.

The business grew – as you might expect – through additional alternative means. On the one hand, it secured repeated endorsement from the Shock-Jock Howard Stern on his syndicated but anarchic *Radio Show*. On the other, the small amount of mainstream advertising deployed a novel and impactful approach which essentially amplified something true about the company. Wendy Kaufman was an employee who had taken it upon herself to answer the waves of customer letters with questions about the product and its ingredients. Wendy the Snapple Lady was depicted in advertising as an unusual straight-talking company spokesperson, answering customer letters in her endearingly idiosyncratic manner. Within American popular culture she came to represent and embody the company's beliefs in a way that a more traditional approach would almost certainly not have done.

Distribution was expanded into New England and California and sales continued to rise. When sales growth reached a 400% annual increase, the original founders sold the business to a Boston investment company, who then sold the business on to a large but ailing manufacturer.

Meanwhile, Quaker realized that their food and beverage business was stuck in low-growth categories and despite millions of dollars being spent on new product development (NPD) programmes, they concluded that their own efforts would be unlikely to change the fortunes of their company. Snapple by contrast represented a very different opportunity – high growth, high margin, with a very strong customer franchise.

So, Dear Reader, they bought it. For $ 1.7 billion.

The acquisition was disastrous. Sales dived and Quaker were forced to sell the business on to another investment company, Triarc, for $ 300 million – less than one fifth of the original purchase price. And a huge discount on the cost of acquiring and managing the business. So great was the scale of this cock-up that Quaker itself was subsequently sold. And many of the managers responsible put out on the street.

The misfits

There are many reasons which have been proposed by people much smarter than me, as to why the acquisition of Snapple went so badly wrong. Of course, in retrospect, the price paid by Quaker for the business seems excessive; equally, Quaker's poor previous track record in M&A and making such transactions work seems to have been ignored by all parties – they just weren't very good at it. The overestimation of the acquiring firm's abilities is not unusual in M&A activities – many academics point to overestimation of our own skills and resources as a key reason for M&A failure.

But talking to those who were watching the farrago at close quarters, it occurs to me that Quaker's attempts to impose its own ways of thinking and behaving on the belief-driven Snapple Corporation are a prime cause of the catastrophe.

Quaker was a conservative manufacturing business, with well-established and well-tried approaches to managing and marketing their businesses. For example, product development – a key to keeping a soda brand vital and interesting in the eyes of its customers – had always been done at Snapple on the basis of belief and ingenuity, not on the basis of segmentation and benefit-led thinking. Coming up with new products had always been both an expression and a reward for the believers inside the company; Quaker made it a chore. Equally while Quaker advertising was always developed to be safe and uncontroversial and more than a little bland (they were strong believers in the transmission/persuasion model discussed in Chapter 5), Snapple had always enjoyed the experience and acted far more from their gut instincts and beliefs. Quaker's social conservatism was irked at the thought of Howard Stern's anarchic and often filthy style.

Quaker acted quickly to impose its behaviours on its new acquisition. This involved changing its marketing communications: they fired Wendy (and the agency that produced the ads she featured in) and dropped the foul-mouthed Stern unceremoniously. But such public acts became symbolic of a bigger struggle to the believers inside the company and out; that of the emerging counter-culture and 'the Man' (the counter-cultural personification of the Western capitalist system). They signalled a fundamental misunderstanding about how belief businesses work and what matters in managing them. Quaker thought having paid their $1.7 billion that they now owned the brand; employees and customers realized that the opposite was the case. The ideas and beliefs that Snapple embodied had become the property of believers and could not be bought and sold, no matter how much was offered.

Curiously, as soon as Triarc acquired the business in 1997, both Wendy and Stern were reinstated, customers celebrated and the sales decline was reversed. Triarc and subsequent owners Cadbury Schweppes both seemed to understand more viscerally than Quaker what kind of business Snapple is and how it needs to be managed. How important the beliefs behind the business are and how the behaviours that bring them alive remain. How unhelpful traditional ways of managing are to such a business and what the cost of forcing them onto a belief business can be.

Relighting my fire

Of course, the story of Snapple is not just a cautionary tale of what can go wrong and the true cost of doing the wrong thing. It also has a positive moral: it *is* possible to relight the fire of a belief- and purpose-driven business. It *can* be done.

But it can't be done by using the traditional ways of thinking, of identifying and seeking to satisfy the needs of identified key customers; of communicating benefits and reasons why; of persuading individuals to buy; of looking for the short term over the longer term; of thinking from the B2C perspective, in selfish relationship terms. And most of all it can't be done in a cold-hearted analytic manner because while beliefs and a sense of purpose can be analysed using the traditional tools, they cannot be animated or managed using these approaches.

The power of dreams

Honda UK is a great case study of rediscovering a long-smouldering fire at the heart of a business. Fantastic communications such as the award-winning Cog and Grrrr commercials, fantastic sales results and a fantastic tale of the defeat of analysis by belief and creativity.

And in one of the better descriptions[3] of what happened behind the scenes of a campaign called *The Power of Dreams*, key participants from Honda's comms team acknowledge the problems a more traditional way of thinking has in dealing with beliefs.

> Our first instinct was to drop *The Power of Dreams* (a line that the company had long used on marketing materials) ... It sounded like the usual car bollocks. Our second instinct was to focus on some simple, overarching value, some territory we could 'own' in the vast accumulation of car marketing pablum. We set about digging into Honda's history and culture to find the inspirational nugget. We soon realised our instincts were rubbish.

Prior to working with Wieden and Kennedy London, Honda had little appeal in the UK.

> The most common reason for someone not buying a Honda was that it simply didn't occur to them. The second most common reason was that the brand doesn't appeal. People bought Hondas despite the brand; for the entirely rational reason that the cars are excellent.

In other words, the business had little in the way of consumer franchise and little sense for both customers and staff of what made Honda special. No wonder the quality of the product was hidden behind me-too behaviours and marketing. Indeed, so weak was the reputation of Honda as a car manufacturer, that both customers and journalists referred to specific models ('I drive a Civic' is how they put it) rather than the company.

Instead, through a highly collaborative approach, the Wieden's team helped Honda UK to see the flame that burned brightly at the heart of the home corporation. As Russell Davies puts it,

> [We discovered that] the *Power of Dreams* was true. It sprang directly out of their culture, not from a series of global focus groups, and that kind of human truth about a company was a powerful weapon.

Note Davies' comment about focus groups – the ready-reckoner of traditional marketing thinking; what 'the power of dreams' represented was the fire at the heart of the Japanese corporation; its driving belief [*sic*]. A belief in doing things better, in going beyond what is expected and asked for, in progressive thinking and engineering and design behaviour. A belief that was entirely personal for the founder of the company, Soichiro Honda, a belief that helped him build the business in Japan.

Soichiro's father had been a blacksmith and all-round technical odd-job man and Soichiro learnt to use his hands and his brain to make things work and then his ingenuity to make them work better. All his life he strove after what seemed just out of his reach – he later told the story of his first sight of an automobile as an emblem for his lifelong passion to make cars better. Entranced and astonished by the rumble of the first car to visit Yamahigashi, a small village in Japan's Shizuoka prefecture, his jaw dropped when he saw it.

> I turned and chased after that car for all I was worth. And when it had driven past me, without even thinking why I found myself chasing it down the road, as hard as I could run.

Dream a little dream

But 'dreaming' and 'optimism' are both rather vague, however true or attractive they might seem. What turned such positive thoughts into driving energy was a recontextualization – finding a way to locate this in the real world of customers and cars. To turn it from a noble thought into a purpose for the company to enact.

In the case of Honda, this was achieved by identifying the enemy that both company and customer could share.

> Spending all that time delving into the restless energy of Honda culture, while simultaneously sitting through reel after reel of car ads, pointed us to a compelling enemy for Honda – the bewildering complacency of the contemporary car industry.

In other words, Honda's commitment to doing things better really started to have an edge when placed side by side with the dull conformity of the rest of the industry.

Wieden's great step forward was embodying this both at a high conceptual level ('OK is not OK' was one early expression) but also in practical terms – Cog celebrates the build quality of Honda's rather dull-styled saloons; Grrrr shows how Honda diesel engines are the result of challenging the downsides of existing engine technology (why do diesel engines have to be so noisy and dirty?). And doing so in a distinctive and memorable manner (or rather a different manner for each commercial – as Davies notes, it was important that the team embraced complexity rather than the reductive thinking of traditional comms thinking. 'Keep it complex, stupid', he quips). This in turn generated a great deal of word of mouth – both Cog and Grrrr were downloaded millions of times from Internet sites both in the UK and around the world, and 500,000 DVDs were dispatched to meet customer enquiries.

The commercial results[4] are astounding for a business in a heavily oversupplied market (each year European-based car manufacturers make some 30% more cars than are bought). The campaign has been shown to be responsible for nearly £400m in revenue for Honda. In the two years from April 2002, sales of new Honda cars since then have increased by 28%, despite a significant decline in media spend, share of voice and PR activity. Moreover, this was achieved at a time when Honda raised its prices relative to both UK customers and overseas affiliates (rather than lowering them).

But perhaps most important of all is the way it has transformed the way the employees interact with each other and with customers around the company and its product.

For the first time, in 2003, Honda made it into 'the *Sunday Times* Best Companies to Work For' list. Entry is based on surveys measuring staff satisfaction and pride in working for the company. Honda made number 18. In 2004, it climbed the charts to 16, when 89% of staff said they were proud to work for Honda. Staff turnover was down to 11% by early 2003, and then just 7% by early 2004.

Vile bodies

It's all very well, you might think, unearthing a founder's driving belief in a business that has almost forgotten it – in an overseas division of a particular company. But can you find and implement a belief approach in a business that has never really had one? Can you take a mature and rather dull business and transform it into one driven by beliefs and a sense of purpose? Is it possible to retrofit belief in a convincing way? Or do we have to limit this approach to businesses that are founded on them and condemn all others to a duller and less successful future?

When Unilever launched a new soap bar in 1957, they named it Dove to reflect the lightness and purity of a soap bar made with 25% moisturizer. Over the next 40 years, Dove grew and grew, partly through organic means as Unilever took the brand to more and more markets around the world, but increasingly it came from new products. So much so that by 2005, soap accounted for only half of Dove's sales. Hair products, deodorants, skincare and even facial care products have appeared in different markets, with differing degrees of success. Part of the reason for these differences in performance are cultural – women's personal hygiene routines are largely culturally determined – partly also because wherever the products appeared, all cultures saw a basic split between soap and these other product categories. On the one hand, soap is about cleaning – about being and feeling clean and spruce; on the other, things like moisturizers and haircare products are about grooming and beauty in the more general sense.

The real challenge to those managing a business with a foot in both camps was to bridge this gap. Dove had to become a beauty- rather than just a cleaning-brand. The only problem being that the last thing the world needs now is another beauty brand. As the team's planning lead, Olivia Johnson puts it, 'The world is awash with them. How on earth could Dove be a distinctive voice in this overpopulated world?'[5]

A familiar situation

Now many of us have faced similar problems. Every market today is over-supplied with equally good options. How can you stand out? How can you engage with customers and staff to provide something worth them interacting around? What can you say or do?

But sharing a problem doesn't necessarily make it easier to solve. If it did then more of us would be millionaires. Rather it is one of those unavoidable choices for today's business. Fortunately, belief can provide some antidote, given that most businesses are still not driven by belief or purpose. Belief can be a way of overcoming the problems of oversupply; indeed, belief is probably the best way to do so.

Girl talk

Unusually for even an advertising agency, the Ogilvy Dove team were almost all female. When they came to ponder the challenge of making Dove into a beauty brand, this proved essential to solving the problem. Not because they had any particular expert knowledge from the accident of their genetic make-up. No, what helped them was their ability to examine and express their own feelings and beliefs about the bigger issues of beauty and its portrayal by corporations in the media and in other behaviour. In other words, they could approach the problem from an entirely personal point of view.

> Each member of the team had the intuitive [sic] sense that the way beauty brands behaved wasn't quite right (in the moral sense, not the commercial sense).

Each of them felt that 'it was the type of beauty promoted by these brands . . . a physical ideal that most of us fall short of'. And each of them was thus able to acknowledge that this left them feeling 'miserable . . . you feel like substandard goods'. In the context of the images presented by the industry, images created by friends and peers of the Ogilvy team itself, this feeling presented a personally felt opportunity to do something different. To avoid further misery and self-loathing.

From this entirely personal perspective and fuelled by conversations with commentators and counsellors working in the area (people such as Susie Orbach, Gloria Steinem and Noami Wolf as well as those working at the coal face of female body-image), the team developed a sense of mission for the brand; rather than being just another beauty brand imposing an impossible ideal on women young and old (or mostly young, as the older ones are ignored and made to feel particularly inadequate), Dove could change the way women feel about themselves.

The danger of missions

In order to be clear about their thinking, the Ogilvy team wrote this down in the form of a statement of purpose for their own view of the brand.

> To make more women feel more beautiful every day, by widening today's stereotypical view of beauty and inspiring them to take great care of themselves.

The global brand director, Silvia Lagnado, was a great supporter of this direction because she had long been a confirmed critic of the beauty industry and how it made women feel. So another personal conviction was recruited to the team.

However, she – and it has to be said the Ogilvy team itself – was concerned about whether or not this could be done credibly by a soap brand. Wouldn't it just end up being a bit preachy and feeling a bit happy-clappy or just over-serious?

Well, naturally it could. And did. Because Ogilvy's first three or so attempts at expressing this mission did feel just that. Lines such as 'Beauty has a million faces one of them is yours' just seemed to be bossy and implicitly criticizing the audience, not trying to offer an alternative. So it was back to the drawing board.

You too can look like this

The team retreated to a specific product – a minor but important product launch of firming cream. For the men among you, let me just say that this kind of product is applied by women to their hips, bums, thighs, and any other bits that run the risk of sagging, and the stigmatizing cellulite – orange-peel skin. Very quickly the team realized that what united the millions of women in the audience was not the product or a perceived need for it but a shared hatred of advertising for such products. All the advertising seemed to feature stick insects in their early twenties who looked as if they had a greater need of a square meal than a firming cream. The 'metamessage' – the message behind the message, as sociolinguist Deborah Tannen[6] calls it – of all the advertising in the category is that thin is the only way to be; that 'slinky little hips [are] the only hips to have', that not only can products like this make you look like a starved 20-year-old but that only by looking so, could a woman be acceptable.

A good thought, you might think. An interesting and refreshing one, you might murmur, if you had sat in the room with the creative team and compared it to the category's communications hung on the walls.

But a thought that ran the risk of more bossy happy-clappy stuff if you didn't *feel* the alternative.

But the way the brand team expressed the brief shifted the way the creative team understood the brief, how they felt about it and the work they did. As Dennis Lewis, the (undoubtedly male) creative director, describes it,

> The first thing Daryl and Olivia said to me to try and help me understand how women felt . . . was simply 'Just imagine every day for 40 years someone telling you your willy's not big enough.'

One of the first ads which emerged was the one shown in Figure 8.1. The team (and everyone outside it who had a sneak preview) instinctively felt that this really redefined current notions of beauty and provided a notable (and talk-worthy) counterpoint to what the industry had been doing for so long.

This woman is undoubtedly beautiful. She is large but more than happy with herself. You see it in her eyes and her body language.

And so did the populations of most European countries when local marketing executives observed the outstanding sales effect in both the UK and Germany (all except Sweden where conservative business practices got their way). And they talked endlessly to each other about it, the story of its

let's face it, firming the thighs of a size 8 supermodel wouldn't have been much of a challenge.

new Dove
Firming Range

Figure 8.1   *Dove ad*
Source: Unilever. Reproduced by permission.

creation with the collaboration of the fashion photographer Rankin. And they did so everywhere – on buses, on websites, in chatrooms and coffee shops and saw the conversation echoed and amplified in newspapers and on TV.

This experience allowed Ogilvy to understand how to create a bigger campaign for Dove in general – the so-called 'campaign for real beauty', which would express the brand's new belief in a compelling and populist manner, the brief for which read like this: 'Question(s) the images pumped out by the beauty industry by showing genuinely stunning beauty comes in lots of shapes, sizes and forms'.

The key to getting this right turned out to be based on understanding which rules of the beauty industry most annoyed women. Lots of work was done in on- and offline research to get a grip on the detail of this. Lots of debate went on inside the team. And lots of work was written, featuring young and old, thin and less so, freckled and dark-skinned women in this way. To encourage women to debate the issues themselves by 'joining the beauty debate' at www.campaignforrealbeauty.co.uk (see Figure 8.2).

More belief

However powerful the team's own beliefs, however strong the work, however powerful the insights, however strong the commitment of the sponsoring clients – Silvia and Klaus Arntz of Unilever Germany – such a high-profile campaign, expressing such powerful and powerfully held beliefs, would need a very high level of support and agreement within Unilever before it would ever see the light of day.

I'm told that the Ogilvy team approached this with the same degree of creativity and commitment that had got them to the work itself. Instead of making a rational argument or an impassioned plea for the justness of their cause or the efficacy of their work, they chose the belief route. They chose to recruit the senior management team at Unilever to their passionately held beliefs about beauty and the language of beauty and what it does to women's self-esteem.

And if the story I've been told is true, they were rather sneaky about it. Using a simple hand-held camera, the team secretly interviewed the daughters and other close female relatives of all the approving board members – including one childless senior executive's beloved pooch – about their views

Figure 8.2 *Example from the 'Campaign for real beauty'*
Source: Unilever. Reproduced by permission.

of their bodies and their relationship with the imagery projected by the beauty industry of what is acceptable and desirable. There was, I am told, a long silence in the room when this film was first shown. The proposal was no longer a proposal; the team had managed to recruit the management of Unilever personal products to the cause. They had made Dove's cause as personal for the approvers as it was and remains for the team itself.

'T ain't what you say

Because of the personal commitment to the cause that Dove championed, the team also realized that advertising and publicity were only ever going to have a short-term effect unless they were backed up by substantial and tangible behaviours by the brand. It just wouldn't cut the mustard if the campaign for real beauty was able to be exposed as empty words, as flim-flam, as mere hype. The campaign had to be embodied in real words, not just some advertising-led petition, if you like. As one industry cynic commented to me, 'Putting a fat bird on a bus-side doesn't change the world.' It didn't even earn many creative awards to salve the consciences of the advertising luvvies (mostly men, it must be said, big believers of the beauty myth) but that didn't really matter to the team. They had already busied themselves with doing unusual things to evidence the brand's commitment to this core belief in real beauty.

So for example, Ogilvy Toronto had already developed a travelling photographic exhibition, 'Beyond Compare', depicting alternative takes on real beauty and the dangers of the beauty myth. Ogilvy London worked with the original photographer, Rankin, to develop educational materials around the depiction of beauty in magazines and on film. Rankin had long refused to use make-up, lighting and the vast array of retouching and post-production technology to create the fictitious images that young girls in particular are exposed to. This he felt was an opportunity to really lift the curtain on the beauty industry's continual lies which the industry peddles to distort how women see themselves and their bodies; lies which create so much misery.

And this misery is palpable. According to the Dove UK website,[7] over 50% of women say their body disgusts them, and six out of ten British girls think that they would be happier if they were thinner.

So the worldwide team created a proposal for a Dove self-esteem fund – a charitable body which supports groups and individuals that work with women to educate them to fight a number of debilitating conditions. Eating disorders are a prime example and sadly very common – it is estimated that 1.1 m women in the UK have some kind of medically diagnosed eating disorder. So in the UK, this area is one on which the self-esteem fund focusses its efforts. In the USA, the DSEF partners with Girl Scouts of the USA to support 'uniquely ME!', an educational health programme which reaches some 70,000 American teenage girls a year. Here's what the USA website has to say about this programme:

> The program consists of an educational curriculum that integrates the latest research from the Girl Scout Research Institute (GSRI) and offers hands-on activities such as mentoring, community service or sports. Three activity

booklets, available in English and bilingual English/Spanish, guide girls through simple exercises that help them understand and build self-confidence. The booklets target two developmental age groups: 8–10 year-olds and 11–14 year-olds. Through sessions led by caring adult volunteers, and the uniquely ME! curriculum, the program includes exercises about recognizing one's strengths and best attributes, handling peer pressure, identifying core values and personal interests, eating disorders, the power of positive thinking, relationships and stress – on an age-appropriate basis.

The fire inside – summary so far

So far we have seen that it is possible to either brighten or darken the flame that drives a belief-driven business. Key to doing so seems to be in the way the business is approached: is belief something which is allowed to shape the behaviours of the business or is the belief reduced merely to some bland brand-positioning statement and caged within the traditional marketing ways of thinking?

Both brand-babble and money-mindedness can conspire against belief, because they depersonalize the belief – for managers, employees and ultimately for customers. The great power of belief in business is that it is personal – it demands engagement and commitment from the internal audiences if it is to express itself in behaviour. A half-hearted semi-belief is not good enough – something that the team or management feel is 'kinda interesting' is insufficient. Belief is a bit like pregnancy – you can't be half-pregnant, nor can you half-believe.

To make the fire burn bright, it is important to find a way to contextualize the belief. It helps to find an enemy or an existing state of affairs to kick against.

Snapple's commitment to natural product ingredients gets a real spin when expressed in the context of the corporate world of food and drink businesses and what they do to us. Honda's commitment to challenging and improving technology for the driver is interesting when considered in isolation but gets more vital when it's compared to the complacency of the rest of the industry. Dove's commitment to natural beauty really sings out when it challenges the rest of the industry and the damage it does.

Once the fire burns bright inside, the next thing to do is to turn the belief into action. In Snapple's case the most visible behaviours were product composition and marketing communications. All of these have to be generated

by and exemplify the belief that drives the business or they will ring false –
that's why the amateurish Wendy the Snapple lady and Howard Stern's
ranting obscenities signalled so much about the brand (and their axing by
Quaker proved so disastrous).

In the case of Honda, communication played a different role – amplifying
and celebrating the behaviours already in place within the business (but
hidden from the British consumer's eyes). But to do this, communication had
also to be as different from the rest of the pack as the belief and the hidden
behaviours that it illuminated were.

In Dove's case, the belief that has taken over as the brand's driving force
is of such social import and is so contrary that the team has had to work
really hard to develop behaviours which substantiate the belief well beyond
communication. It is hard to conceive that even five years ago a major consumer goods company like Unilever would be making a public commitment
to address social needs. Oh, and the advertising had to do more than just
sell products by transmitting for use by 'real women' (though this was an
important element): it had to do a different job – that is, start a debate around
the issues of body image that women were most concerned about.

It is no surprise that all three cases have very high-profile communications
– all of them generate tremendous debate and excitement, but not through
the tricks of word-of-mouth marketing. No, their communication is interesting to both professionals and 'civilians' (as TV production people call us
normal folk) because it is an authentic expression of the belief that drives
the business. The communication is interesting because the business is.

Where next?

So far we have discussed how to light or relight your fire of belief – how to
identify and shape your core beliefs and how behaviours need to be aligned
to these beliefs if your business is to be truly belief-driven. I've described in
passing three different brands' successful efforts to do so and made it all seem
fairly straightforward (I hope). Almost as if these things happen without
effort.

Any of the people who were involved in these or the examples of found-
ing-belief businesses we discussed in the last chapter will tell you that it just
isn't so. That after the fact things seem straightforward and logical but the
reality is much messier and much tougher (even the most entrepreneurial

business person knows the allure and the temptations that Mr Dury describes – the daily temptation to compromise, the struggle to find new and interesting things to do and to make them happen).

The rest of this chapter explores three big issues in implementing this belief- or purpose-led model of business:

1. How to work out what to do.
2. Why you really need to do this.
3. What happens if you don't (a repeat, I know, but it's fun . . .).

How to work out what to do?

One of the least useful ideas adopted by business in recent years is 'benchmarking'. That is the analysis of competitors, what they do and how they do it. Actually it's not the analysis that's such a problem, it's more the application of the analysis. More often than not what company A does following its benchmarking of its competitive set is copy everyone else. And if company B does the same analysis – and company C – then very quickly all the companies in a particular market end up doing exactly the same thing. Some years ago, McKinsey – a key proponent of this kind of approach – demonstrated through a study of the German telco market how quickly this destroys value for the companies (and, I'd suggest, the consumer).

Now I'm not denying that it is useful to know what your competitors do and how they do it, but only as a guide for what you are going to do differently. Keeping the flame of your driving belief or purpose alive will make it harder for you to just copy others (however tempting this may seem – particularly when distributors and suppliers encourage you to do so). Beliefs keep you true to yourself – they help you be authentically different. As the guys from howies show, every time you do something that doesn't live up to your belief you damage what makes you truly interesting. Ian Dury again, 'You know what that'll make you be.'

More behaviour thinking

Another angle on this is the 'strategic canvas' developed by Kim and Mauborgne[8] in their book, *Blue Ocean Strategy*. This tool of analysis encourages you to depict visually the things and behaviours that cost your business in terms of their significance to your customers – *and* in the content of what your competitors do.

This may seem a little simplistic, but being forced to audit everything that you take for granted in your market (the things that all your competitors do) and identifying the cost of each of these as well as the value that they create for your customers makes you be tough on your own business and its behaviours, to ask how your behaviours really bring your beliefs alive. How can you tell from the pattern of significant (and expensive) actions that your business believes anything different from your competitors?

Kim and Mauborgne use the example of the Canadian circus company, Cirque du Soleil, to explain the concept. While Cirque's original competitors spent money on animals and animal acts, most customers either didn't appreciate or actively disliked such things. Cirque chose to spend the money on live music and storylines. Equally, while competitors tended to spend money on their own portable venues (which customers often found uncomfortable, grubby and draughty), Cirque chose to use fixed theatrical and music venues, which made the experience of a Cirque show more comfortable and at the same time more attractive to non-circus fans.[8]

Show, don't tell

'All character is action' is an old adage of movie makers. 'Show, don't tell' is its equivalent in the communication world. Both of these show the importance of doing rather than speaking about it. Pretty words and pretty pictures are much less convincing than deeds. We learn to trust people – politicians, lovers or colleagues – through their actions, not through their assurances and promises. And yet most businesses still haven't got this.

One of the reasons why marketing has long struggled in the boardroom is that the marketing world has become obsessed with the pretty words and pretty pictures of communication, rather than actually doing things differently (or at all!). As the IT marketing guru, Regis McKenna,[9] has observed of marketing in his sector, most marketing jobs have become marketing communications jobs rather than proper marketing jobs.

One of the worst culprits for this is the brand-babblers. Some ten years ago, some smart design folk realized that branding and rebranding could be a great space to play in. Many millions of dollars have been spent changing or reinventing logos and livery to create or polish the 'image' of companies and their products; all at the expense of doing anything different. In the UK, the leading telephony company BT has spent a fortune on rebadging itself and its divisions each time a new corporate strategy document appears and precious little on enacting the strategy in terms of new behaviours. As the IT journalist John McNaughton of the *Observer* newspaper has noted, it is now 20 years since BT started promising broadband for all. And it has only just got round to doing it.

Brand-babble is the delight of petty bureaucrats – the lance-corporals of business – suits who like to check that everything looks the same, sounds the same and feels the same. It wouldn't occur to these so-called 'logo-police' to believe anything or to act on beliefs, because that would be messy and personal. They prefer to stick at the surface veneer because there are always rules to make and enforce there.

Brand-babbling clients have told me many silly things over the years, but one of the silliest was that a particular brand targeted at teenage boys couldn't run a funny ad because 'humour is not one of our core brand values'. We fought, my agency got fired, the client got moved on and guess what? The next agency produced a string of award-winning funny ads.

How a business behaves is *really* important. It tells the audience – internal or external – what the brand believes or the degree to which it believes what it claims to believe. I have often encouraged my clients and colleagues to think without money – the zero budget game, I call it – to think harder about what the brand can *do* to be interesting in its own right. To change hiring policies or guarantees or whatever; to align the company's actions with the beliefs it claims to have. Not only – as in the case of Dove – does this lead to substantive stuff that might get ignored by McKenna's kind of marketing communications people, but it also leads to greater clarity about the belief itself.

A remarkable book, *The Pragmatics of Human Communication*[10] – a strange collision of late sixties system thinkers and psychology – underlines how important this is (the 'pragmatics' of the title refers to the ability of human communication to change behaviour). The most powerful form of behaviour-changing human communication is behaviour. Imagine you come home from work. Your cat greets you with purring and by rubbing itself against your legs. You assume he is pleased to see you, that he loves you, that he's missed you, that he's trying to tell you so, that his mews are his feline attempt to say so.

How wrong this is! The cat is a cat. Cats don't talk. Cats just do. Your cat is only doing what cats do from an early age. That is acting in a way that encourages you to behave like their mother. And feed him.

The moral of the tale (!) is this: if you want people to behave differently, you have to behave differently yourself.

Interlude: Beyond Petroleum

It is no surprise that Lord John Browne is repeatedly cited in the list of top business leaders; he is serious about his business; he is one of the great visionary leaders of modern business. As Group CEO of British oil giant, BP, he is at the helm of one of the largest companies in the world at the heart of the current debate around global warming, the burning of fossil fuels and the conservation of our natural world. You and I (and most environmental experts and NGOs working in the area) might expect him to follow the example of the tobacco company chiefs and deny the impact of his industry in general and his business in particular.

But he is made of sterner stuff. In good faith, he endorsed a $200m corporate rebranding exercise such as I described above to position BP as *beyond petroleum* (advertising only really ran in the USA, but the corporate identity, the green and gold sun logotype, the so-called 'helios' appears everywhere in the world). Wind-engines started to appear on the top of the range BP gas stations; a lot of extra funds were ploughed into alternative energy resources and curiously BP joined up with New York's Urban Park Rangers to release four bald eagles into the wilds of Upper Manhattan.

The intention it seems, according to his then Group VP for marketing, Anna Catalano,[11] is to present BP as 'the company that goes beyond what you expect from an oil company – frank, open, honest and unapologetic'.

But this change in direction appears to be something very personal for Browne. In 1997, he gave a notable speech at Stanford University in which he admitted that there was now an 'effective consensus' among leading scientists about humankind's role in generating climate change. This was not a speech that you'd expect from an oil baron, a representative of the old industrial sector, a denier of global warming who asked for more research on the effects of his industry on global warming (as his counterpart at Exxon Mobil and that nice man in the Oval Office have done). BP were effectively blackballed by the American Petroleum Institute. A big bold move. Five years later, he returned to Stanford and again expressed a radical point of view. 'Climate change', he said,

> is an issue which raises fundamental questions about the relationship between companies and society as a whole, and between one generation and the next . . . Companies composed of highly skilled and trained people can't live in denial of mounting evidence gathered by hundreds of the most reputable scientists in the world.

In other words, he personally aligned himself and by implication the company he led with the central charge made by environmentalists and accepted responsibility for going beyond this.

An incredibly brave move for such a business leader – particularly in the face of such persistent peer pressure to keep silent on the subject. And the hard line being pursued by the Bush Administration on the Kyoto treaty. However, despite the bravery, despite a continuing dialogue with NGOs and expert forums such as the Pew Center on Global Climate Change, despite the openness to criticism even on the company website and of course despite the striking and powerful rebranding programme, BP are today probably just as unpopular a business as ever they were with the environmental lobby.

Some company defenders point to the complexity of the environment and the very slow build of practical application of alternative energy sources as the reasons why this is the case. Some others point to the high price of oil (and petrol at the pumps, more particularly) combined with BP's headline-grabbing continuing profit growth (it is a phenomenally well-managed business) to explain the unpopularity. But my hunch is that the behaviour of the company does not *appear* to have been changed since Browne and his team started to reorient BP, guided by his deeply held convictions.

For the average citizen, BP remains an oil and petrol company. It continues to make record profits as we have to pay much much more to fill up our 4×4 s. The forecourts are cleaner and brighter (and the coffee at the strangely named Wild Bean Café is certainly tastier) and the staff better dressed, but BP hasn't changed. We don't know that BP has cleaned up its act on its core business dramatically – by 2002, BP had exceeded its target for reducing its own greenhouse gas emissions by 10% of its 1990 figures. Nor that it continues to press for greater reductions. But I'm not sure how interested we would be.

In addition, while the newer cleaner energy sources that BP hopes to develop are still a minority business, BP continues to need to explore for new oil sources in virgin territory such as in Alaska's Arctic National Wildlife

Refuge. And this brings the brickbats of the environmental lobby: Green-peace have honoured Browne with a special award for 'Best Impression of an Environmentalist'. And journalists have joined in the cynicism, openly con-trasting the 'green pretensions of the leader' (according to the *Independent*) with his company's support for what many see as the despoliation of one of the last great wildernesses, a designated conservation site. Equally the busi-ness is still not as clean as it would like to be; in 1999 the company was fined $7 m because a contractor had dumped hazardous waste when working for BP in Alaska. Equally, BP has been found in contravention of federal clean-air laws in eight US states. Refinery fires (such as the one in 2005) do not help the cause either; indeed, they just provide more excuses for the detrac-tors to confirm the negative existing view the general public have of the corporation.

It seems quite unfair that BP should be so criticized when its heart is in the right place. Exxon Mobil continues to flout the scientific consensus on global warming and still refuses to pay the $5 billion damages ordered by an Alaskan court for the 1989 Exxon Valdez disaster. Shouldn't they be singled out for real boycotts and protests? Shouldn't they be the object of hardline criticism? Shouldn't BP have an easier ride?

No, the thing is this. If you say you believe something, you have to behave accordingly, if you want to get the benefits of belief. Or rather, you have to be seen to be behaving accordingly, by both the public and the many com-mentators and experts who fill in the gaps in our knowledge for us and provide us with stories to tell each other. Because belief and cynicism are two sides of the same coin. With one comes the need to watch out for the other.

Belief in a cynical age

Cynicism seems more common nowadays than in previous eras. Cynicism about business, brands, marketing, politicians and the media. Not only are consumers and citizens more educated about what we do (many of us in the behaviour-change world have made a nice little living from telling the world about our tricks), but they are also more demanding of us (we have told them they are in control – you might say we have created a 'have it your way' culture, thanks to our obsession with customer orientation, focus groups and opinion-polling). And yet we've also failed to live up to the grand promises we make – and given them the means (e.g. via the Internet) to check up on us and to share their views with each other.

It's not just the series of scandals which has rocked Western capitalism – it seems to be an ideal breeding ground for dark deeds and deceptions, from Enron to Martha Stewart to the brother of English footballer Gary Lineker, recently jailed for currency offences. Nor is it just our obsession with image over substance as exemplified in UK politics by the Blair–Campbell spin machine and across the pond by the Bush–Libby Rove team.

All across society, we see traditional sources of authority being found less than trustworthy, as the Edelman Trust Report discussed in Chapter 5 shows. Whether we in business and in politics are any less trustworthy than before is not clear to me at all – every era of Western history has had its political and financial scandals, from South Sea Bubbles to WorldCom to Nixon and our own dear Jonathan Aitken and his 'sword of truth'. The point now is that the degree of transparency makes it hard to conceal anything bad, indifferent or downright kooky (why *was* the British Prime Minister seen wearing a bracelet from the wierdy Kabbalah sect that Madonna likes so much?)

And the degree to which we can share our rumours and concerns has increased dramatically. In psychological terms, we know that it is easier to be cynical and dismissive than to believe. It also makes the cynic look smarter; one study of academic peer reviews suggests that those who make negative comments about someone else's work are seen to be smarter than those who make a positive or neutral comment.

Cynics and dogs

The etymological roots of the notion of *cynicism* are worth pondering for a moment because the etymology of the word adds extra spice about what's really going on in our modern world with regard to the behaviour we call 'cynical'.

A modern cynic is someone who doesn't believe what is told them, doesn't trust those in authority and sees only the worst in others' motivations and intentions.

The original Cynics were a school of philosophers in Ancient Greece (although they enjoyed a revival later in imperial Rome) – Diogenes remains their most famous member. This school became infamous for rejecting the social mores and accepted practice of their times on principle and often in a striking and offensive manner, rather than through argument. At the heart of their system of thought is an insistence on our animal nature – hence the adoption of a dog as their symbol and their name (cynic derives from the Greek word for 'dog' – *kuon*) as well as the stories of members urinating in public places to deliberately offend the masses.

So when we talk about 'cynical' people or 'cynical' behaviour, what we seem to be saying is this: urinating like a dog rather than a man.

Thinking about it this way perhaps illuminates the real cause of what we think of as cynicism in the modern world. A cynic you might say is a disappointed idealist. Someone who has been let down. Individuals 'piss' on what corporations tell us, because they suspect that corporations are 'pissing' on them. Talking sweet words but picking our pockets while doing so.

But nobody would act this if they felt they were able to trust and believe. Make no mistake: they really do want to believe. Many people believed Blair and Brown in 1997; many Bush and Cheney in 2000 and in 2004. We know from previous chapters that humans want to belong to a group that is aligned with their own passions and beliefs and ally themselves to larger bodies that also share these things. As Victor Frankl puts it, we have been programmed to quest for meaning and purpose.

It's just harder to sustain belief today, what with the very real history of being misled and deceived by business and politics and the new easily accessed means to spread stories about misdeeds and discuss them with each other. That's why conspiracy theorists abide, both at the water cooler, in the media and on the Internet. Dan Brown's *Da Vinci Code* is so successful not because we are interested in the theological debate nor really in the mysterious mind of Leonardo himself. No, we love a good consipiracy theory – particularly one with gender politics, men in cassocks and international travel.

And that is why cynicism is not something that any one of us trying to change mass behaviour can ignore. Particularly if we are building our organization around beliefs.

Spotting cheaters

Actually it's a lot more serious than you might think. Cynicism seems to be hardwired into us. As we have seen many times before in this book, the modern age is not revealing some new-fangled aspect of human behaviour; it's just allowing us to be more and more our – super-social – selves.

It turns out that spotting cheaters is something we humans are very, very good at. Indeed, we are bloody good at it because it's very important to us. Without this ability, we would not be able to build very stable social structures.

This is the curious finding of a series of psychological studies designed to resolve an issue that only a small number of professionals could be concerned about (whether or not our brain is organized around specialist modules of intelligence or by a general intelligence). We – the super-social apes – are programmed to spot cheaters. In a series of cross-cultural studies, the evolutionary psychologists Cosmides and Tooby[12] have demonstrated that humans score equally – and consistently – well on tests designed to spot cheaters in social exchange. Whether or not the individuals show any prowess at more formal abstract logic versions of the same problems (and the more primitive peoples are undoubtedly poor at abstract logic games), humans – be they from the Kalahari or Connecticut – are very good at spotting those who cheat.

That's why you might think that building or rebuilding your business is really playing with fire. The fire within, the fire without and the risk of unfriendly fire from employees, customers or the media when you fail to live up to the fire within.

But it is, as I have shown, more than worth it.

Conclusions

It *is* possible to light or relight the fire of belief in an organization that has gone cold. Which is just as well, given that most businesses are desperately in need of beliefs to animate them. However, if you do choose this path for your brand, organization or business, beware. Given the transparency of the modern world and the rising tide of cynicism, you need to really make it personal to live your beliefs. Otherwise cynicism, within or without, will unpick your vestal virgin impersonation.

Questions for marketers

1. What did the founders of your business believe? What drove them to shape the business as they did? Why did the belief fade? Why did the fire go out? Is it to do with 'best practice' or some such management or

marketing wisdom? Or is it that the wrong kind of people took over control? Or got recruited? Or you got distracted?

2. How does a belief business challenge marketing notions such as positioning and propositions? Where's the fit and the lack of fit? What other ideas might you have to question?

3. What really matters to you and your colleagues? What do you believe in? What would provide sufficient drive to get you out of bed in the morning (and don't say, 'the money')?

4. What can you do to avoid a cynical response? Who or what are likely to be the biggest sources of cynicism? What should you do about them?

5. Who are the vestals of your business's flame? Are they inside or outside the firm? What are you doing to honour and nurture them? What happens if they let the fires go out or burn low?

9

Key Principle No. 6:
Co-Creativity

What this chapter will cover

Being interesting (to yourself and thereby to others) is not enough. It can get
the herd to interact around you short term but there is one more thing you
have to do to make the most of yourself: use the herd's desire to co-create.
However, this is fraught with difficulties for most organizations as it
challenges some central assumptions about our organizations and ourselves:
assumptions about creativity, originality and the role of the firm in value-
creation. Co-creativity is no new phenomenon – it is part and parcel of our
human herd nature.

> *'Men work together,'* I told him from the heart,
> *'Whether they work together or apart.'*
>
> 'The Tuft of Flowers'
> Robert Frost

Unlikely popstars vol. 103

Peter Kay is an unlikely popstar. He is definitely overweight, he can't really dance, he sweats at the slightest exertion ('like a couple of pregnant nuns' he avers) and his taste in music seems to be that of a northern club singer approaching retirement rather than of anything the record-buying demographic might appreciate. While he has a half-decent voice, it is nothing to write home about. Yet somehow he holds the record for most consecutive weeks at number one in the British singles charts (more even than that execrable Bryan Adams' 'Everything I do'); an achievement which many self-styled musicians would envy even though Peter himself didn't write or sing a note on the single. So how did it happen then? How did this unlikely northern lad do so well?

Kay is the outstanding British comedic talent of his generation, with hundreds of sell-out live shows (including 180 on his 'Mam wants a bungalow' tour of 2004–5) and four hit TV series, all before he reached his thirties. His wry and affectionate take on the mundanities of provincial life have captured the hearts of audiences both young and old. His loving celebration of ignorance, social ineptitude and small town prejudice ('garlic bread . . . it's the future' is one catchphrase) have entered British culture in a number of ways, not least through TBWA's advertising for John Smiths (I particularly like the diving competition commercial – very serious v/o comments on the technical performance of other divers until Kay appears as the British entry and 'bombs' into the pool, showering everything with his chlorinated backwash).

So how is it that Peter Kay holds the UK singles chart record? How did he manage to beat Elvis and the Beatles, Oasis and Michael Jackson? And without singing or writing a note? And what does his success have to tell us about business and mass behaviour?

Charidee, my friends

The UK's annual charity telethon *Comic Relief* is the brainchild of a number of luminaries in the entertainment industry, not least Richard Curtis, writer of *Blackadder* (TV) and movies such as *Four Weddings and a Funeral*, *Notting Hill* and *Love, Actually*. As is the way with these kinds of thing, each year the team sets out to beat the previous year's achievements in terms of both profile and fundraising. Favours are called in, arms are twisted and egos stroked in order to get an even better show on air than the previous year's efforts.

This year, Peter Kay was asked to contribute something – a short three-minute section – maybe a song or something that could be released to raise further money for charity. Rather than invent something new, Kay chose to steal from himself – to steal something that he had already stolen from himself, in fact.

On his record-setting UK tour, Kay had climbed on stage to the old Tony Christie number, '(Is this the way to) Amarillo', which reached 18 in the UK singles charts back in 1971 (a version by Neil Sedaka only reached 44 in the Billboard charts when it was released there some six years later). The choice suited his sing-along, club-singer persona (and the culture he celebrates in the TV series *Phoenix Nights* in particular). Every night of the tour he would sing the first chorus with his tour manager and any friends around from the wings – out of sight of the audience – to warm them up with a sing-song. As a little twist to get the audience to play along, the sharp horn stabs in the chorus become handclaps. Sha-la-la-la-la-la-la-la CLAP CLAP! Sha-la-la-la-la-la-la-la CLAP CLAP! (Not sure this helps if you don't know the song . . .)

Which is an idea he stole from himself. In 2002, in the second series of the Kay sitcom, *Phoenix Nights*, nearly unemployed nightclub bouncers Max (played by Kay) and Paddy find themselves transporting a crowd of devout

Muslims to the local mosque but get stuck in traffic. To raise spirits, they start singing along to 'Amarillo' and clapping in the appointed place in the chorus.

So what Kay did for *Comic Relief 2005* was produce a video of himself and various second- (and third- and fourth-) rate British TV entertainers (from *Bullseye's* Jim Bowen to *Rainbow's* Bungle) miming the song and pretending to walk across the desert and along lonely roads suggested by the lyrics of the song.

And what a hit it was – the switchboard was jammed with requests immediately and in subsequent days, thousands of downloads were made from related sites. And for seven long weeks, 'Amarillo' sat comfortably at the top of the British singles charts, raising millions for charity and revitalizing the career of one A. Christie (outside Germany that is, where he has long been a hero for women of a certain age). 'Amarillo' was an unlikely hit – not just as a piece of music but as a popular phenomenon. Jonathan Ross, the self-admiring front man for the telethon, put the feelings of the nation into words, 'I love this . . . almost more than I love myself.'

Number one and everything after

Now normally tales of such surprising success end at this point so that we can pick the bones out of them (one particularly boring culture show laboured the point about record-breaking number ones needing to appeal to a much larger section of the population than that which usually buys singles – no shit, Sherlock . . . to sell unprecedented amounts of anything we have to bring in light and non-buyers . . . *doh!*).

But this story is different. The momentum that was created by Kay was continued by other hands. (Note to readers: don't make the techno-error again as you read. While the technology of the Internet and high-powered laptop computers enables some of this to happen, it is not responsible for all of it. Moreover, what the technology enables is that our herd instincts – sharing, interaction, communication – can be embodied as behaviours, rather than remaining hidden).

So how does the story continue then? First, there is the army connection. On 13 May, the computer system of the Ministry of Defence (the UK armed forces computing network if you like) crashed because one quite substantial file kept being sent back and forth across it. What was that one file? A spoof of the *Comic Relief* video, with the original Tony Christie voice track but the mime this time performed by the men of the Royal Dragoon Guards in their base at Al Faw in Southern Iraq. Squaddies being squaddies, each MOD user wanted to share the fun with their mates – other squaddies – and they chose the only means to do so, which was the MOD computer system, despite the fact that the regiment concerned was one of those directly involved in combat operations at the time. When the minister responsible was challenged by the press as to whether it had been a wise thing to do to send this video file around in times of war, he was advised to agree but praise the morale and ingenuity of the soldiers concerned.

Second, there is the overseas connection. Armies are nothing if not competitive. So it should be no surprise that, as the Al Faw version of 'Amarillo' circulated around the Internet (yes, it got outside the closed walls of the MOD system within minutes), allied regiments chose to do their own version. A very long (and moderately amusing) Dutch version and an excruciatingly unfunny German version were both made, circulated and recirculated. Which is curious, given neither could have appreciated the original Peter Kay version's irony and humour, so culturally specific were they. But that didn't stop the squaddies of other nations from having a go.

Third, Peter Kay reappeared to vamp his creation again at Live 8 in Hyde Park on 2 July. As the crowd became restless, waiting for the headliners – the long promised reunion of the members Pink Floyd after more than 20 years of feuds and quarrels, lawsuits and sulkiness – Kay marched on stage. Rather than make any pretence at introducing the band, he proceeded to start the sing-song 'Sha la la la las' all over again, doing a version of the marching dance which features in the video. Apparently unperturbed by the pressures of timing and TV schedules or the anticipation of musos in the crowd at the dream of a reunited Waters, Mason, Wright and Gilmour, he carried on and on and on before being virtually manhandled off stage.

Finally, my own little role in this story. I told this tale a few times over the summer of 2005 to client meetings and at conferences. At the end of July, I found myself in a conference room at the AAAA Account Planning Conference talking to about 200 US planners about co-creativity, telling the story again. And as we went along, I thought it would be fun to have some audience participation. Why not? After all, it would seem strange to be totally uncollaborative in a session about co-creativity. So I risked it.

And 190 or so joined in (Steve, you are too cool for school, honestly). 'Sha la la', they sang. Clap clap. On and on. As the game spread through the room, I saw more and more smiles appear (clearly this is something that conference speakers should do more of . . . people enjoy joining in). And I thought no more of it, until later that evening, when Mike Hall and I fell out of some bar or other in downtown Chicago, I caught the plaintive cries of drunken planners singing 'Sha-la-la-la-la-la-la-la'. And then came the proof that I had played my part, the unmistakable *clap clap*! On they went: 'Sha-la-la-la-la-la-la-la *clap clap*! Into the night.

'My work is done here', I thought to myself. 'I have shared the magic of the Bard of Bolton and watched it spread across this great nation.' (Actually I just made up that last bit, but I wish I had felt so noble. The point was I felt that I had passed the game on to a new set of players. It felt good. They appreciated the gift and the game itself. Some of them would even remember it, a handful its significance and a few even buy this book. You never know. A boy can dream, can't he?)

So what does the 'Amarillo' syndrome teach us?

I'm sure each of us can think of similar (if not quite so spectacular and enjoyably successful) phenomena as Peter Kay's ubiquitous 'Amarillo'. But the whole story (not just Peter's part of it) is bigger than most such crazes. How did he do this? What was it that makes this different from the run-of-the-mill charity single? From the average comedian's attempts to win popstar status? And what does this tell us about business and the human herd?

First, let's consider Peter himself. Peter Kay is undoubtedly interesting. He is clear about who he is and he appears authentic; he is a funny, self-confessed 'fat lad' from Bolton. His behaviour is aligned completely with his beliefs. And entirely consistent over time.

That said, the concerns of his humour are not particularly original in themselves (as say Bill Hick's or Richard Pryor's or even the *Monty Python* team's were in their time), but it *is* honest and free of the cleverness that so much television and stand-up comedy have been infected by in recent years. You've also got to say that the format for his comedy is actually quite old-fashioned – stand-up and sitcoms (albeit sitcoms with the excruciating honesty of recent shows such as *The Office* or *The Royle Family*).

That's not to say that his comedy is indifferent. Kay is a master performer and writer.

No, what makes Kay's comedy so successful is his ability to make something for us to do together; with him and – long after he's left the stage – with each other. He understands co-creativity. He practises co-creativity. He encourages us – the army lads and the USA planning crowd included – to practise co-creativity. This is what makes Peter Kay so unusual. And is the most important thing behind the phenomenal success of the 'Amarillo' syndrome.

Originality and creativity

I'm not sure that he'd ever talk about things this way, but Kay's notion of originality is also strikingly different from his contemporaries' (and from much of the culture of creativity in which he works).

To start with, the 'Amarillo' syndrome is based on somebody else's work – Tony Christie sang on the original single and the words and music were written by Howard Greenfield and Neil Sedaka. The essence of the 'Amarillo' experience is recycling someone else's creativity. Equally, as noted above, Kay steals from himself – again and again. And again. He doesn't even respect his own originality.

Now this contrasts very strongly with what our culture and all too many other entertainers think about originality and creativity. Too many of those who think themselves creative, or need to do something creative, retire to some lonely place (windswept cliff tops or lonely moors are in tune with our romantic notions of the creative artist) in order to create something of unique and stupendous value. Theirs is the unique contribution, theirs the raw material, theirs the artistry; the object itself comes out perfect and unimprovable. It is to be appreciated, admired and valued – but not touched or changed or fiddled about with. That – it is very clear – is the job of the artist. Whether this is scriptwriting, painting, composing, gag-writing or advertising, the same rules apply.

What Peter Kay instinctively understands and what distinguishes him from his contemporaries is his recognition that creativity – value-creation we call it – is not a one-man show. Real creativity is the work of many, *many* hands and the more suitable an assembly is to manipulation by these many hands, the greater the resonance and value it will have.

(Value) chain of fools?

One of the most important things that Kay's genius challenges in our thinking about business is how we think about the company and its interaction with audiences outside.

First, we assume that it is the company (or department or function within the company) that creates value for customers – it then exchanges this with customers for money (hence 'value' chain). While this may work for old manufacturing businesses (the source of much of our thinking about business), it doesn't work for 'Amarillo' and it doesn't work for most businesses today either. Clearly Kay is not the exclusive author of all value here – the Royal Dragoon Guards and I both recycled Kay's original recycling to create value for ourselves and our own audiences.

In effect, 'Amarillo' encourages us to see that the company itself is not the sole value-creator; indeed, the company must learn to respect and encourage other value-creators in the network of parties in what it does.

To see how this 'Amarillo'-thinking is different, we need to see what one well-worn way of analysing companies tells us: that is 'value-chain' analysis. This is an attempt to lay out the activities of the business in a sequence (or 'chain') to identify what it is the company does to create value for its customers.

Imagine you have a company that makes candy bars. If you lay out every one of its activities – from sourcing raw materials, to marketing and advertising – it becomes easy to see where in the production process the company 'adds value' beyond the basic costs (of what the materials and the process itself involve). This is particularly useful when you compare the value chains of different businesses. For example, some candy businesses pay more for the ingredients (say the organic chocolate firm, Green and Black); others look to pay less (a more mass market business like Nestlé for example) (Figure 9.1).

'Amarillo' encourages us to think of value creation beyond what the company's own activities involve; it also encourages us to see beyond the company's interaction with its own immediate suppliers and customers. Instead, the value chain for a co-creative business *includes* an extensive network of other parties; it also recognizes that value is created by all of these parties (Figure 9.2).

In particular, what is clear is that each time an individual refers to or re-enacts or even just passes on the 'Amarillo' sing-along, a social (peer-to-peer)

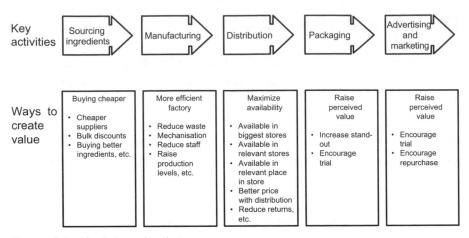

Figure 9.1 *Candy bar value chain*

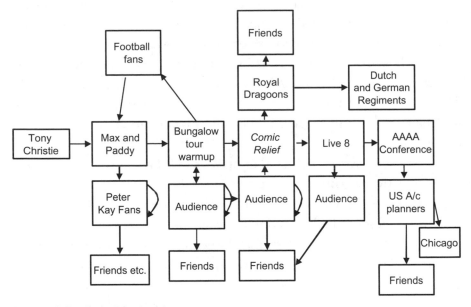

Figure 9.2 *'Amarillo' value chain*

value-exchange takes place. If you like, where Peter Kay differs from other entertainers is that he recognizes that while E2C (entertainer-to-consumer) interactions are important, it is the far more widespread C2C (consumer-to-consumer) interactions where the majority of value is created, or rather co-created. '(Is this the way to) Amarillo?' is the success that it is, purely because it encourages consumer-to-consumer co-creative interactions.

Is this new news?

In his latest beautifully written book,[1] the Indian-born business guru C.K. Prahalad suggests that this is a new phenomenon. He uses the example of the changing market context of a firm that manufactures pacemakers to argue that this way of seeing things is now unavoidable. Prahalad points to the explosion of the Internet (which lifts the curtain on information which was previously denied to customers/patients) and the decreasing trust in authority that individual consumers now have to show how the pacemaker manufacturer now has to deal with a very different strategic landscape. From being a fairly simple business with links to the medical profession it now finds itself embedded in a shifting network of businesses and organizations that all interact with each other in different ways. As anyone who works in the medical sector will attest, the patient groups are themselves now of critical importance; they – and online medical dictionaries – arm patients much better for the interaction with the medical profession. Or at least they feel more confident going into the interaction.

But are we right to see this as a new phenomenon? Is this a major shift in behaviour or something more interesting?

Hi-tech co-creativity

Those who work in the computer industry know all about co-creativity. For a long time, users and technical advisors were pushing computer manufacturers to abandon their proprietary systems, which stopped different makes of computer from working together properly (or indeed at all). Subsequently software manufacturers have changed the way IT looks at software and other such developments. Rather than keep software source code (its DNA) secret so that software products can hit the market fully formed, software firms now tend to see their software development as a co-operative activity with their key corporate customers. From beta-testing to the support of user communities who discuss, debate and share improvements to the product, the whole way of thinking about making software has been rewritten.

Central to this is the recognition (as with 'Amarillo') of the importance of the users in creating the total value of the product (in software terms this means that users are going to know much more about the product in use than the manufacturer). In turn this means that the value that users create in their interaction with each other is just as important as that which the company creates in its interactions with users. If – that is – the company wants its products to be widely supported and continuously improved.

This ability of co-creative networks to develop and debug software collaboratively has led not just to a completely open-source operating system (Linux was originally published by one Linus Torvald but is really the product of hundreds of thousands of code-writers around the world – the only condition of the licence to use it is that all amendments are to be shared freely with other users); but also, to a whole new kind of computer-based entertainment – co-creative co-created computer games.

Welcome to SIM City[2]

Last year, sales of the video and computer gaming industry eclipsed those of the film industry. As the new entertainment colossus flew to the sunshine of LA, the old one scuttled in to Cannes, wearing dark glasses and a pashmina to hide the post-operative scarring from its latest round of cosmetic 'enhancement'. The gaming industry has exploded largely through co-creation of this sort, but on a grand scale. How companies approach the issues of creativity, ownership and collaboration in this space is instructive for the rest of us.

Perhaps the best-known company is Electronic Arts Games; and one of their best-known titles, The Sims, grew in precisely this way.

The Sims is a simulation game (as opposed to a 'shoot-' em up' or a 'quest' or similar). In other words, it lets you create a world, manage and direct it. It grew out of a terribly addictive game called Sim City in which players designed a city and watched it grow, prosper or otherwise. Too soon and too often otherwise, when I played it.

Where Sim City took a whole society, The Sims is a whole lot more intimate. It focusses on a small number of individuals – a family – that interacts based on how you programme them and nurture them. Individual characters live, die, eat, sleep, fight, make love, kill each other and so on according to your instructions. The original version – developed through beta-testing (that is a lot of potential customers played with early versions and suggested improvements and corrections until it was ready for launch) – quickly built an online community (or rather an online community built itself) around the game. Players swapped hints, tips, tools, software and artefacts to put in their virtual homes. Some 90% of the content of the game is now player-created rather than just created by the people at Electronic Arts Games.

The follow-up[3] – 3D Sims online – was designed from the get-go as a co-creative venture (EA still had to stump up some $ 15 m to get the core of the game robust but the rest is player-developed). So much so that, shortly before the launch in 2004, EA produced a set of tools for players to produce their own characters and content. At launch some 50,000 such items had already been created. In some ways, 3D Sims online has redefined EA's role from a games company to a host for gaming co-creators: the new game is really just a platform – an expensive one to maintain at that (information requests come through fast and furious) but one which can only be kept interesting by the rolling co-creativity of the player community itself. Not by the extraordinary creativity or ingenuity of the longhairs at EA itself.

Rewriting history (together?)[4]

From the way software people talk, you might imagine that distributed or herd co-creativity was a new phenomenon. If you believe the new business gurus and prophets of co-creativity, you might imagine that this is the coming thing. But history tells us otherwise. While our culture of individualism may have shielded us from this (as from other herd truths), the evidence is clear: real creativity has always been a herd game; real innovation and value creation is the work of many hands.

Every generation has its boom towns – places which are such a hotbed of economic activity that innovators are attracted and find traction for their ideas. in madly competitive environments the ingenuity of the few can really be harnessed to find new and better solutions to old problems. In the late 20th century, Silicon Valley was one such, but in the 18th century rural Cornwall was the equivalent, thanks to its vast natural wealth of tin and copper. However, the mines were deep (well before the Romans they were being exploited to the full) and thus prone to flooding. A vast amount of coal was needed to keep them pumped dry and safe to work.

A number of engineers and inventors proposed solutions with a range of success but the most successful was the engineer James Watt. His 1769 engine design cut the fuel costs by two thirds and thus changed the economics of mining, even for the deepest and dampest mines. Watt's innovation, heavily protected by the laws of patent, spread quickly through the Cornish mines and for 15 long years, Watt and his business partner Matthew Boulton made money hand over fist. Given the advantages of the Watt design, mine owners were compelled to buy it to keep up with their neighbours despite the legal straitjacket which stopped them adapting and improving the basic design in position.

For 15 years until 1800 when the patent ran out, Watt and Boulton just had to sit back and count their money. There was no incentive for them to improve the patent-protected design, even though customers wanted improvements to get ahead of their competitors and wanted it badly. But after the patent ran out, Watt and Boulton sold not a single engine more. Not one. Because their customers were already improving on the design itself, swapping stories and experiences.

Just a few years later, this community (a 'user-group' we might call it nowadays) started a journal of its own to better share these ideas. For 100 years from 1811, *Lean's Engine Reporter* (named after one of the leading engineers, Joel Lean) published discussions and proposals on every aspect of engine design. Indeed in one of the early issues of *Lean's* a new design was announced, a design by Richard Trevithick and Arthur Woolf. One which quickly swept through the Cornish mining world and replaced the earlier patent-protected original. Unlike Watt's design, this one was not patented; indeed Woolf and Trevithick encouraged other mines and other mining engineers to copy and improve their original. The journal was soon bursting with ideas, suggestions and thoughts for how to improve on the basic idea. And in the 30 years of co-creative improvement that followed, the community managed to improve efficiency by 300%.

Galileo, Newton and Einstein

Even in the world of scientific discovery, the old story of brave individuals overturning accepted wisdom is widely discredited nowadays. No one working in science today believes that changes in ways of seeing the world are the result of a heroic loner – a Galileo, a Newton, an Einstein – seeing and laying out the truth for colleagues to admit the superior argument or superior evidence and chair the discovering hero from the room, with a volley of cheers from the new converts and a volley of headgear heading skywards.

It's more than 40 years since Thomas Kuhn[5] published his masterpiece on how scientific revolutions happen. Unlike others who have theorized about how the big changes in science come about, Kuhn bothered to go back to the original sources – to find out what actually happened. What did Galileo or Newton or Einstein's contemporaries actually think about the ideas proposed by these shapers of our scientific tradition?

Curiously, Kuhn discovered that the cheering crowds of converts, heads turned and hearts all a-flutter as a result of having the superior evidence laid before them, didn't gather. Nobody sang. Only a few stragglers feted the hero who'd lifted the scales from their eyes.

The sad truth, Kuhn points out, is that most of the big breakthroughs of science have been rejected or at least heavily criticized by those already practising in the field. It's only when the new way of thinking about or seeing the world (hence 'paradigm') is seen by enough practitioners to provide a more useful field to work in – to provide, as Kuhn puts it, more interesting problems to wrestle with – that scientific paradigms shift and the new way of seeing things gets adopted.

Sometimes it can be as small as a detail in the new explanation which provides some more interesting questions on a particular subject (Newton's gravitational theory was given a boost because of its explanation of the retrograde movement of the planet Mercury, not because of the beauty of the argument Newton laid out). Science then is a co-creative activity; scientific knowledge is the result of many hands working together and against each other. Behind 'peer review' – both in the strict sense that modern science uses to ensure that work is done properly, that evidence is properly accrued and hypotheses properly tested *and* in the broader sense that Kuhn describes – is the means by which the individual's contribution is maximized: herd co-creativity.

Another 'pencil squeezer'?

Equally, Kuhn's counterpart in the study of creativity – the psychologist Professor Howard Gardner – makes it clear that most new ways of seeing things are the result of a group of people working together. Gardner's study[6] of the great minds of the 20th century shows how each of those studied (from Freud to Gandhi) did their most powerful work through a 'field'; that is, a group of people to discuss, elaborate and educate the world outside about the big idea. (Martha Graham, the woman credited with the invention of contemporary dance, actually held classes to teach the critics she had recruited what on earth she was on about. The bitter infighting between the various collaborators, relatives and protégés of Sigmund Freud is best understood similarly as a necessary function of this same co-creative team.)

Co-creativity – summary so far

What Peter Kay's 'Amarillo' success reveals to us is that co-creativity is not a new or new-media-led phenomenon. Rather it is rooted deep in our human herd nature. Most of the knowledge, technology and ideas that have shaped our world are the work of many hands; are the work of the herd.

The ideas of originality and individual creativity that our culture has lifted up and celebrated are largely illusory. They mislead us in our personal lives, in our cultural lives, how we think about business and in our view of what underlies all of these things: mass behaviour.

One tradition that runs counter to this received wisdom is that of *play* – that is seeing our species first and foremost as a playful one (humans like most primates spend most of their time not being serious but being playful with others). The Indian guru, Osho, put it this way: 'You will be surprised to know that all that you see has been invented by playful people.' Pat Kane[7] – popstar turned social commentator – suggests that in the 21st century we need to rethink our relationship to play; indeed, he suggests we abandon the 19th-century notion of the 'work ethic' – the Calvinist empire-building cultural imperative – and replace it with a 'play ethic'. In so doing, our personal and professional lives will undergo significant changes and our experience of life be transformed.

However well-meaning these two visionary play-advocates are, it remains extremely difficult to know quite what to do to harness our herd nature in the area of co-creativity. There are so many barriers to doing so – personal, professional, financial and cultural. Where can we start to put the co-creativity of our species to play? What do we focus on first?

Let's start with something really simple and on a really small scale. A meeting.

Meetings, bloody meetings

The late great economist, J.K. Galbraith, was searing in his disdain about many of our foibles in business but he reserved particular scorn for the cult of meetings. Meetings, he noted, 'are indispensable when you don't want to do anything'. Apart from fill my diary up with meetings, that is. I don't know why it is but I think some of my colleagues and clients exist only to have meetings. They don't actually do anything apart from sit in meetings. I certainly feel a bit Dilbertish at times when another meeting is called by the meeting monitors; it seems the real purpose of the meeting is to have a meeting. No one really preps, nothing ever changes afterwards. Or worse, the really important thing about meetings for those who love them is to check up on the progress of the work done by those who actually do stuff outside meetings.

I remember with horror the stories one colleague, Susan, used to tell me about her meeting monsters one-on-one meetings to prep for team meetings, which were in themselves to prep for management meetings, which were a dry run with the no. two client before we went to the meeting where we were supposed to discuss the analysis that Susan was trying to do (in between all the meetings to discuss it). Yikes!

But my point here is not about the volume of meetings (I think we all can agree that fewer meetings would be a good thing for all of us – apart from the meeting-less meeting monsters. I can imagine them running around like dogs that had forgotten where they had previously buried the bones). No, my point is this: *how rarely are meetings actually that – a meeting of minds?* More often than not meetings seem to me to be anything but co-creative. More combatative more like (however civilized the veneer).

So think back for a moment over your own experience, over the meetings you have attended in the last year or so. They could be small scale 'team-meetings' to large-scale high-octane set pieces. And they could range in number from a handful to hundreds or even thousands. Ask yourself this: how many of these meetings revealed any sign of our co-creativity and how many were really just an opportunity for various individuals to attempt to impose their agenda on the other 'participants'? More '*Gladiator* than Gladys Knight (and her charming Pips)'.

Think about it this way: in order to feel prepared for the meeting, you have to prep yourself like Maximus. You have to craft your skills, your weapons; you have to gird yourself and face down the other guy. No surrender, no giving of ground. We all hate it when people do it to us so why does each of us do this again and again? To our colleagues and our clients. As an agency planner, I know I conspire for this to be true – both inside and outside the agency. Too often, I don't go into meetings with creative people with a clear mind and a willingness to do something interesting and new together. No, I've got a strategy or a brief or a tacit agreement with the client to defend. Or, with the client it's the same but worse: I've got a strategy to convince him of, or work that we have created to get him to buy, or a proposal I want him to sign off.

I've always got something to sell – it wouldn't feel right, I wouldn't feel prepared if I didn't have an agenda. But when I realize that you and almost everybody else has their own stuff to sell too, the noise and the psychic testosterone is unbearable. It takes a special kind of person to co-create in these circumstances. And I think I'm a very collaborative and co-creative kind of fella, but I find it hard. No wonder that I've often sat in meetings high above Canary Wharf, gazing out of the window as I fantasize about smashing the safety glass and leaping 10 storeys to freedom.

So even reducing the number of meetings you attend is not enough; it seems important to change the way we approach some (or all) of them. Sometimes, the best way is to deliberately not prepare. I've tried this with hilarious results. Other times, I've just asked questions. Other times, I've made sure that we waste no time and energy transmitting via a presentation, and focus instead on questions/queries/challenges. For example I make sure that my agenda item is circulated, read and discussed one-to-one prior to the meeting, so that we can clear the airwaves for actual discussion and interaction.

Kick-off

But perhaps the most important thing is that those who run the meetings do their jobs and ensure that the meeting is about exchange and interaction and not a war of PowerPoint and spreadsheet agendas. The best version of this I have come across was enacted by Guy de Laliberte, the co-founder and abiding genius of the Montreal Circus troupe, *Cirque du Soleil*. Some 20 years ago, Guy was a homeless fire-eater who slept on a park bench outside the Dorchester Hotel on his one trip to London (this is why he always stays on the other side of the glass on his return trips to London). Today, he is a multimillionaire inspiration to entertainers around the world: he has four shows running continuously in Las Vegas and 10 troupes touring the world at any one time. He collaborates naturally – this is what circus skills (both old and new) demand.

So when a new multimillion-dollar production project starts, Guy might open the huge all-hands meeting with a request for all those who think they know the answer to the problem on the table today to leave the room. 'On our own,' he explains 'we may well create something very good – each of us is extremely talented in our field. But together we will create something extraordinary.'

What use are people on your team who are not going to work with you? Who are not going to co-create? Who are not going to harness the power we share? Who are going to insist on pressing their own ideas – however powerful – on us?

At the theatre

Joan Littlewood[8] was probably the greatest theatre director (or facilitator as she would prefer to be called) of our or any age. Short, with bad teeth and hooded eyes, she dominates the theatre world of her generation and subsequent ones. For her vision, her passion and her working method.

Staunchly socialist, an unreconstructed radical, she worked outside the mainstream for all of her career – indeed almost until the end of it, the theatre establishment rejected her (or studiously avoided supporting her). Money was always tight. Personal commitment was required from company members – and this sometimes proved too much, so company membership churned a number of times. And even then, Joan and her colleagues were very tough on who might and might not join them. At the same time, she encouraged them to recruit those with no apparently relevant skills or talents, but Joan always found ways of using them that exploited previously hidden skills.

And yet her legacy of co-creative improvised productions have shaped much of modern British theatre practice with her Theatre Workshop. Everything was co-created, even though one individual had the responsibility of going away and writing the show down (rarely Joan). It all arose from frequent and passionate improvisational physical work sessions, rooted in the work of Rudolf Laban.

Of course, Joan was supremely talented. She could act, sing, dance, direct and do most other things in the group. But it was her approach to co-creation which seems to have made all the difference. And the strong personality and courage which encouraged others to follow her lead.

Key to this was the simple adage of trust. Trust the show (it will emerge). Trust the players. Trust the audience. Trust yourself. But don't expect it to be easy – co-creativity always involves hard work.

An excellent guide to all kinds of co-creative ventures. In the theatre and way beyond. Write it down.

Co-creative marketing attempts to change mass behaviour

As I have already suggested, most marketing campaigns are based on the assumption that it is what the company does to the customer/consumer that matters, what it makes each individual do or what it makes them think. Herd theory by contrast suggests that what really matters is what the company can get customers to do to each other.

Sometimes we might describe this as marketing which generates C2C interaction such as word of mouth or recommendation; sometimes it is a non-verbal form of influence – we create the impression (true or false) that people like me (or me as I would like to think of myself being) love this product. Sometimes indeed as in the case of the Boeing World Design Team – which encourages everyone from geeks to frequent travellers to get involved with the design of Boeing's next generation of passenger aircraft. I know that my colleague Rory Sutherland is now a particular advocate for an aircraft that is still many years from commercial flight.

But the most powerful of all herd-marketing approaches does something slightly different: it encourages customers to do something together to create their own value. One little known example of this is Motorola's sponsorship of the first series of *American Idol*. You may think this not an unusual choice of sponsorship for a teen-targeted product brand but the thinking is much more profound and the effect more widespread. Put simply it is this: at the time US consumers were largely ignorant (and scared) of the SMS text facility on their cell phones. Motorola needed to find a way to get the mass of their user base over this hurdle, so using the TV audience vote as a means to try SMS and get used to it seemed a fantastic opportunity. Several million American consumers tried texting for the first time, thanks to Motorola.

Another example is the so-called 9644 campaign for South African Breweries' Castle Lager created and managed by Ogilvy South Africa. Following the transition to majority rule in South Africa, Castle's sales had slipped as its associations with the old South Africa became increasingly anachronistic and out of tune with the spirit of the new vibrant multicultural country. While mainstream marketing and advertising was created to address this problem, the real reversal of the brand's fortunes seems to have come largely from a programme of C2C marketing. A small number of community leaders were invited to be flown to Jo'burg for the launch of a programme celebrating the new cultural movers and shakers of SA – from designers to musicians. While there, SAB offered the audience and their friends and colleagues practical (and beverage) support for any social, cultural and community events and gatherings organized by these individuals. The programme proved hugely successful and now – after a full year of national implementation – the long-term sales decline has reversed and the brand is culturally relevant again.

I saw this and I thought of you

In this and many other cases it seems that using marketing communications activity to encourage an audience's creativity – to encourage them to do something to each other or make something together – is more powerful a lever for bringing about changes in mass behaviour than the traditional 'think differently' approaches.

One striking example is that for Royal Mail[9] (1996–2001). Outside the direct marketing fraternity where variants on a letter is bread-and-butter stuff, letter-writing has declined massively over the last 20 years, largely but not exclusively in the face of newer more immediate media like email and mobile telephony. A number of 'persuasive' marketing communication programmes had attempted to reverse this long-term decline in both the UK and just about every postal market in the Western world ('Remember what a Valentine card means?' etc.) but with little demonstrable effect (I suspect this was more to do with the approach to the programme rather than its measurement although my short experience of the international postal marketing community suggests that measurement was pretty poor, too).

What changed things for the Royal Mail was a campaign called 'I Saw This and Thought of You', by the now defunct Bates Dorland agency. Thanks to the planner's insight that people wanted to communicate with each other, would happily use the post but were intimidated by the idea of the formal letter, the creative team came up with a programme which focussed on encouraging consumers to send all kinds of things to each other – as a means to build and reinforce existing and new relationships. 'I saw this and thought of you' became both a reminder of the usefulness and openness of the letter within these primary (C2C) relationships and also a source of suggestions and prompts to encourage their creativity.

I suspect that this tells us another bigger story about marketing communications in general. As herd theory would insist, it seems that what matters most is what consumers pass to each other (in terms of behaviour or belief, rather than any message we transmit to them or behaviour we incentivize. Robin Wight of WCRS has developed the idea of 'memetic' creativity, that is creative communications that are specifically designed to have elements that pass through the population. His agency's award-winning work on the telephone directory service 118118 is one such piece of work. Their website[10] has numerous other examples which are worth visiting.

In the online space a number of folk have got excited about the concept of 'stickiness' – that is something which keeps getting played with by individuals and passed on to their peers, long after the campaign has stopped. While this is undoubtedly a good thing, the herd theorist in you (as in me) may well feel the sense that this is something new – a new piece of technology if you like – is itself somewhat misleading. Hasn't it always been the case that successful marketing stuff gets into our real lives, into our conversations and our interactions with each other? Isn't that what buzz really means – becoming useful for us in our real lives with each other rather than just for the company or the category's sake?

Using co-creativity to change internal audience mass behaviour

Co-creativity might well turn out to be the thing that's missing from many of our attempts to change the behaviour of our internal masses. Take CRM implementation for example, a common frame from many of today's internal change programmes. Whatever one thinks of the philosophy itself, it is clear that most implementations do not live up to the billing. A recent article[11] suggests that behind many bad CRM implementation stories are bad assumptions about employees' attitudes and motivations towards any behavioural change the organization tries to bring about. For example, that employees will adopt new behaviours if the system and its benefits are explained, that the organization's interests are always seen to be more important than the employees' own ones, that different functions and departments share a common view of what is best for the organization. This latter one always makes me laugh – imagine a fashion firm run by accountants or an accountancy firm run by HR(!) or anything at all run by the IT department. IT people tolerate (barely) the users they are there to support and have little real interest or understanding of the nature of the business and how it creates value. A bold statement, I know, but I am prepared to be proved wrong. Too much of it is top-down implementation with individual users being trained to comply with new operating procedures rather than being encouraged to do anything to redesign, adapt or enhance the system descending from on high.

Anyway what Corner and Rogers suggest – these are two respected practitioners of CRM implementation, after all – is the opposite: a more consultative approach based on user–user interests; encouraging more honest discussion and co-working of the prototype system to meet all stakeholders' needs. Which makes a lot of sense, even if it seems to run counter to the mechanistic view of business operations that underpin most CRM systems thinking. The same seems to be the case with any kind of change programme – from CRM to HR, from brand-led to M&A; indeed, even the notion of setting some kind of strategy at the high level which is then enacted – loyally, dutifully and gratefully – by those on the front line falls into the same trap.

With CRM or any other enterprise-wide change programme, what it all comes down to is this: do you see the organization as a machine with dumb operators? Or do you see it as an adaptive system of smart interactive agents? The former is a denial of the basic premise of herd theory and this is why approaches to internal change driven by this kind of thinking are bound to fail. As most do.

The Hawthorne effect[12] and after

In the Cicero, Illinois, in the heart of the old industrial Midwest, is the famous Hawthorne plant. Of course, now with the shift in the industrial base away from the great industries of the past, it is rather less impressive than it was in its peak, in the early part of the 20th century, when 40,000 workers were employed there. So important was it that an army of organizational scientists from the great American universities, from Harvard and MIT, would frequently descend on the plant to test new working practices and report on their likely effect on productivity and profitability.

Out of these many studies came the curious – and I would argue misleading – phenomenon known as the 'Hawthorne effect'. What these academics discovered was that no matter what change was proposed, so long as the staff were consulted prior to the change, their productivity seemed to improve. If the proposal was that lighting be increased, then productivity went up. Ditto, if lighting was progressively decreased, then up and up went productivity.

Now some use this as an argument for this kind of one-way consultation generally in business – do what you want, just tell them beforehand – but most of us know that this isn't likely to bring about the change you want, because today's employees are rather more self-assured. Modern workforces are – unionized or not – likely to argue, because they think they can do better than the managers from head office in working out what to do. And often they are right.

No, internal change programmes need to harness the co-creative powers of the internal herd if they are to have lasting success. Of course, as with external audiences, the interactions are already going on – the herd is already doing its thing, so if you don't harness its power it is likely to work against your change ambitions. And this gives us some important clues about ongoing business leadership, too (see next chapter).

Co-creative innovation

In Peter Kay's view of the world, his own resources are not sufficient to do all of the innovation necessary to create the 'Amarillo' syndrome. So it is with most businesses today. We do not have the time, expertise or levels of resource to innovate in most markets – we have to look outside for help to keep up with an ever-accelerating market.

Now, the traditional route through this has been to hire some third party – an NPD agency or software house or similar to innovate for us. Sadly, they too face the same limitations on resources and speeds and are unlikely to be able to keep us supplied with the right kind of innovations over time (innovation is nowadays a constant and continuous activity, not a five-year rethink opportunity).

So more and more businesses are looking outside of this to tailor-made networks of different collaboration partners who can and will co-create innovation with them. This opens up huge opportunities. Long before Steve Jobs of Apple went to PortalPlayer – Apple's key technical design partner in the development of iPod – PortalPlayer had already built up just such a network of disparate but highly specialized technology companies to solve just the kind of problems that the iPod design raised, such as how to deliver high-quality audio from small, frequently handled and light devices.

Unfortunately most executives and most businesses have unhealthy ideas about managing such networks (many of them reminiscent of engine designer James Watt's own problems) that stop them embracing the power of such co-creativity to create real value for both the firm and its innovation partners. Unhealthy ideas such as control, ownership, value creation, originality, etc.

Two types of co-creative networks

McKinsey's two experts[13] in this area have identified two types of co-creative networks and their definition is very useful to grasp. On the one hand is what they call 'practice' networks or nets. That is, networks of practitioners with similar practical skills and interests. So for example, in the world of extreme sports, practitioners work together to develop the means to surf the biggest wave, board the highest glacier and so on. Equally, open source software development, such as Linux or the SIMS example discussed above, or even the Cornish mining engineers that put Watt out of business, are all examples of networks with similar interests and skills. The community of volunteers who build Wikipedia, the online encyclopedia, would also probably qualify for this typology (despite the Republican interns who were recently caught 'spinning' entries); as are most scientific and academic journals.

By contrast, 'process' networks are those that mobilize participants with very different expertise and experiences. PortalPlayer is one example. So are the apparel networks assembled across the Asian region that so many of our famous Western fashion businesses, both design and retail, tap into for our benefit.

286 HERD - HOW TO CHANGE MASS BEHAVIOUR

By and large, practice networks are more loosely managed (with real effort going into ensuring the ground rules are established early on). Process networks – by virtue of the disparate nature of the participants and the specific deadlines – require more continuous overseeing.

Key to the success of both kinds of network appears to be feedback loops, participant–participant as well as host–participant, and clarity and transparency on performance standards. Without this the essential power of interaction and co-creation is either hindered or unfocussed (in which case continued participation is often seen to be costly and therefore is abandoned).

The *Ocean's 11* dream team

Andy Bryant[14] is one of those visionary people in the world of television who's making co-creativity a reality. He uses the metaphor of *Ocean's 11* – the criminal dream team assembled by the fictional Danny Ocean in the movies which bear that name (either as played by Frank Sinatra or George Clooney, depending which generation you belong to). Andy is Director, Creative, Red Bee Media (formerly BBC Broadcast Ltd), a creative company which specializes in promotion and design for media brands. Red Bee creates high-profile work for clients including the BBC, UKTV and Discovery Networks Europe, channel identities for ITV and other broadcasters, Discovery Channel and SciFi Channel in the USA and elsewhere.

Bryant has written an interesting review of how the television industry is beginning to use external innovation networks to develop fascinating new programming and promotional ideas which can work in the modern, multi-platform world (in other words, in a world in which broadcast TV, online and mobile telephony all interact). It must be noted that the industry has long used such networks for production, particularly here in the UK following recent regulatory changes.

He cites Alex Graham, CEO of the award-winning Wall to Wall, in why the industry is moving this way. The answer it seems is talent, or rather the lack of it.

> Talent is the key to all really interesting innovations and some of the best talent these days increasingly wants to work outside the bigger, traditional organizations – either as free agents or as part of much smaller, 'boutique' companies. If a project demands a distinctive configuration of skills, it would be rare to find all the right expertise in one organization at the same time.

Bryant makes the point that such collaborations are difficult and require the creation of an atmosphere of mutual trust and benefit, with shared goals and a shared understanding of what outcome is desired. Strong leadership and clear ownership of the project need to be in place as well. Much as McKinsey would suggest.

And it seems when you get it right, collaboration has a reward all of its own. Mary Beer (formerly of Flextech) tells Andy, 'Collaboration is not just a means to an end. It's something to be treasured, like doing a play.'

Like the great co-creator he is, Andy is typically modest about his own experiences. But I know he treasures them, too.

Co-creativity and market research (1)

John Griffiths is an experienced and talented account planner and market researcher. A significant part of his work involves designing, conducting and interpreting focus groups. Which – as you might imagine – can pall after a while, whether you agree with my view of them or not (see the Introduction for more details on my perspective, if you missed it first time round). There are only so many times you can discuss the intricacies of a new piece of advertising with the general public. There are only – forgive me – so many times you can sit in the same front rooms in Slough and listen to people's attempts to make sense of the nonsense the creative department handed you as you went out the door.

So John decided to experiment, to see if a co-creative approach to interpretation of such data could produce more interesting results. He experimented with using various combinations of experts in other disciplines (such as a semiotician, an ethnographer and a literary critic). For one project[15] – to help the drinks company Diageo learn how to help stop binge drinking – he not only assembled the crew but also encouraged them to synthesize their individual interpretations into something more illuminating and more insightful. He also had a lucky bounce – open-mindedness really helps if you want to be lucky. He took the risk of letting the respondents get drunk during the research and record their own experience. This revealed a huge inconsistency with what the respondents told him in the conventional focus group format, what they told each other, what he heard and what his collaborators heard.

And this willingness to co-create has earned him the respect and adulation of his peers and clients alike. His record of this particular project won the award for Best New Thinking at 2005 Market Research Society Conference. And his clients love it, too.

Co-creativity and market research (2)

Another market research company, Opinion Leader Research, has developed an approach for co-creating solutions for government, for business and for communications companies using a panel of co-creative consumers. The 'social influencers network' is made up of individuals from all walks of life who are – as discussed in Chapter 5 – those who are most active disseminators of news and information through the rest of the population. Using a combination of larger groups and smaller working teams, the approach has addressed issues for government, business and education.

One of OLR's directors[16] has even proposed that this is the future of market research; rather than being a pure information-gathering function, MR, he suggests, can become a co-creative innovation function.

A similar approach has been applied by particular public sector service providers to co-create innovative geriatric care systems[17] or general practice services.[18] The advantage in all cases is beyond the receptiveness of the audience to the finished proposals or the speed of prototyping (both are features of all co-creative networks' outputs); rather it is in the sheer innovative nature of the solutions, much more so than might otherwise be dreamt up by individual experts or task-forces.

Some ideas that co-creativity challenges

Co-creativity – in theory and in practice – is anathema to our existing ways of thinking and doing. It challenges and overturns so many of our most important ideas – originality, creativity and ownership. It challenges our view of the company as the source of value-creation and insists that we view consumers and business suppliers (and even competitors) as partners in the creation of value.

But most of all it challenges our assumption of control; the warm, comforting feeling that we are in control and that we can retain control of who does what, who thinks what and indeed what the outcome might be.

It is not easy to do so. Surrendering control can be painful; the more that we relinquish it, the scarier it feels. And the scarier it feels, the more we want to control it. This is why businesses and organizations experimenting with co-creativity often fluctuate in their attempts to retain control, from loose to tight. From open to closed. From carefree to anxious. From open-handed to white-knuckle.

And so it is for each of us, in our private lives as in our business lives.

But the really scary thing is how our co-creative partners respond to the fluctuations. Think of it this way: if you say to your children, 'Let's work this out together. I don't have all the answers. I need your help to crack this problem' and then go back to a more authoritarian stance the next day – telling them their ideas are childish – what is their reaction to you going to be? Once the cat is out of the bag, there's no getting the furry feline back in the sack.

Some questions for marketing

1. To what extent is your market co-creative? To what extent is your business co-creative? And to what extent do they seek to control and exploit interactions with each other? Draw a map of all interactions, first between your company and outsiders and second within the company.

2. How does your personal behaviour and that of your peers encourage or discourage co-creativity? What behaviours could you focus on to bring about maximizing co-creativity in your interactions? How could you change the way that meetings and project design change to do this?

3. How does the notion of co-creativity change your view of creativity and innovation? And of creative and innovative people? Draw up two lists: first for the old way of thinking, second, for co-creativity.

4. How do you feel about letting go of control? Does it make it any better to know that control was an illusion all along?

10

Key Principle
No. 7:
Letting Go

What this chapter will cover

The final principle of herd theory: letting go. In trying to change mass behaviour, we have to let go of our illusions of control. This is illustrated by examining the received wisdom about managing and leading business and teams within business. Given that human herd behaviour is complex and systemic, the illusion of control is both largely unhelpful and misleading. The alternative approach that herd theory proposes chimes with Buddhist teachings about attachments.

*Kirkpatrick to Williams. This is great stuff. Phil Bennett
covering chased by Alistair Scown. Brilliant, Oh, that's
brilliant. John Williams, Bryan Williams . . . Pullin,
John Dawes. Great Dummy. David, Tom David,
the halfway line. Brilliant by Quinnell. This is
Gareth Edwards. A dramatic start. What a score!*

Cliff Morgan, BBC Sport[1]

What a score!

This was undoubtedly the greatest try in the entire history of the game of
rugby. Cardiff Arms Park, 27 January 1973. The Barbarians vs. the mighty
All Blacks. An invitation scratch team who refused on principle to practise
together vs. the highly tuned and rightly feared New Zealand national
side.

The most outrageous move I have seen in any sport – ever – ends with
Gareth Edwards, the Barbars' scrum half, going over in the corner. Still today
when I watch this, I marvel at the ingenuity, the flair and the sheer bravery
of the players involved. I shiver with excitement – at the sheer impossibility
of the move. My heart races and my breath is short. And yet I cannot believe
– however many times I watch this short passage of play – that it will end
as it always does, with Edwards' full-length dive into the cold Cardiff mud.

Here's what actually happened:

The match was barely a couple of minutes old when Ian Kirkpatrick, the
great All Black flanker, passed to Brian Williams, his winger. Hemmed in

just by the touchline and about halfway between the two sets of posts, Williams lofted a high kick down into the Barbarians' 22. Bang in front of the posts.

Phil Bennett, the diminutive Barbarians' fly-half, wearing the red socks of Llanelli (Barbar players always wear their normal club socks but Barbar shorts and shirts), scurried after the ball which was bouncing and bobbling towards his posts, as ominous All Blacks chased.

With his back to the rest of the players, Bennett picked up the ball cleanly but just 10 yards from his line as the powerful All Black flank Alastair Scown approached with murderous intent clear in his eyes.

Bennett turned on a sixpence, moved to his right, and in doing so out-flanked the advancing Scown. But as he did so All Black centre Ian Hurst came hard at him from the outside. Like a matador, Bennett jinked to his left. Whiting charged at him from the other side. Bennett jinked again, this time to his left. Then Ian Kirkpatrick charged at him. Again Bennett jinked out of harm's way but burly man-mountain Ron Urlich came at him. In a trice Bennett passed to his left, to fullback JPR Williams. Not just four tackles evaded through nifty footwork but a clean and accurate pass to a teammate when the opponents could no longer be evaded.

Almost the same moment that JPR – with his distinctive mutton-chop whiskers – got the ball, All Black Bryan Williams tackled him viciously and dangerously high around the neck, but JPR stayed on his feet, twisted round and gave the ball to Barbarian hooker John Pullin. Pullin made a few yards on his own. He passed left to John Dawes who raced over the Barbarians' 22. What audacity! A break-out from defence seemed possible now. Dawes dummied and went on the inside of Kiwi Grant Batty, then slung a silky pass to young Tommy David (the uncapped player in the side) who went over the halfway line – still the Barbars were going forward! David got rid of the ball as best he could – he threw a quick, dipping pass at big Derek Quinnell on his left.

Quinnell – running at full pace or what for him counted as full pace, somehow managed to reach down to pick up the low ball, then threw his own pass out left towards the sizzling speed of John Bevan on the left wing. But the ball never reached Bevan because Gareth Edwards intercepted it – racing up from the Welsh line to join the game. Edwards stepped on the gas and sped 30 yards or more downfield, evading as he did Batty's diving tackle to score in the corner.

The limits of my powers

Even though I didn't play my first game of rugby until nearly 10 years later, my family – being Welsh – had a passion for the game that they passed on to me. My memory tells me that I watched the game on our TV in Wembley (though my mother tells me otherwise), that I sat enthralled by it, that I cheered at every sidestep and the sheer brilliance of young Phil Bennett (standing in for the great Barry John at the last minute), jinking again and again to avoid the tackles which would have surrendered the ball to the opposition in front of his own posts. At the amazing way that the big burly forwards and the fleeter-footed backs and half-backs inter-passed at speed. And the way that the tiny tyro Edwards raced through to intercept the pass meant for his colleague, before racing downfield, with All Black Batty in hot pursuit, before diving full length in the corner. The entire stadium erupted. And only five minutes gone.

If you want to take a break now and really get a sense of what I mean, go watch the video on your computer. Any number of sites host it, from the BBC[7] to a range of club and enthusiast sites[3] to the Barbarians own club website.[4] Or you could get a copy of the video or one of the many rugby 'greatest tries' DVDs that are now available through the likes of Amazon.

Watch it. Then watch it again, more closely. And ask yourself, how did this supreme piece of sporting co-creativity come about? What was the game plan? What was the team briefing all about? How did the coach get the players to do something quite so outrageous?

The loneliness of the touchline

Ah, the coach. The legendary Carwyn James. A chain-smoking and ruminating rugby genius who also happened to be a recognized Welsh-language poet. Born in 1929, and like so many of the old breed the son of a coalminer, in Cefneithin in the Gwendraeth Valley. He loved the Eisteddfod platform (the great celebration of Welsh-language poetry of the classical sort) as much as the rugby field.

He loved his country dearly – he was the unsuccessful Plaid Cymru candidate for Llanelli in the 1970 General Election – but also loved his rugby. Sadly he played only twice for Wales in 1958. But he was probably the greatest thinker and teacher of rugby that the game has ever seen. But there – on the touchline – wrapped in a dark overcoat, he stood on that January afternoon, smoking and admiring his charges and their extraordinary invention and co-creativity (though I'm not sure he would have used that word).

One of the things about being a rugby coach is that you cannot make your players do anything; nor can you do it for them. Once they step on the field, bar a few well-aimed shouted instructions and a solid half-time talk, you have little means to shape how your team play. Sure, in most sports you can make substitutions and in some call time-outs when you need to, but the coach is essentially impotent on the field of play.

More so, the coach of the Barbars. This club is invitation only – theoretically, injuries and availability permitting, the coach can select the world's top players (apart from the club's rule of always fielding one non-capped player). But more than this, the coach has little scope for preparing his charges to do what he wants; until recently, the club eschewed training, on the good old English assumption of amateur superiority. So how did James pull it off?

How did he get his players to play that way, to beat the best side in the world, without intensive training sessions and without the help of repeatedly drilled and sweatily honed set moves?

Well, on the one hand, he had coached a number of the players before – he prepared the Llanelli team that pulled off the outrageous defeat of the all-conquering All Blacks in 1971. He also coached the Welsh side and the combined British and Irish Lions in the winter of 1972 which had inflicted the first series defeat for the All Blacks on home soil. So he knew most of the players, believed and trusted in their talents, and they knew him and how he believed the game should be played – fast, attacking and collaboratively; everyone should link with everyone else, rather than grinding out a controlling game of forward-play, so popular at the time in England.

In addition, James was helped by the ethos of the Barbarian club – it was for a long time the bastion of fast and attacking play. Amateurism emphasized flair and opportunism rather than dreary well-rehearsed drills. (Curiously close to the All Blacks whose playing motto has long been to 'play rugby like it has never been played before'). All the Barbarian players knew this was why they had been selected; this was the kind of game Carwyn wanted them to play and all of them aspired to play this way.

What Carwyn did and didn't do

But all of this still doesn't explain the audaciousness, the sheer unadulterated beauty of the move that ended with Edwards going over in the corner.

And the truth is that Carwyn didn't tell them to do this precise move. There was no chalkboard discussion marking out the move. (Imagine, 'Right, Phil. When you pick up the bobbling ball in front of your posts, I want you to jink past their tackles, say three or four times . . . and you Gareth, I want you to prepare to intercept this pass and head off for the corner . . .'). No pre-planning of this specific move. No specific instructions.

No, what Carwyn did was remind them of how the game should be played, encourage certain rules of interaction within the team and give each of them the self-belief to play within these rules beyond the limits of their own previous behaviour – to each of them, whatever their skill-level or speed – all of them, from the twinkled-toed Phil Bennett who started the move to the giant Derek Quinnell who made the final intercepted pass.

And then he was able to take his place on the touchline and watch the magic unfold. And – drawing on one cigarette after another – watch the complex system that his team now was developing: its own patterns of behaviour. To co-create a winning performance. Yes, including that glorious move which set the tone of the remaining 75 minutes.

The loneliness of the manager

This is the central lesson of this chapter. If, in your capacity as a manager, you want to embrace the truth of our human herd nature, you have to learn to let go. To retire to the touchline if you like, having done your work.

Because a rugby team like a company is not a machine – predictable and pre-programmed to execute specific moves – but a complex adaptive system. The best you can do is light the fire of purpose and belief, establish the rules of interaction and then set the distributed intelligence of the system free to create its own patterns. Sure you can correct some things at 'half-time' – make substitutions or tinker with the rules of interaction of one or two players, but at heart you know you have to let go.

And of course, the same is true of how the company interacts with its customers and its other stakeholders. And we will deal with this in the second half of the chapter.

Of course, businesses don't play for just 80 minutes – even if our obsession with quarterly financial reporting makes it feel this way, the game goes on and on. But I promise you this: if you manage to let go of control fully – the grand illusion – of the behaviour of your people and of your customers, you might even be able to enjoy – yes, *enjoy* – the journey.

The company as machine

Most of our thinking in business derives from earlier eras with other concerns and other insights into what was seen as true or desirable about human nature in the workforce. From an age when machines and humans were first thrown together. An age when machines were worshipped.

And much of our thinking is still influenced by the man who has been and continues to be the most influential thinker of the machine company point of view. That said, Frederick Winslow Taylor is an unlikely intellectual hero. He was an American college dropout who suffered lifelong bad health and bad eyesight, a poor public speaker who was poor at communicating his ideas even face to face – a real burden later in his life as he struggled to explain himself again and again (to suspicious Congressional Labour Committees).

His central concern was to develop 'scientific' approaches to managing the workplace which might enable businesses to apply the same engineering precision to the human workforce as they were already doing to the machinery operated by the employees. This, he hoped, would replace the very informal arrangements about what to do and how to do it that factory workgroups agreed among themselves.

Reducing the human element[5]

At heart,[6] Taylor was concerned with reducing the variable human element of factory work. He observed individuals – the best-performing individuals – and specified through analysis and detailed note-taking the best way to do a particular job.

In 1881 Taylor studied metal-cutting and optimized the process in one factory. Later he studied coal-shovelling, experimenting with different designs of shovel to specify the best practice and best tools to shovel different substances (from 'rice' coal to ore). Through this he was able to cut the number of people shovelling at the Bethlehem Steel Works from 500 to 140, increasing total output by 200% with only a 50% increase in individual pay.

A decade later he perfected his incentive theories (an annual bonus was rejected for shorter-term incentives). And then in 1909, he published his most famous book, *Principles of Scientific Management.*[7] Some key principles of Taylor's approach included:

1. Breaking down the work of all the factory's employee activities into specific tasks so that humans worked as efficiently as possible, according to precise instructions.
2. The development – through strict, scientific observational means – of a 'best-practice instruction' for each individual's job.
3. The scientific recruitment, training and development of workers to fit the job specified rather than allowing workers to choose their own jobs and their own training.
4. Functions matter more than people. This created the need for specialized clerks to monitor, report and control the performance of specific tasks.

Taylor saw humans in the workplace as less reliable than the machines that lay at the heart of every factory. Humans, he felt were unpredictable and variable, if left to their own devices. And not just intermittently lazy. He was convinced it was only if their work and their jobs were scientifically specified – right down to the level of every individual – that they could deliver the efficiencies that mass production promised. Only if the business dictated, monitored, incentivized and disciplined – albeit it on rational, evidence-based principles – what each individual did, could it hope to succeed in reducing the imperfections that human workers brought to manufacturing and other industries.

Children of the lesser god

Taylor's ideas garnered much support at the time in all kinds of places – Lenin was a tremendous fan. It has been suggested by some historians that one of the reasons behind the failure of collective planning in Soviet Era Russia is that it was based too closely on Taylor's scientific management ideas and practices.

But the ideas are alive and well today. The tendency all managers seem to have of specifying their staff's behaviour is hard to avoid – micro-managing we call it. The notion of lazy, ignorant or just downright unreliable human 'assets' is equally widespread. And the need to check and recheck performance that Taylor recommended also. Equally, the goal of machine-like efficiency – and the possibility that it can be achieved – still plays a big part in every manager's thinking about his operational team.

As with any distinctive line of thinking, Taylor's intellectual children added to the legacy (they co-created it, if you like). Others developed tools and ideas to help scientific managers do their thing even better. Henry Gantt developed Gantt charts, originally for the visually impaired, which help us manage timelines for all kinds of projects and in all kinds of situations. He also contributed to the creation of management systems such as PERT and CPM (critical path method) that are both – in developed forms – around today. Some of the more bizarre additions to the scientific manager's toolbox include the work of Frank 'father of motion studies' Gilbreth and his wife Lillian 'first lady of management' Gilbreth. These include among other things the chroncyclegraph (which used stop watches and strobe lights to help observers identify precise hand actions and a host of innovation in, of all things, factory whistle blasts).

But the greatest legacy of Taylorism is that humans can be treated as rational machine parts (why do we draw organograms of our organizations that resemble the wiring diagrams for my computer?), their work capable of fine-tuning and re-engineering, and that in order to bring about change in a workforce's performance detailed specifications of each job could and should be made. And thus the managers and owners of a business could – if only they used the right 'scientific' tools and methods, control their human capital and get the maximum from them.

Another point of view

Clearly to the herd theorist this is nonsense. It misunderstands much of our nature – we are not rational, we are not isolated individuals, we do not live our lives (inside the workplace or outside) except in the company of others (real or imagined).

Certainly, some of Taylor's contemporaries disagreed with his underlying theories and his specific remedies. One of his loudest contemporary critics,

Elton Mayo, claimed that 'alienation', which he observed in the American workforce in the 1920s and 1930s, stemmed from industrialization and the factory system championed by Taylor and his gang; in particular Mayo pointed out the effect these innovations in the workplace had in breaking down the social structures which were essential to human happiness.

Moreover, the studies of the workplace at the Hawthorne works in Cicero, Illinois (see Chapter 9 for more details) provided a good counter to Taylor's mechanized vision of the company. They reveal much of what we in the herd corner would insist on in understanding the herd in the workplace.

Key principles of what later became known as the 'Human Relations' movement include the following:

1. Organizations are social systems, not technical machines.
2. We are not logical or motivated only by money.
3. We are interdependent – particularly with our work group.
4. Local – workgroup – influence is often stronger than that of management.
5. Jobs are often more complex and thus not reducible to the simple tasks that Taylorism suggests.
6. Job satisfaction often leads to higher productivity.
7. Management requires effective social – not just technical – skills.

Human remains

Now, you may think, this chimes all very well with the kind of approach to organizing that Carwyn James might have adopted. Or that I might well be about to recommend to you.

And that's where you'd be wrong.

Because – as the name of this group of organizational experts suggests – it gave rise to the HR function in business. And I know of too many businesses in which the HR function is a hindrance rather than a help in doing better things or doing things better. It's not that HR folk are intentionally unhelp-ful, it's rather that their discipline doesn't tend to have a firm grip on the practicalities of the business either. In many businesses, HR is set up as a counterweight to the bullies of command-and-control scientific management. It invokes protocols and procedures in order to meet the prevalent approach in a fair fight. And it has become the repository of HR practice – similar to the supervising clerks of Taylor's companies, rather than embedding sound humanist and good legal practices into the managers and employees it tends to create its own army of overseers and experts.

And as for the nature of the individuals who in my experience gravitate to this part of most big businesses, I think the name says it all.

Interaction businesses

No, however close our underlying assumptions about people in the workforce are, Herd theory points in a different direction for developing strategies and plans for changing employee behaviour. Let me lay out three principles for you to be clear.

First, most businesses in the Western world today are what McKinsey[8] call 'interaction' businesses – that is, businesses whose success depends on distributed intelligence and the interaction of employees with each other and with customers and suppliers/partners.

Second, the most that can be done is what Carwyn did to his victorious Barbarian side: to put the fire of belief in an employee base, encourage the desired rules of interaction and then trust in their distributed intelligence to find the solutions to local problems and challenges.

Third, the sense of control and predictability which the old post-Taylorist view gave managers is an illusion and should be abandoned.

A different kind of job

I observed above that most of our ideas about the company, our workforce and how to manage it come from a different age, an age with different views and insights into human nature. In particular, too much is derived directly from the machine-age thinking of Taylor and co. which sees humans as unreliable machine parts, much more so than the machines they served.

Increasingly, it is clear that most of our businesses are of a different kind. According to one estimate,[9] 80% of all non-agricultural jobs in the developed economies are 'interactional'; that is, they involve complex problem-solving and collaboration. Only 20% are in such traditional activities as performing simple predefined tasks as Taylor described on factory floors and production lines (even then, many manufacturing businesses, such as the Japanese automotive manufacturers, encourage the kind of collaborative activity between the production workers that Taylor would have recognized, designers and engineers to seek out ways to improve both product quality and efficiencies in manufacturing practice). And this four to one ratio is exactly the reverse of what Taylor would have observed in his studies, thanks to the growth of other kinds of businesses (particularly the service sector) and the decline of other sectors and the success our predecessors had in improving productivity for those businesses that have survived.

For most workers in the West then collaborative, complex problem-solving, using the exchange of information, the need to call on many different kinds of knowledge while doing so (with customers and co-workers alike) is the essence of their work. Health workers and M&A specialists, insurance sales-people and software engineers, advertising executives and movie producers all rely on what economists call 'tacit' interactions of this sort. McKinsey estimate that while 63% of all insurance company employees now experience tacit interactions as the central character of their job, this is also true for some 30% of all utility workers. As a rule of thumb, it is suggested, between a quarter and a half of all jobs are now primarily concerned with tacit interactions.

Of course, the problem for those of us looking to improve the performance of a given employee base is that the old management ideas and tools (either the ones handed down by Taylor or the Human Relations gang) are no longer relevant. The tasks that are involved in tacit interaction businesses are not predictable or (often) scalable. They depend on the context in which they emerge and the success of an employee or group in dealing with these is largely determined by that context.

Technology can be a big help – providing for example updated and integrated patient records to a doctor or surgeon will give her a much better chance of a swift and accurate diagnosis; a PDA which gives an insurance salesman access to the right kind of information for the specific customer will also give him a great advantage. Indeed the best-performing companies of those whose business is primarily based on tacit interaction give their employees five times as much IT support per person as the worst performers. They also happen to be increasing their investment in IT per person 40% faster than their counterparts.

It is clear from McKinsey's work, though, that there is huge scope for improvement in how business approaches the needs of this new reality, how it seeks to manage and enhance its people's interactions. In a study of 8,000 US companies which were biased towards tacit interactions, they found that there is an enormous gap in terms of productivity – and a very big difference in management practice – between the best and the worst performing companies. And this compared badly with those companies studied in the low- and middling-interaction sectors.

> The level of performance variability (defined as the standard deviation of performance divided by the mean level of performance) was 0.9 for companies in sectors with a low level of tacit interactions (e.g. in mining or extraction). Among companies in sectors with a middling number of tacit interactions (e.g. transformational businesses such as manufacturing) it was 5.5, rising to 9.4 in sectors with a high level of interactions.[10]

In other words, the performance of companies in industries in which successful interactions of their staff really mattered actually varied much more than the performance of companies in industries in which interaction was less important (say manufacturing). And the reason is that the old ways of thinking about business and the tools of management just don't work in the fastest-growing sector of the economies of the developed world: people businesses. The time has come to think again. To follow Carwyn, perhaps?

Back to the drawing board?

OK, let's start again. A business is not a machine with – more or less – compliant human components. A business is an organism – a complex adaptive system of individuals interacting with each other and third parties such as customers all of the time.

This means that we have to turn many of our existing ideas on their heads if we are to influence the system successfully.

First we have to recognize that innovation is more likely to come from collaboration somewhere in or on the edge of the distributed system that is the firm, rather than at the centre. Again and again, management writers have shown the weakness of centrally driven and managed innovation.

Companies *can* increase their chances of their business producing valuable innovations if they incentivize this kind of behaviour among the workforce. 3M have traditionally done this informally and most of us know the story of how not-very-good adhesive led to the ubiquitous post-it note but Google encourages its software engineers to spend one day a week doing their own stuff for new products and services. Google Earth – the mapping application – is one such and it has been tested in a co-creative manner through Google

Labs (log on to this if you haven't already; some fascinating stuff here). Nokia have long had a market in 'by-product' ideas – that is, it incentivizes its people to develop new ideas and rewards them if they are a success for the company or the company sells them on. Other companies are learning the value of encouraging innovation at the margins.

Second, we have to change our notions of how management and strategy interact. All too many companies – and M&A proposals – are still driven by top-down strategies. While it is understandable for those at the top (or their advisers) to want to suggest grand strategies (what else do they do? You might otherwise ask) most of these grand strategies never get implemented. Of course, this does not mean that management gives up its role for strategic guidance entirely; both at the level of purpose-idea or core belief and at the more practical level of clear objectives these are both essential, but we must stop writing strategies which, like Napoleon's battle plans, never survive the first contact with the enemy. All too often, we try to legislate – to write the rule book – to hard-wire behaviours in our staff that are too simplistic to deal with all the situations that arise. It seems that in implementing grand strategy we really do want to Taylorize our workers – to remove the last shred of intelligence, intuition and simple old-fashioned gumption from their jobs – and replace them with robots who just do exactly what we tell them to do.

One interesting alternative approach to this is a management style that has been used to explain[11] the repeated ability of Japanese companies to come back from the brink of economic disaster. Essentially the job of the manager is to give the team thematic goals and coach or support them in their attempts to reach them together, rather than dictate the means by which they choose to do so. A far cry from the dictatorial bosses of too many Western businesses and the interfering senior managers I too often encounter. Indeed, Collins and Porras have suggested much the same notion in their review of the data from *Built to Last*. It seems that far from a charismatic leader being a positive help in creating value- or purpose-driven businesses, it is a hindrance. Charismatic leaders are negatively correlated with such businesses. What matters – as discussed in Chapters 7 & 8 – is making the organization's purpose really clear (what McKinsey call 'providing a magnetic north'), encouraging individuals to feel it personally and then setting precise project outcomes and parameters for how they get there rather than detailed strategies. Much as Carwyn did.

Third, we have to recognize that traditional tools are actually working against the collaborative ethos required in interactive businesses. Let's just abandon them. One obvious example is the individual bonus-able objectives. How can an individual truly work with his colleagues, freely and whole-heartedly, if he is set on a different and conflicting agenda with them? One agency manager I know all too well delighted in the 'creative conflict' that he claimed this produces. Right.

Fourth, we have to admit that we cannot make anyone or any group do anything. We cannot communicate with them in isolation or hope to 'persuade them' (as the old advertising models would have it); they influence each other. Only by getting individuals and groups to choose to do something for their own reasons – often largely social – will change in behaviour come about. And even then to different degrees with different groups – maybe the pitch for behaviourial change has to be different to different groups, but if this works, then what the hell? Remember most behaviour-change programmes fail.

So what can you do?

It might seem that everything is fired with difficulty. That all your traditional tools are being denied you. But there are ways of thinking about this which can help; there are things that herd theory can do to help you bring about behavioural change within the company beyond lighting or relighting the fire. Many of the ideas articulated earlier in this book can help you approach the problems constructively and confidently, I have applied them in different ways to different change problems for both the companies I have worked for as well as those who have paid the bills.

More human physics

In Chapter 4, we saw how mass behaviour could be understood using the tools of particle physics. That is in terms of rule-based interactive particles. Just as with the example of crime, we can divide any mass population (say of your company) into three groups – the 'saints', 'floaters' and the 'crims'.

Let's say this corresponds to those who buy totally into your beliefs and the changes you want to see (believers), those who aren't sure yet (the fence-sitters) and finally those who don't like what you believe and will resist or try to ignore your programme (the resistance). If you look around your team, you will quickly be able to sort people into these three groups but a word of warning: most companies have tried to change any number of times and most of these programmes have failed. Thus it is that quite a lot of people have developed a good toolkit at avoiding and undermining change. They smile, they nod, they tell you how much they agree. But like St Augustine, who asked his God to make him good, but *just not yet*, they will find any number of reasons why change has to be taken at a slower pace in their part of the business.

In any change programme, the resisters are going to resist. The question is the extent to which you allow them to shape the context for the floating voters. If you remember the crime stats example, the key thing is the extent to which the majority of 'floaters' perceive that criminal behaviour is acceptable in their local environment. So you have to be tough on the resisters and their kind of behaviour. Think again of Broken Windows and the NY Transit Authority. How you are seen to deal with aberrant behaviour – even of the most minor kind – really helps to communicate your message to the floaters. It also has the advantage of unearthing hidden resistance groupings.

Of course, you will need to work with the believers (your *saints*), to encourage and support them publicly, but the real work is to be done with the floaters and the resisters. Remember to keep monitoring your employee base as you go through this though, as metastable states can suddenly emerge through the interaction of individuals and you could be suddenly flooded with new resisters.

Crisis, what crisis?

Another aspect of this physics approach is to be found in all management textbooks on change: it really helps if you create or highlight a crisis (to change the perceived context for employee–employee interaction). This provides a real impetus to change. Key to the ability of St Luke's[12] – the creative collective which burned so brightly at the end of the 1990s – to implement so much change in a conservative industry were the close personal bonds formed by the crisis which gave birth to the company. The somewhat loopy ideals behind the business were embraced by so many on the back of a real crisis. Employees' jobs and mortgages were on the line as a result of the American owners of Chiat Day selling to another network. Employees were asked if they wanted to go their own way or 'cross the line' (literally a line drawn on the floor) to a new kind of business.

Crisis (or a sense of crisis) seems to provide a good spurt to innovation. Motorola became a phone company because the business was in meltdown.[13] ARM[14] stopped manufacturing microchips and focussed instead on designing and licensing them to others, because the management team faced another round of redundancies and heartache as the economic cycle drove the industry into panic yet again.

Let them all talk

Another approach you might use (in addition to or instead of the physics one) is to harness the power of word of mouth inside your company. In doing so, it is important to remember two things: first, people will always talk and not always positively about you and your aims. They will gossip about who's in and who's out. This is an important part of the social activity that we are programmed to indulge in – it is, as Chapter 1 suggests, entirely and necessarily human. Even the negativity and the obsession with company politics seem to be important for building social groups.

You cannot stop people talking – they always will. To whom they choose and in the contexts in which they choose. So don't be misled into assuming that they will obey the gagging orders you might want to enforce, through legal or other means. The challenge for you is finding ways to get the talk that builds the social networks to work for you and your objectives.

A lot of the talk will not be flattering even before you start. An unusual film[15] at the 2006 Tribeca Film Festival reveals how difficult it is to suppress disrespect and affront, even in totalitarian states. From the poorest and most downtrodden to the party members and even the secret police and the party's leaders, Soviet communists all told each other jokes about communism – jokes about the surreal realities of everyday life, of the madness of Soviet bureaucracy and the leaders of the party. While Stalin sent many to the Soviet labour camps, just for telling or hearing a joke, other leaders such as Khrushchev and Gorbachev both loved and collected these jokes (Gorbachev is shown in the film telling one such to a British chat show audience).

Not all of the jokes told are that funny, but this one gives you a flavour of the better ones:

A man dies and goes to hell. He is confronted by a choice between two options: capitalist or communist hell. Outside the door of capitalist hell stands the devil, who bears a striking resemblance to Ronald Reagan.

'What's it like in capitalist hell?' asks the newly deceased.

'Well,' says the devil, 'in capitalist hell, they flay you alive, then they boil you in oil and then they cut you up into small pieces with sharp knives.'

'Wow! And in communist hell?'

Here he finds a huge queue of people waiting to get in. He waits patiently. Eventually he gets to the front and there at the door to communist hell is a grizzly old man who looks a bit like Karl Marx. He asks Karl the same question.

'Here it's the same as down the road,' quips Marx impatiently, 'they flay you alive, then they boil you in oil, and then they cut you up into small pieces with sharp knives.'

Clearly the same deal. 'But why the long queue?' he asks.

'Oh that,' sighs Marx, 'Sometimes we're out of oil, sometimes we don't have knives, sometimes no hot water . . .'[16]

The film suggests that in some ways joke-telling was seen as some kind of – indeed the only possible – resistance to the tyranny of the state and its agents; it seems no coincidence that Poland, the first country in the Soviet block whose citizens successfully overthrew their communist government, was also the first country to allow anti-government and anti-establishment humour on television.

While I am sure that your regime is nothing like that endured by the Soviets, I am convinced that ribald and disrespectful rumours and stories are told in your workplace about the company and its leaders. It's par for the course so don't exercise yourself too much about it.

Equally it is now well established that in online environments – e.g. on your office email system – negativity is the norm.[17] During one change programme I was involved in, I discovered that some of my team had developed a website spoof of our CEO, which likened him and his behaviour with that of the scurrilous salesman Swiss Tony from Paul Whitehouse's TV series, *The Fast Show*. We both found it very funny and refused to clamp down on it.

There is academic interest to be had from the kind of epidemiological studies of how fast such jokes or rumours pass through a given population (*Hammer and Tickle*[18] also reveals the story of a clerk in Bucharest, Calin Bogdan Stefanescu, who spent the last 10 years of Ceauşescu's era collecting political jokes. His careful observations on political events, which jokes he was told about each and when enabled him to plot the velocity of Romanian anti-establishment jokes and assert the link between joke-telling and the fall of the regime. Jokes against the leader apparently doubled in his last three years.)

It seems highly inappropriate for any Western business to bother with such analysis. And frankly humourless in the extreme. If you are upset by people telling jokes about you, then I suspect you were not made for a leadership position. I have always seen it as a sign of a healthy company culture that it tells jokes about itself, but then I am very British about these things. I have always encouraged the 'alternative' workplace news-sheets and gossip sites.

Indeed, with the advent of online bulletin boards and blogging by employees, you can learn an awful lot about the experience of the front-line staff by monitoring these things for yourself. They add colour and context to the things managers report in more formal staff surveys. I have in fact taken clients to such sites to show them what their staff are telling friends and family about the company and its policies. And often with eye-opening effect for them!

It is also pointless to try to stop your people doing so as — legalities such as slander or defamation aside and the release of commercially confidential information — you cannot control what employees say to each other. Just as you cannot control what your customers say (if you close down one channel, another will emerge).

The question instead is this: how can you harness the power of word of mouth among employees and their families to bolster the kind of change you want to see in your business?

Talk with the talkers

One of the least helpful hand-me-downs of Taylor's view of the firm is his insistence, in thinking about and describing the structure of a business, that function is more important than people. If you draw a Taylorist organogram, your picture will be about functions and the jobs that lead or manage those functions. This makes an awful lot of sense if you see the firm as simply in Taylor's terms but if you see it as a social phenomenon first — a series of shifting herds and groupings within and around the functional system — then it is plainly inadequate for describing the nature of the organization (or 'organism-ization', if you like).

The alternative way of approaching an organization is often much more helpful in working out who you might want to lead the worker–worker discussions. Some of the models from Chapter 6 can be applied to this problem.

On the one hand you might take the 'Influentials' approach: find those people (Keller's 10%) who are the ones that everyone else turns to for advice on matters surrounding the workplace (and if Keller's right, most other things). These are unlikely to be drawn exclusively from senior or even middle-ranking positions but they are likely to be more involved in the workplace community.

On the other, you might take the 'super-connector' or 'social influencer' approach; there are some individuals who are always going to be more net-worked than others, passing on opinions and information to their peers. You can easily identify these types, though again they are unlikely to be your most senior managers.

Alternatively if you are looking at a specific sub-group whose behaviour you want to change (and if you have the time and energy) you could take the DecisionWatch approach: identifying the networks of influence which have affected a specific individual and then planning accordingly to influence this.

In my experience any of these approaches can be overlaid and combined with the physics approach to understanding. Even a rough-and-ready – back of a fag packet – calculation will help you avoid the usual bland and ineffective broadcasts from the chairman's office.

What do they talk of?

But don't expect bland repetition of your messages and your actions from your colleagues (as certain advertising researchers would have you believe is important). This is another of the Taylor-era misunderstandings of how mass behaviour comes about.

No, the key thing to look for is how the system operates on your behalf. How employees influence each other. How they work on your behalf.

And the same things that matter here are the same as we've discussed before with regard to customers and external audiences. Things like being clear about and articulating your driving beliefs. Making sure you really, *really* believe what drives you and then acting accordingly. If you want to signal a change in behaviour, you have to behave differently. You have to encourage the business to be different.

And finally . . .

Let's admit that we do not control what our employees and colleagues do. We can't do what Taylor promised – enforce particular practices – because the truth is employees won't *obey* anymore (if they ever did!). And most of the rules we try to impose are rightly seen as pompous and petty-minded. And that often works counter to our intentions.

Control of our employees is an illusion that we in the boardroom could well do without. Nor, in a complex adaptive system, can we predict precisely what people will do (and nor should we waste our time doing so). Of course, organograms, Gantt charts and 6-sigma processes all make us feel more secure. But this security is based on just the same illusory roots as our own individual volition and sense of self (see Chapter 2). Or on the marriage vows that fewer and fewer of us take. 'Forsaking all others, in sickness and in health . . .' Fine words but they don't make a difference to the length of the modern marriage, it seems, unless you really believe them.

As inside, so outside

While this chapter has been almost exclusively devoted to applying herd theories to internal management problems, the same issues arise when thinking about how you relate to the outside world of customers and (hopefully) collaborators and co-creators.

We spend so much time counting, keeping the score, dissecting and interrogating the budgets and plans of those that report to us that it's a wonder that some of us get any work done at all. And the only real benefit I can see is that it makes those of us who have to 'face the beak' in the holding company or at the shareholders' meetings feel more confident. But it is all an illusion.

We have to accept that – once the game kicks off – we have to retire to the touchlines, just as Carwyn did that glorious January afternoon. Even as we plan how we want things to go – say a marketing campaign or the kind of co-creative project that Andy Bryant describes (Chapter 9) – it is worth leaving the illusion of control at the door. Our mechanistic and individualist ways of thinking about mass behaviour encourage us to believe that everything is controllable and predictable – that we can make people do things, that we can impose our will upon them directly, whether or not what we are trying to impose is scientifically based, as Taylor would suggest. But as inside, so outside; this illusion has no value to us apart from making us feel better about ourselves. The truth is that in the complex systems that are human herds, we don't have, have never had and never will have control of the herd.

The end of management

What this means for those of you who have job titles such as 'director' or 'manager' or 'supervisor' is quite plain. You have to get used to being out of control. If you're a director, you don't direct anything (and in the modern world, you'd better learn to co-create with those outside, both clients and their customers and even your competitors, particularly if you are the corner-office creative director type). If you're a manager, you don't manage anything either. You have to accept that your powers are strictly limited and less important than the swirling seas of colleague-networks and customer interactions. If you're a supervisor, you should put away your stop watch and clipboard. And if you sit in the higher echelons of business (you have VP or SVP prefix on your business card, maybe) you'd better get used to the fact that you don't control anything inside or outside the company.

No, the best we can hope to do is cast a pebble on the water. Choose the pebble wisely, choose how to throw it but once the stone leaves your hand we have to let go. Watch its flight, by all means, but then sit back and watch the ripples that it creates roll across the water.

Buddhist teaching suggests that our 'attachments' to particular outcomes are spiritually and psychologically unhelpful. Indeed, they are the source of all our suffering in this world. My friend, 'Dr Jim', has suggested that what I'm arguing for here is some kind of business Taoism (an interesting thought, admittedly) but you don't have to be religious or in any way spiritual to see the truth of this.

'Relinquishing control with dignity', wrote Kevin Kelly,[19] co-founder and editor at large of the DotCom bible, *Wired* magazine, 'is the greatest challenge in the 21st century.' So sit back, smoke like Carwyn if you like, but let go for God's sake. The game is about to start.

Some questions for marketing

1. Control is one of the central assumptions behind the marketing ethos; we like to pretend we can manage all sorts of things. Processes, people, customer relationships and so on. But control *is* an illusion. We cannot make anyone do or say anything – at least not without heavy-handed and expensive coercion. How does it feel to know this for sure?

2. How deep does the Taylorist model go in your view of yourself in business? How deeply is it embedded in your business? And in your approach to marketing? Where are the 'hot spots' – the behaviours and concepts – which reveal your model most clearly? What could you do otherwise?

3. What needs – in yourself and in your business culture – does control satisfy? Why do we cling to it so tightly?

4. How does the application of 'marketing physics' and the influence approach change what you do? Does it change how you feel about control?

Part Three

Making Sense of the Herd

11

Conclusions

What this chapter will cover

Why seeing the world through someone else's beliefs can be strange. Why 'I' and 'We' perspectives are so different. Conclusions and implications of the herd theory for those trying to bring about changes in mass behaviour. Some closing thoughts.

It's turtles all the way down.

(anonymous)

Life, the universe and giant aquatic reptiles

There's a story that you may have heard about what it feels like to encounter someone with what you may feel is a strange belief system.

In the different versions I have heard, the hero has been variously identified as William James, brother of novelist Henry and one of the founders of modern psychology, Albert Einstein, Galileo and a number of other great scientific minds. Of all of these, I prefer to imagine William James. I picture him in frock coat and cravat, earnestly lecturing a room of well-bred Boston ladies on what science has to tell us about the planets and our solar system. As in his writing, he chooses clear and simple language to bring to life complex and sometimes difficult subjects and make them understood by the generalist.

'So you see, contrary to what was long believed, we now know that the earth is like a ball which, far from being the centre of our solar system as the Roman Church once taught, is merely one of many planets rotating around the biggest and fieriest ball of all – the Sun.'

Most of his audience nod, their bowed heads acknowledging his scientific authority. However, one rather grand lady looks perturbed.

'That's all very well, Mr James,' she sniffs, 'but you and I both know that the earth is nothing of the sort.'

'No, madam?' enquires James politely, suspecting he might have a flat-earther on his hands but not wanting to be seen to be rude or patronizing. 'Pray tell, what *is* the earth then?'

'No, the earth is no mere ball, floating in space. It is a solid crust. Solid beneath our feet as our daily experience confirms.'

Silence. He draws himself up, smiling his broadest smile. 'So madam, what does this crust rest on? On what is it built?'

'Why, I'm surprised you have to ask, Mr James. You should know that it rides on the back of a giant turtle.'

James raises his eyebrows at this suggestion – a signal failure to tolerate superstition in his fellow human clear for all to see, despite his best efforts at concealment.

'And on what does this giant turtle rest, may I ask?'

'Why on the back of another giant turtle, of course. It's turtles all the way down, Mr James. Turtles all the way down.'

Seeing things differently

When you look at the world through the lenses of someone else's belief system (or 'paradigm' as Thomas Kuhn[1] calls it), the world can seem very strange. You do not see the same world as that which is clear and vivid when you look through your own lenses. Some things become more important and salient; others recede or even sometimes transform themselves; black can become white. But mostly it seems downright strange to see the world in the way some people do. And slightly disconcerting. I'm sure that this was how William James, the mighty scourge of ignorance, the popularizer of modern science, the great communicator, must have felt when confronted by the lady with the turtle obsession.

This, Kuhn points out, is why evidence-based thinking can only change the existing state of affairs to a certain degree. Unless the new way of seeing things raises more interesting questions to grapple with, unless it explains some big issues better in order to pose those more interesting questions, unless it is useful to a large enough number of people, then the best-evidenced argument can work only so hard to change how we think about things, how we see the world.

I am happy to acknowledge this may well be the case for you with this herd theory of mine but I hope that I have managed to give you enough to see things from my perspective (and do so turtle-free). I hope that I have managed to show you how ungrounded the 'I' paradigm is, how unhelpful it is in explaining mass behaviour, because this I think highlights the value of my approach.

Perhaps you are even convinced enough of the argument I have laid out to begin to share the sensation I have when I hear others talk about human nature and mass behaviour from the individualist perspective. I sense the splish-splosh flip-flop of giant turtles when I hear 'I' think and talk. I do hope you do too.

This aside, I still feel the need to pull the conclusions together, to make really clear what the herd theory says and what the practical implications are for anyone trying to change mass behaviour (which I suspect is the reason why you tell yourself you bought this book – the truth is probably different but let's leave the 'bigger boys made me do it' explanation to another day).

It is customary to boil these conclusions down to a handful – 10 seems a good round number. Any more than 10 and the list becomes too long; any fewer and the conclusions seem less weighty. So 10 it is then.

To make things even easier to digest, I have tried to separate out the conclusions from the implications for marketing and other mass behaviour change agents. I hope this makes a difference.

(Deep intake of breath)

Conclusion 1: Our species is first and foremost a social one

This is the first and most important of the insights in this book. We are designed to be social – the super-social ape – we and our behaviour are made and shaped through our interaction with others, from the moment we are born to the day we die. We seek out the company of others; most of the context of our individual lives is made up of other people (not brands, business or political concerns) and most of what we do is determined by this context. This context is the correct place to understand and harness the power of mass behaviour.

Implication 1: Stop thinking and talking with words that conjure the 'I' perspective

Forget the notion of the consumer (an aggregate for lots of individuals or just the one we spotted in a focus group). Stop counting lots of individuals, assuming that they exist in isolation from each other. Instead we should conceptualize human behaviour in terms of social systems and tribes; of 'Us'. And a shifting 'Us' at that.

Conclusion 2: Individuals are unreliable (if not largely irrelevant) witnesses

Individuals are not good guides to understanding or shaping mass behaviour. Individuals are not just unreliable witnesses to their own behaviour and to the motivations that lie behind them because their memories are faulty or just because a lot of what they do is driven by their unconscious. No, the real reason that individuals are unreliable witnesses to mass behaviour is that mass behaviour is the result of a mechanism that is largely hidden to the individual. This is equally as true about past behaviour as it is about future behaviour.

Implication 2: Ignore them

They cannot really tell you – however convincing it seems when they sit in focus groups, or when you corner one at the supermarket fixture and ask them why they just bought a particular brand. They cannot know how they came to do what they did. So don't bother. Or if you do ask them, remember the illusory nature of their answers to you. Instead consider their reports and opinions for what they are: answers to your questions that might or might not indicate more useful things that lie beneath the answer. But these answers are not the truth about what they do, or why.

Conclusion 3: Interaction is everything; interaction is the 'big how'

Mass behaviour is the result of rule-based interactions of individuals, which happens within certain conditions (real and perceived), rather than the aggregate of individual independent decision-making or, as some suggest, the result of some kind of collective madness.

Implication 3: Understand the how-mechanic and use it

Human-to-human interaction within certain conditions and based on simple rules is how mass behaviour happens. If you don't understand and grasp this insight, you will struggle – as so many of us do – to change mass behaviour. Or do so, despite yourself. Broadly speaking there are two ways to do so: either shape the conditions of interaction (real or imagined) or shape the rules of interaction. Or both.

Conclusion 4: C2C, not B2C

In seeking to generate mass behaviour, remember that what individuals do to each other is much more important than what we do to them. However much the powerful corporation struggles with this insight (largely to protect its view of itself and its executives), however uncomfortable this makes you feel, it is nonetheless true. So embrace it.

Implication 4: Get the system to work for you

Be more humble. Cast aside the illusions of power and persuasion, the egotism of business and marketing thinking, the sense that what you are is big, and customers and citizens are small and isolated and weak. Instead, start to recognize the human systems that create mass behaviour; your job is to shape how that system works. And to balance out your need for short-term sales (the low-hanging fruit which one-to-one-ers would prefer to focus on) with the need to create long-term sustainable mass behavioural change, which can largely be done only by influencing the social systems which drive mass behaviour. While you're about it, develop useful means to understand and monitor the system rather than monitor individuals and your effect on them.

Conclusion 5: MIC vs. MVC

None of us has infinite resources to bring about the changes in mass behaviour we seek; none of us will ever have enough. So we have to prioritize in some way, normally by focussing our efforts on certain parts of our audience or our market. However, it is essential to remember that the most valuable customer (what one-to-one-ers call the MVC) is *not* the one who spends most or who is most 'loyal' to you. If you have to prioritize some customers over others, seek out those who have the most influence over their peers (either in terms of the number of people they influence or the degree or manner in which they influence others). The MICs (most influential customers).

Implication 5: Rethink targeting

There are many models that can help identify influence within any given social network, from the influentials and social influencers, to the super-connectors and the many different kinds of influencer which DecisionWatch suggests. It's up to you but remember that the greatest influence on individuals is other people (and at the same time also the greatest filter on your attempts to have direct influence over individuals).

Conclusion 6: B2C communication, not information transmission

We misunderstand how B2C communication works and this is a big handicap in using these potentially powerful tools. We like to imagine that it is essentially a means to transmit persuasive information from the business to the brains (and sometimes the hearts) of individuals. How the individual responds and processes the communication is not relevant (but clearly it's not even primarily as information-processing). It's what individuals make of the communication in their real-life interaction with other individuals in their social system – the context of mass behaviour – that is important to worry about in seeking to generate an effect on the system.

Implication 6: Rethink communication as action

We spend an awful lot of time, energy and money trying to find the right (most persuasive) messages, the right creative vehicles to transmit them and the most efficient channels to do so. All of this can go out of the window if instead you see communication as behaviour, as a form of action. The informational content is really very unimportant compared to the power of the communication to affect changes in the way the system operates – if it alters the mechanism behind mass behaviour.

Equally, this changes how you judge and evaluate communications, either in market research or in other discussions around the table. Or indeed in the way you go about creating them. It doesn't matter so much what you say or what they tell you that you are saying, as what they say to each other. It doesn't matter if individuals recall or recognize or admit to being personally persuaded or not by your communications. The important questions to ask yourself are these: to what extent does this communication affect the mechanism that lies behind the mass behaviour? What indications might there be? Does this create energy, talkability or something else? Does this upset or rebalance the system's equilibrium? Does it draw the herd's attention to the issue or behaviour that you are concerned with? (Remember those out there cannot tell you the answers to these. You have to read the runes for yourself). Perhaps *herdability* is what you should ask of your communication as of the other behaviours your business enacts.

Conclusion 7: Word of mouth is the most powerful sales tool

The most obvious and easily observed form of C2C influence is word of mouth. Real people chat to each other all of the time and this creates a particular strong and valuable form of C2C influence.

Implication 7: Make WoM the real goal of all actions and not just WoM campaigns

All significant actions and behaviours of a company or product can generate word of mouth; indeed, it is useful to view the goal of all activities in terms of word of mouth and to use recommendation (the *one number*) as a key metric for the company as a whole.

However, it is important to distinguish between superficial (exogenous) word of mouth and the more sustainable (endogenous) form. Too many practitioners think that stirring up a bit of buzz or hype (the former kind of

WoM) is sufficient; it is not and often runs the risk of being seen as yet more marketing trickery, and can be self-defeating as a result.

Conclusion 8: Be more interesting

The only way to generate consistent long-term C2C influence – to influence the herd to work for you to generate sustainable long-term mass behaviour – is to be interesting. And to be so authentically, true to your self.

Implication 8: Find your beliefs and live them

The key to this is to build your business around what you truly believe: to make your business an entirely personal crusade, or a vehicle for it. For you and your people. And to align your business's and your staff's behaviours not just to be consistent with your beliefs but to positively express them. If there's any doubt, work out which behaviours matter most to customers and which ones cost you money. If these are the same, then you are fine; if not, rethink. The things that cost you most should be the things that create the greatest (perceived) value.

But don't just try on beliefs for size. Dig deep and make sure you are really serious about them and prepared to live them truly; only this way will your business be seen as *authentic*. Equally, be wary of the many temptations to compromise your beliefs by doing something *cut-price*. They will raise their ugly little heads each and every day.

Conclusion 9: Co-create

We have to learn to co-create value with staff and customers, rather than extract it. In particular it is essential to give your co-creators something that is useful for them in further co-creative exchanges: employee–employee; employee–customer; customer–customer. The rise of consumer confidence and the transparency of the modern world (thanks to the Internet) means that you have no choice but learn how to co-create.

Implication 9: Learn to be a great co-creator

Consider yourself and your business not as an isolated world but instead as part and parcel of the larger system in which you operate through co-creation. Be more open and learn how to work with other people (rather than trying to control them or impose your own needs or desires on them). But more than this, be more generous: think and evaluate all of your actions in terms of what they give your audience to do with their co-creators. Sometimes, this might be as simple as lubricating their social exchanges – a joke, a pleasantry they can talk about. Sometimes this can be more practical, being something they can do with their peers (think of Royal Mail's campaign in Chapter 9 or the decision markets). But the best place to start is with your colleagues: do you go to meetings with an agenda to impose or are you looking to co-create?

Conclusion 10: Letting go

The real game is out there: in the distributed intelligence of your employees and colleagues, in their co-creative distributed interaction with customers and in your customers' distributed interactions with their peers. You cannot control what happens (not that you ever could do – that was just a convenient illusion) or what they say, so stop trying. So once you have prepared the team, let them play and retire to the touchline. (And smoke if you want to.)

Implication 10: Rethink 'management'

You cannot control your people, your customers or your competitors, so stop trying. Too much time and energy is spent in the wrong place – in 'managing'. Managing relationships, customers, people, accounts, journalists and so on. Managing is a polite way to say 'controlling'. Banish this idea and you're off to a start. Equally stop pretending you can make something happen in the future. Recognize you are the coach and not the team; coach your team in how they interact with each other and with customers and with business partners; in how your customers interact with each other to create sales behaviour; in how plans get enacted; in what kind of game you want to play. And why it matters.

Just as you cannot manage what people say to each other – inside or outside the firm – so you cannot manage what they do. Sure you can prepare for the kick-off, but once that whistle blows, it's the touchline for you. Sit back and watch and revel in the patterns created. And wait for the oranges and the half-time team talk.

Postscript

And it's goodnight from him . . .

So there you are.

My attempt – through a number of co-creative experiences – to develop and articulate what the truth of our human nature means for those of us who are trying to change mass behaviour is finally done. This is where I stop (for now anyway).

I hate protracted goodbyes (so there's no epilogue for you to wade through) but I did want to say a few things before I go.

First, I hope the journey has been fun for you. I've tried to make it so. I also hope I've managed to get you to feel how I and an increasing number of colleagues are seeing mass behaviour, the mechanisms that lie behind it and what seem to be emerging as the kinds of solutions and tools which work within this picture. I hope you've found the evidence convincing and credible and the suggestions and challenges useful.

But more than that, I hope I have stimulated some thoughts of your own. This is no canonical text that is fixed and closed, clutching tightly its truths and insights forever to its breast in the safety of a published book. No, this is just the start of what I hope is a larger co-creative rethinking of what we do in changing mass behaviour. It's my latest contribution to a system-wide change that is already underway. New information, new learning and new insights into mass behaviour are coming to light everyday (as I revise the manuscript for this book, I receive a couple of handy tip-offs each day).

It's over to you now. For you to take my version of things, steal, rebadge, remix, transform, re-articulate if you like; but only if you want to, that is. If you find these ideas useful for whatever reason and in whatever context, then I'm glad; if so, then I've done my job.

The conversations and interactions that I have had in writing this book have shaped the thinking it contains in ways I'm not sure I'll ever understand.

Nor have I always been able to see what effect the conversations have had on my conversational partners and how their interactions with others have changed as a result of our interactions. Similarly, I won't see what effects this book will have on your interactions with your peers and your customers. That is unless you tell me about them: if you'd like to share your thoughts, post them on my blog at http://herd.typead.com or email me at markearls@hotmail.com (if you would prefer one of those one-to-one experiences!).

Maybe this will lead on to other conversations and other interactions . . . *which would be all too human, wouldn't it?* Until then, I hope you at least share my marvel and wonder at the amazing thing that is our little naked super-social ape. And the things we – you and I and the rest of our species – can do together. From flowers to rugby to the miracle (or so it seems to me) of this little book. And all that comes after.

O brave new world, That has such people in't!

Shakespeare, *The Tempest* (V, i)

Endnotes

Acknowledgements

1. M. Earls (2002). *Welcome to the Creative Age: Bananas, Business and the Death of Marketing.* John Wiley & Sons, Ltd.

Introduction

1. S. Pinker (2003). *The Blank Slate: The Modern Denial of Human Nature.* Penguin.
2. http://www.banksy.co.uk
3. M. Collins (2005). *The Likes of Us: A Biography of the White Working Class.* Granta.
4. B. Morrison (2005). 'Saying it with flowers', *Guardian*, Thursday 3 November.
5. KPMG reported in *Sunday Times*, 22 January 2005.
6. J. Ward (2005). 'Why mergers and acquisitions don't work', *Market Leader*, Summer, pp 56–58.
7. A. Bonde (2006). 'Is CRM dead?' Darwinmag.com (USA), online. 3 January.
8. Editorial (D. Holder and R. Fairlie) (2004). *Interactive Marketing*, 6:2.
9. R.E. Nisbett (2005). *The Geography of Thought: How Asians and Westerners Think Differently – And Why.* Nicholas Brealey.
10. A. Miller (1995). *The Drama of Being a Child: The Search for the True Self.* Virago.
11. C. Fine (2006). *A Mind of Its Own: How Your Brain Distorts and Deceives.* Icon.

Chapter 1

1. D. Wallace (2003). *Join Me: The True Story of a Man Who Started a Cult By Accident.* Ebury Press.
2. Online http://www.join-me.co.uk/story.
3. P. Lambourn and B. Weinberg (eds) (1999). *Avant Gardening: Ecological Struggle in the City.* Autonomedia, NY.
4. Red Pepper Online at http://www.redpepper.org.uk/sept2004.
5. R. White (2005). 'The death of demographics', *Admap*, September.
6. Goldie Lookin Chain (2003). *Greatest Hits*, Atlantic Records.
7. '"Big Brother" eyes make us act more honestly' (2006), *New Scientist*, 28 June.
8. 'Pay up, you are being watched' (2005), *New Scientist*, 19 March.
9. I. Sample (2006). 'Closer to man than ape', *Guardian*, 24 January.
10. Andrew Rambaut of Oxford University, quoted in *Sample* (2006).
11. D. Morris (1967). *The Naked Ape: A Zoologist's Study of the Human Animal.* Jonathan Cape.
12. C. Bromhall (2004). *The Eternal Child: How Evolution Has Made Children of Us All.* Ebury Press.

13. R. Dunbar (1998). 'The social brain hypothesis', *Evolutionary Anthropology: Issues, News, and Reviews*, 6:5, pp. 178–190; see also R. Dunbar (2004). *Grooming, Gossip and the Evolution of Language*, Faber & Faber.
14. 'Mindless imitation teaches us how to be human' (2006), *New Scientist* (UK), 1 April.
15. 'Mindless imitation teaches us how to be human' (2006), *New Scientist*.
16. C. van Shaik (2006). 'Why are some animals so smart?' *Scientific American*, April.
17. M.D. Salter Ainsworth and J. Bowlby (1991). 'An ethological approach to personality development', *American Psychologist*, 46:4, April, pp. 333–341. Also: I. Bretherton (1992). 'The origins of attachment theory: John Bowlby and Mary Ainsworth', *Developmental Psychology*, 28, pp. 759–775.
18. E. Waters, S. Merrick, D. Treboux, J. Crowell and L. Albersheim (2000). 'Attachment security in infancy and early adulthood: a twenty-year longitudinal study', *Child Development*, 71:3, May, pp. 684–689. Gay C. Armsden and Mark T. Greenberg (1987). 'The inventory of parent and peer attachment: individual differences and their relationship to psychological well-being in adolescence', *Journal of Youth and Adolescence*, pp. 427–454.
19. L.A. Kirkpatrick and C. Hazan (1994). 'Attachment styles and close relationships: a four-year prospective study', *Personal Relationship*, 1, June, p. 123.
20. L. Cosmides and J. Tooby (2005). 'Neurocognitive adaptations designed for social exchange'. In D.M. Buss (ed.), *Evolutionary Psychology Handbook*. John Wiley & Sons, Inc.
21. F. de Waal (2005). *Our Inner Ape: The Best and Worst of Human Nature*. Granta.
22. R. Dunbar (2004). *Grooming, Gossip and the Evolution of Language*. Faber & Faber. S. Pinker (1995). *The Language Instinct: The New Science of Language and Mind*. Penguin.
23. S. Baron Cohen and P. Bolton (1993). *Autism: The Facts*. Oxford University Press.
24. M. Haddon (2004). *The Curious Incident of the Dog in the Night-time*. Vantage.
25. V. Ramachandran (2006). 'Autism: the search for Steven', *New Scientist*, 17 May.
26. Editorial (anon.) (2005). 'Autism linked to malfunctioning "mirror neurons"', *New Scientist*, 10 December.
27. M.A. Flood (1958). 'Some experimental games', *Management* Science, 5, 5–26.
28. R. Axelrod (1984). *The Evolution of Cooperation*. New York: Basic Books.
29. P. Ball (2005). *Critical Mass: How One Thing Leads to Another*. Heinemann.
30. Cited in P. Ball (2005). *Critical Mass*.
31. A. Smith (2004 edn). *The Theory of Moral Sentiments*. Kessinger Publishing.
32. S. Bowles and H. Gintis (2003). 'The origins of human cooperation'. In Peter Hammerstein (ed.), *The Genetic and Cultural Origins of Cooperation*: MIT Press.
33. P. Seabright (2004). *The Company of Strangers – A Natural History of Economic Life*. Princeton.

Chapter 2

1. J. Steinmeyer (2003). *Hiding the Elephant*. Arrow Books.
2. A.A. Hopkins (1995). *Magic, Stage Illusions and Trick Photography*. Dover Books.
3. *The True History of Pepper's Ghost* (1890) is his own account. Also a good description of the illusion's technical side online at www.acmi.net.au/AIC/PEPPER_BIO/html or a model version at www.phantasmechanics.com/hotel.html.
4. S. Pinker (2003). *The Blank Slate: The Modern Denial of Human Nature*. Penguin.
5. C. Kaufman and M. Gondry (2004). *Eternal Sunshine of the Spotless Mind*, shooting script. Nick Hern Books.

6. Sceptical Enquirer online at http://www.csicop.org.si/9503/memory. False Memory Syndrome Society at http://fmsonline.org/reliable.html.
7. American Psychiatric Association Statement on Memories of Sexual Abuse (1993).
8. Royal College of Psychiatrists' Report on Recovered Adult Memories of Childhood Sexual Abuse (1997).
9. Canadian Psychological Association Position Statement on Adult Recovered Memory of Childhood Sexual Abuse (1996).
10. A true story illustrates how easily we fabricate memories about things which are clearly not true. An acquaintance recently wanted to find out what his old school mates were up to. The most obvious means to do this was to visit http://www.friendsreunited.co.uk. However, Eddie (real name) didn't want to reveal his hand to everyone in his class and so he invented an avatar: a false friendsreunited identity. He became a she, with a fictitious name and a photograph downloaded from somewhere else on the net. What shocked him/her was to discover the number of people who claimed to remember this entirely fictitious female schoolmate. Again and again.
11. T. Grandin (2004). *Animals in Translation*. Bloomsbury.
12. D.J. Simons and C.F. Chabris (1999). 'Gorillas in our midst: sustained inattentional blindness for dynamic events', *Perception*, 28, pp. 1059–1074.
13. C. Fine (2006). *A Mind of Its Own: How Your Brain Distorts and Deceives*. Icon.
14. D. Kahnemann and A. Tversky (1982). 'On the study of statistical intuitions'. In D. Kahnemann, P. Slovic and A. Tversky (eds.), *Judgment under Uncertainty: Heuristics and Biases*, pp. 493–508. New York: Cambridge University Press.
15. J.A. Paulos (2004). *A Mathematician Plays the Stock Market*. Basic Books.
16. B. Libet (2004). *Mind Time: The Temporal Factor in Consciousness*. Harvard University Press.
17. S. Blackmore (2005). *Conversations on Consciousness: Interviews with Twenty Minds*. Oxford University Press.
18. D. Wegner (2003). *The Illusion of Will*. MIT Press.
19. I. Berlin (1953). *The Hedgehog and the Fox*. Wiedenfeld & Nicholson.
20. P. Halligan and D. Oakley (2000). 'Self as necessary illusion', *New Scientist* (Australia), pp. 35–39.
21. T. Nagel (1974). 'What is it like to be a bat?' *Philosophical Review*, LXXXIII: 4, October, pp. 435–450.
22. S. Blackmore (2002). 'The grand illusion', *New Scientist*, 22 June.
23. Online at http://www.bbc.co.uk/health/conditions/mental_health/index.shtml.
24. DAK insurance survey online at http://news.bbc.co.uk/1/hi/world/europe/4456087.stm.

Chapter 3

1. N.K. Humphrey (1976). 'The social function of intellect'. In P.P.G. Bateson and R.A. Hinde (eds.), *Growing Points in Ethology*, ch. 9, pp. 303–317. Cambridge University Press.
2. R.E. Nisbett (2005). *The Geography of Thought: How Asians and Westerners Think Differently – And Why*. Nicholas Brealey.
3. D. Tutu (2000). *No Future Without Forgiveness: A Personal Overview of South Africa's Truth and Reconciliation Commission*. Rider & Co.
4. Youth League of the African National Congress policy statement (1944).
5. D. Tutu (2000). *No Future Without Forgiveness*.
6. T. Marathi (unpublished). *Practical Peacemaking Wisdom from Africa Reflections on Ubuntu*. PhD Programme in Peacemaking and Preventive Diplomacy. United Nations

Institute for Training and Research (UNITAR). http://www.bath.ac.uk/~edsajw//monday/Ubuntu.htm

7. www.hoffmaninstitute.co.uk
8. B. Cova and V. Cova (2002). 'Tribal marketing: the tribalisation of society and its impact on the conduct of marketing', *European*, 36: 5–6, June, pp. 595–620.
9. B. Cova and S. Pace (2006). 'Brand community of convenience products: new forms of customer empowerment. The case "my Nutella the community"', to be published in *European Journal of Market Research*. Paper first given at joint conference on marketing trends by Università Ca' Foscari Venezia/Ecole Supérieure de Commerce de Paris-EAP, June 2005.
10. T.T. Ahonen and A. Moore (2005). *Communities Dominate brands – Business and Marketing Challenges for the 21st Century*. Future Text.
11. S. Pinker (2003). *The Blank Slate: The Modern Denial of Human Nature*. Penguin.
12. G. le Bon (1895). *La psychologie des foules* (unknown publisher).
13. S. Freud (2004). *Mass Psychology*, tr. J. Underwood. Penguin.
14. A. Rosenberg and W. Weiß (1927). Reichsparteitag der NSDAP Nürnberg 19./21. August. Munich: Verlag Frz. Eher.
15. E. Bernays (1923, reprinted 2004). *Crystallizing Public Opinion*. Kessinger Publishing.
16. Margaret Thatcher (1987), talking to *Woman's Own* magazine, 31 October.
17. D. Reisman (1950). *The Lonely Crowd: A Study of Changing American Character*. Yale University Press.
18. R.M. Farr (1996). *The Roots of Modern Social Psychology 1872–1954*. Blackwell Publishing.
19. F.H. Allport (1924). *Social Psychology*. Houghton-Mifflin. Cited in M. Farr (1996). *The Roots of Modern Social Psychology*.
20. G.W. Allport (1937). *Personality: A Psychological Interpretation*. Holt. Cited in R.M. Farr (1996). *The Roots of Modern Social Psychology*.
21. F.H. Allport (1924). *Social Psychology*. Cited in M. Farr (1996). *Roots of Modern Social Psychology*.
22. Interviewed by J. Lannon (2005). 'Unilever champions the power of big brand ideas', *Market Leader* magazine, Winter.
23. See my paper 'Rethinking prediction: were you still up when Bob called it for Kerry?' MRS Conference Papers (2005) for more details and a more thorough exposition of the methodology and the implications for market research and other attempts to predict human behaviour.
24. J. Surowiecki (2004). *The Wisdom of Crowds: – Why the Many Are Smarter Than the Few and How Collective Wisdom Shapes Business, Economies, Societies and Nations*. Little Brown.
25. Popbitch at www.popbitch.co.uk.
26. J. Goebbels (1931). Wille und Weg (later Unser Wille und Weg). Monatsblaetter der Reichspropagandaleitung der NSPAD. Online at http://www.calvin.edu/academic/cas/gpa/wille.htm.

Chapter 4

1. T.C. Schelling (1980). *Micromotives and Macrobehaviour*. W.W. Norton.
2. To understand how the science of this works, the following may help. When oil and vinegar in French dressing separate, what's really happening is that the oil droplets are

becoming larger and larger, eventually becoming a separate layer. Mayonnaise uses an emulsifying agent (the egg) to keep the two apart. It helps if you combine the egg and lemon-juice/vinegar first, only slowly dropping the oil in and whisking as you go. Adding too much oil at once will undermine your efforts to keep oil droplets apart from the egg. Also, it makes things a whole lot easier if you use ingredients that are at room temperature; if the ingredients are cold, the eggs won't emulsify so well and the oil won't spread so evenly. More of this kind of stuff at http://www.science.demon.co.uk/handbook/11.htm.

3. http://www.red3d.com/cwr/boids/.
4. http://www.helbing.org.
5. *Nature* (2002), 419, 12 September. www.nature.com/nature.
6. Online at http://www.helbing.org.
7. See M. Earls (2002), *Welcome to the Creative Age: Bananas, Business and the Death of Marketing*, John Wiley & Sons, Ltd for more details.
8. K. Fox (2004). *Watching the English – The Hidden Rules of English Behaviour*. Hodder & Stoughton.
9. M. Gladwell (2000). *The Tipping Point – How Little Things Can Make a Big Difference*. Little Brown.
10. Cited in Gladwell (2000). *Tipping Point*.
11. P. Ball (2004). *Critical Mass – How One Thing Leads to Another*. Heinemann.
12. Ball (2004). *Critical Mass*.
13. Gladwell (2000). *Tipping Point*.
14. ABC news online at http://www.abc.net.au/news/.

Chapter 5

1. S. Freud (2004). *Mass Psychology*, tr. J. Underwood. Penguin.
2. M. Sherif (1936). *The Psychology of Social Norms*. Harper Brothers.
3. S.E. Asch (1956). 'Studies of independence and conformity I: a minority of one against a unanimous majority', *Psychological Monographs*, 70: 9.
4. S. Schachter and J.E. Singer (1962). 'Cognitive, social and physiological determinants of emotional state', *Psychological Review*, 69, pp. 379–399.
5. M. Earls (2002), *Welcome to the Creative Age: Bananas, Business and the Death of Marketing*, John Wiley & Sons, Ltd.
6. From John Naughton UK Marketing Society annual lecture (2006), 28 February.
7. S. Milgram (1992). *The Individual in a Social World: Essays and Experiments*. 2nd edn (eds. John Sabini and Maury Silver). McGraw-Hill.
8. Cited in 'Neophiliac', *New Scientist*, 19 June 2006.
9. Cited in 'Neophiliac', *New Scientist*, 19 June 2006.
10. P. Eveliegh (2004). *Marketing to Women*. Ogilvy.
11. E. Keller and J. Berry (2003). *The Influentials – One American in Ten Tells the Other Nine How to Vote, Where to Eat and What to Buy*. Simon & Schuster.
12. E. Keller and S. Chadwick (2006). 'Word of mouth: the next big thing, or just a buzz?' MRS Conference Papers.
13. M. Gladwell (2000). *The Tipping Point – How Little Things Can Make a Big Difference*. Little Brown.
14. 'Annals of Society' (1999), *New Yorker* magazine, 11 January.
15. F. Blades and S. Phillips (2005). 'Decision Watch UK'. MRS Conference Papers.
16. Blades and Phillips (2005). 'Decision Watch UK'.

Chapter 6

1. It is interesting to note how the music industry has long seen the Internet as a competitive (commercial) distribution channel – a threat to existing ones – rather than a new means to drive the mechanic behind mass behaviour. Hence the heavy-handed repression of Napster (and other file-sharing technology) in recent years. It's almost as if they think that our natural urge to share our favourite music was a novel thing – who hasn't made some kind of compilation tape or CD for their friends/lovers?

2. J. Finch (2006). 'HMV boss is first victim as internet price war batters the high street', *Guardian*, Friday 13 January.

3. Jarvis Cocker quoted in 'Arctic Monkeys make chart history', 26 January 2006. http://news.bbc.co.uk/1/hi/entertainment/4660394.stm.

4. http://www.arcticmonkeys-remixed.com/.

5. 'In era of consumer control, marketers crave the potency of word-of-mouth' (2005), *Advertising Age*, 28 November.

6. E. Keller and S. Chadwick (2006). 'Word of mouth: the next big thing, or just a buzz?' MRS Conference Papers.

7. J. Bloom (2006). *Advertising Age*, 30 January.

8. http://www.womma.org.

9. See E. Keller and J. Berry (2003), *The Influentials – One American in Ten Tells the Other Nine How to Vote, Where to Eat and What to Buy*, Simon & Schuster; or E. Keller and S. Chadwick (2006). 'Word of mouth: the next big thing, or just a buzz?'.

10. E. Katz and P.F. Lazarsfeld (1955). *Personal Influence*. New Brunswick.

11. Cap Gemini Ernst & Young Study (2003). Cited in 'Study: TV ads don't sell cars', *Ad Age*, 13 October.

12. E. Keller (2005). 'The state of WOM, 2005: the consumer perspective' presentation to the Word of Mouth Marketing Association, 29 March. Available online at http://www.womma.org.

13. Edelman (2005). Annual Trust Barometer online at http://www.edelman.com.

14. Edelman (2005). Annual Trust Barometer.

15. MediaEdge CIA (2005). *Where's Debbie?* online at http://www.mecglobal.com.

16. In J. Bullmore (2006), *Apples, Insights and Mad Inventors: An Entertaining Analysis of Modern Marketing*. John Wiley & Sons, Ltd.

17. E. Keller and S. Chadwick (2006). 'Word of mouth: the next big thing, or just a buzz?'.

18. R. Reeves (2006), quoted in *Sunday Times* 'Culture' magazine, 21 May.

19. 2 April 2006.

20. http://www.girlsintelligenceagency.com.

21. Brian Deer of the *Sunday Times* and C4 has long documented this case. See online at http://briandeer.com/wakefield-deer.htm. Also Ben Goldacre, GP, who writes the 'Bad Science' column for the *Guardian*, and blogs at http://www.badscience.net.

22. A.J. Wakefield, S.H. Murch, A. Anthony, J. Linnell, D.M. Casson, M. Malik, M. Berelowitz, A.P. Dhillon, M.A. Thomson, P. Harvey, A. Valentine, S.E. Davies and J.A. Walker-Smith (1998). 'Ilead-lymphoid-nodular hyperplasia, non-specific colitis, and pervasive developmental disorder in children', *Lancet*, 351, 28 February.

23. Online at http://briandeer.com/wakefield-deer.html and http://www.badscience.net

24. I. Hargreaves, J. Lewis and T. Speers (2003). 'Towards a better map: science, the public and the media'. Economic and Social Research Council online at http://www.esrcsocietytoday.ac.uk/ESRCInfoCentre/Images/Mapdocfinal_tcm6-5505.pdf.

25. B. Goldacre (2005). 'The MMR skeptic who just doesn't understand science', *Guardian*, 2 November.

26. R. Dunbar (2004). *Grooming, Gossip and the Evolution of Language*, Faber & Faber.
27. S. Pinker (1995). *The Language Instinct: The New Science of Language and Mind*. Penguin.
28. *Scientific American* (2005), January.
29. J. Pfeffer & R.I. Sutton (2006). *Hard Facts, Dangerous Half-Truths and Total Nonsense* HBSP.
30. D. Godes and D. Mayzlin (2002). 'Using online conversations to study word of mouth communication'. Yale SOM Working Paper No. MK-13; Harvard NOM Working Paper No. 02-32; HBS Marketing Research Paper No. 02-01.
31. F. Reichheld (1999). *Loyalty Rules! How Leaders Build Lasting Relationships*. Harvard Business Press.
32. F. Reichheld (2003). 'The one number you need to grow', *Harvard Business Review*.
33. P. Marsden (2006). 'Measuring the success of word of mouth'. MRS Conference Papers.
34. F. Reichheld (2006). *The Ultimate Question: Driving Good Profits and True Growth*. HBS.

Chapter 7

1. Interview with author, July 2006.
2. D. Atkin (2004). *The Culting of Brands: When Customers Become True Believers*. Portfolio Press.
3. Victor E. Frankl (1973). *Psychotherapy and Existentialism*, Pelican, London; Victor E. Frankl (1946). *Aertzliche Seelsorge*, Franz Deuticke, Vienna, translated as (1955). *The Doctor and the Soul*, Alfred A. Knopf, Random House, New York.
4. Internal document, howies ®.
5. Online at www.jamieoliver.com.
6. Interview by author, May 2006.
7. J. Collins and J. Porras (2000). *Built to Last: Successful Habits of Visionary Companies*. HarperCollins.
8. S. Bedbury and S. Fenichell (2004). *New Brand World: 8 Principles for Achieving Brand Leadership in the 21st Century*. Penguin.
9. J. Bick (2002). 'Inside the smartest little company in America', *Inc.* magazine.
10. C. Thompson (2004). 'The play's the thing', *New York Times* magazine.
11. J. Sculley and J.A. Byrne (1987). *Odyssey: Pepsi to Apple: A Journey of Adventure, Ideas, and the Future*. HarperCollins.
12. I. Dury and C. Jankel (1977). *Sex and Drugs and Rock and Roll*. Copyright Blackhill Music Ltd. All rights administered by Warner/Chappell Music Ltd. Reproduced by permission.
13. A. Morgan (1998). *Eating the Big Fish: How 'Challenger Brands' Can Compete Against Brand Leaders*. John Wiley & Sons, Ltd.

Chapter 8

1. H. Whetstone Johnston (1903, 1932). *The Private Life of the Romans*. Revd by M. Johnston Scott. Foresman & Co. More online at http://www.novaroma.org/religio_romana/deities.html.
2. M. Earls (2002). 'Learning to live without the brand'. In M. Baskin and M. Earls (eds.), *Brand New Brand Thinking*, Kogan Page.
3. R. Davies (2003). 'Honda – isn't it nice when things just work?' APG Creative Planning Awards Papers.

4. S. Smith (2004). 'Honda: What happened when Honda started asking questions?' IPA Advertising Effectiveness Papers.
5. O. Johnson (2005). 'How Dove changed the beauty game rules', *Market Leader* magazine, Winter.
6. D. Tannen (2006). *You're Wearing THAT?* Virago Press.
7. Dove internal study (2002). More info on Dove at http://www.campaignforrealbeauty.co.uk.
8. W. Chan Kim and R. Mauborgne (2005). *Blue Ocean Strategy – How to Create Uncontested Market Space and Make Competition Irrelevant.* Harvard Business School Press.
9. R. Mckenna (1997). 'Real time: preparing for the age of the never satisfied customer', *HBSP.* Also interview online January 2001 at http://www.mindspring.com.
10. P. Watzlawick, J.H. Beavin and D.D. Jackson (1980). *Pragmatics of Human Communication: Study of Interactional Patterns, Pathologies and Paradoxes.* W.W. Norton.
11. A. Catalano quoted in *New York Times* magazine, 8 December 2002.
12. L. Cosmides and J. Tooby (2005). 'Neurocognitive adaptations designed for social exchange'. In D.M. Buss (ed.), *Evolutionary Psychology Handbook.* John Wiley & Sons, Inc.

Chapter 9

1. C.K. Prahalad and V. Ramaswamy (2004). *The Future of Competition: Co-creating Unique Value with Customers.* Harvard Business School Press.
2. Online at http://www.thesims.ea.com.
3. Online at http://thesims2.ea.com.
4. C. Leadbetter (2006). 'The user innovation revolution – how business can unlock the value of customers', online at http://www.ncc.org.uk/intellectualproperty/publications.html.
5. T. Kuhn (1962). *The Structure of Scientific Revolutions.* University of Chicago Press.
6. H. Gardner (1994). *Creating Minds: An Anatomy of Creativity Seen Through the Lives of Freud, Einstein, Picasso, Stravinsky, Eliot, Graham and Gandhi.* Basic Books.
7. P. Kane (2004). *The Play Ethic: A Manifesto for a Different Way of Living.* Macmillan. See also online at http://www.theplayethic.com.
8. J. Littlewood (1994). *Joan's Book: The Autobiography of Joan Littlewood.* Methuen.
9. S. Fisher (1996). Royal Mail APG Creative Planning Awards Papers 1995.
10. Online at http://www.wcrs.com/.
11. I. Corner and B. Rogers (2005). 'Opinion monitory qualitative aspects of CRM implementation', *Journal of Targetting, Measurement and Analysis,* 13: 3, pp. 267–274.
12. P. Marsden (2006). 'Measuring the success of word of mouth'. MRS Conference Papers.
13. J. Seely Brown and J. Hagel III (2006). 'Creation nets: getting the most from open innovation', *McKinsey Quarterly.*
14. A. Bryant (2006). 'The Ocean's 11 approach'. In B. Clarke (ed.), *New Language for the New Medium of Television.* IDS/UKTV/Flextech Television and Premium Publishing.
15. J. Griffiths, G. Rowland, S. Salari and J. Beasley-Murray (2005). 'Qual remix'. MRS Conference Papers.
16. G. Traynor (2006). 'Open source thinking: from passive consumers to active creators'. MRS Conference Papers.

17. C. Foote and C. Stanners (2002). *An Integrated System of Care for Older People – New Care for Old – a Systems Approach*. Jessica Kingsley Publishers.
18. C. Leadbetter (2006). 'The user innovation revolution – how business can unlock the value of customers', online at http://www.ncc.org.uk/intellectualproperty/publications.html.

Chapter 10

1. Reproduced by permission of BBC Sport.
2. http://www.bbc.co.uk/wales/walesonair/sport.
3. For example, http://www.uidaho.edu/clubs/.
4. http://www.barbarianfc.co.uk/videogallery.shtml.
5. D. Nelson (1978). 'Scientific management in retrospect', *Academy of Management Review*, 3, October, pp. 736–749.
6. 'Employee motivation, the organizational environment and productivity', essay. Online at http://www.accel-team.com/scientific/scientific_02.html.
7. F. Taylor (1947). *The Principles of Scientific Management*. Harper & Row. (Originally published 1911.)
8. P. Butler, T.W. Hall, A.M. Hanna, L. Mendonca, B. Auguste, J. Manyika and A. Sahay (1997). 'A revolution in interaction', *McKinsey Quarterly*, 1.
9. S.C. Beardsley, B.C. Johnson and J.M. Manyika (2006). 'Competitive advantage from better interactions', *McKinsey Quarterly*, 2.
10. Beardsley, Johnson and Manyika (2006). 'Competitive advantage from better interactions'.
11. I. Nonaka and H. Takeuchi (1995). *The Knowledge-Creating Company: How Japanese Companies Create the Dynamics of Innovation*. Oxford University Press.
12. A. Law (2001). *Open Minds: 21st Century Business Lessons and Innovations*. St Luke's Texere Publishing, USA.
13. A. Morgan (1998). *Eating the Big Fish: How 'Challenger Brands' Can Compete Against Brand Leaders*. John Wiley & Sons, Ltd.
14. See M. Earls (2002). *Welcome to the Creative Age: Bananas, Business and the Death of Marketing*. John Wiley & Sons, Ltd.
15. B. Lewis (2006). *Hammer and Tickle – The Communist Joke Book* (written and directed by Ben Lewis).
16. B. Lewis (2006). 'Hammer and tickle', *Prospect* magazine, 122, May.
17. J.H. Huang and Y.E. Chen (2006). 'Herding in online product choice'. *Psychology and Marketing* (USA), 23:5, pp. 413 428.
18. Lewis (2006). 'Hammer and tickle'.
19. K. Kelly (1995). *Out of Control: The New Biology of Machines, Social Systems, and the Economic World*. Perseus Books.

Conclusions

1. T. Kuhn (1962). *The Structure of Scientific Revolutions*. University of Chicago Press.

Index

Note: illustrations are indicated by *italic page numbers*, endnotes by suffix 'n'

3M 304
15 (Jamie Oliver's) restaurant 214–15, 216
80:20 rule 147

AAAA (American Association of Advertising Agencies), Account Planning Conference 266–7
A/not-A logic 80
accident avoidance behaviour 64
action, rather than talk 228, 311–12
Adams, Douglas 156, 193
African cultures, mass behaviour 8
African National Congress, Youth League, policy statement 77, 81–2
AIDA (awareness–interest–desire–action) model of behaviour 65
airline loyalty cards 147
akrasia ('weakness of will') 228
alertness to danger 31
Alexander, Whit 223
Allport, Floyd H. 92
Allport, Gordon W. 92, 151
alternative medicine 41–2
altruism 27
'Amarillo' song
armed forces versions 265–6
at AAAA co-creativity session 266–7
as example of co-creativity 268
Peter Kay's version 264–5
value-chain analysis 269, 270
American Psychiatric Association, on memory recovery 60
Anglo Saxon approach to human behaviour 78, 84
apartheid system (South Africa) 154
apes
closeness to humans as species 28
humans as successful 28–9
naked, humans as 32–3
social behaviour 31–2
in suits 193
see also chimpanzees; orang-utans
Apple Computers 207, 224–5, 285
approximateness of day-to-day thinking 62, 74
Arctic Monkeys 12, 169–71
awards 169

background 170
lessons to be learnt from success 173–4
performances 170–1
reaction of music industry 172–3
recordings 170, 171
US reaction 171, 183
word of mouth recommendation 170, 173–4, 184, 189
ARM Holdings 308
Arntz, Klaus 246
Asch, Solomon 138–9, 151
conformity research 139–40
Asperger, Hans 43
Atkin, Douglas 86, 207
attachment theory 9, 38–9
attention, ways of getting 157, 206, 241, 242
attitude change (to match behaviour) 65–6
attitudinal surveys 92–3
audience interaction 136–7, 145
autism 42–5
characteristics 43, 44, 61
as defence mechanism 44
diagnosis 43
EEG mu wave patterns 44
mirror neuron explanation 44
MMR vaccine and 185–8
automobile *see* car . . .
Axelrod, Robert 48
axolotl (water salamander) 33, 34

B2B (business-to-business) marketing 178
word of mouth used 178, 179
B2C communication 324
Babelfish 193
Ball, Phillip 119, 120
Barbarians vs. All Blacks match 293–5
Barr Gazetas (architects) 114
Bateman, Melissa 27
Bates Dorland agency 281
beauty industry, criticism of 244, 245, 246, 248
Bedbury, Scott 222
Beer, Mary 287
behavioural markets 128–9
belief 14, 203–30
acting on 226–8, 326
questions for marketing 229–30
see also personal beliefs

belief-led businesses 207–8
examples 209–19, 221–5, 236, 240
implication(s) 326
misunderstanding of how they work 238
performance compared with other companies 220–1
practical advice 226–8, 251
reasons for success 208
believers/fence-sitters/resisters model 306–7
benchmarking 251
Berlin, Sir Isaiah 67
Bernays, Edward 89
betting markets 94
'bigger boys made me do it' excuse 5
binge drinking project 287
bipedalism
disadvantages 32
supposed advantages 35
Blackmore, Susan 66, 69
Blades, Fiona 162, 164
Blair, Tony 117
blogging 310
Bloom, Jonah 174
BLTT (big long-term trend) 4
Blue Ocean Strategy (book) 251–2
BMW drivers 103–4, 115
board games industry 222–4
body language 42
Body Shop 221
Boeing World Design Team 280
boids (computer simulation) 110
Bolan, Marc 2, 3
bonobo (pygmy chimp) 29, 32
Boulton, Matthew 274
Bowlby, John 9, 38, 39
BP 254–6
environmental lobby and 255, 256
rebranding exercise 254
brain
energy requirements 36
factors affecting size 36–7
readiness potential 67
brainwashing 137–8
conformity and 138–9
brand, meaning of term 235
brand-babble 235, 249, 252–3
Bratton, William 118, 119

'broken windows' theory (of crime)
    117–18, 119, 307
    applications 118–19, 126
Broomhall, Clive 35
Brown, Derren [illusionist] 141–2
Browne, Lord (John) 254, 255,
    256
Bryant, Andy 286–7, 312
BT 253
Buddhist teaching 313
Built to Last (book) 220, 305
built-to-last approach to clothing
    211
Bullmore, Jeremy 179
Burdett, Richard 218
Bush, George W. 97
buzz-marketing 174–5, 282

C2C (consumer-to-consumer)
    influence 137, 150
    implication(s) 323
    Internet used 149
    measurement of 198–200
C2C (consumer-to-consumer)
    interactions, value creation
    through 270
C4 Creative 218–19
Cachelogic, on peer-to-peer
    networking 149
Cadbury Schweppes 238
Campbell, Colin 156
Campbell, Michael 120, 121
candy bar manufacture, value-
    chain analysis 269, 270
Cap Gemini study (on car
    purchasing) 176
car driving example 64
car purchase, influences on 162–3,
    176, 239
Cardigan Bay 209–10
    see also howies (clothing
    company)
celebrity gossip 95–6
celebrity marketing 157
cell phones see mobile phones
'cellotaphs' (floral memorials) 1–4,
    5, 144
Chabris, Christopher 61, 62
Chadwick, Simon 174, 180
Chalmers, David 68
change programmes 306–7
    co-creativity and 282–3, 284
change spotting 64, 127
Channel 4, inhouse
    communications agency
    218–19
channel tunnel vision 148
charismatic leaders 305
charity sector, use of database
    marketing 146
charity telethon 264–5
chatrooms
    infiltration by company agents
    183
    word-of-mouth measurement 197
chatter 191–2
cheaters, humans' ability to spot
    40, 258–9
'checking out' 143

chimpanzees
    author's interest in 30, 31
    biological classification 30
    closeness to humans as species
    28, 29–32
    group size 115
    intelligence testing 79
    as social creatures 31–2, 115
Chinese/Confucian culture 79
    compared with Greek culture
    80–1
Chinese medicine, view on cause
    of depression 72
Christie, Tony (singer) 264, 268
Churchill, Winston 70
Cirque du Soleil 252, 278
class system 4
Claydon Heeley Jones Mason
    agency 162, *163*
Clift, Simon 93
climate change, BP's viewpoint
    254–5
clothing
    ecologically aware 211, 213–14
    influence of others on choice
    143
Cocker, Jarvis 173
co-creative consumers 288
co-creative innovation 284–5
co-creative marketing 280–1
    Motorola 280
    South African Breweries 281
co-creative networks 285–6
co-creativity 15, 261–89
    'Amarillo' example 268, 269
    computer industry 271–2
    in creativity 275–6
    ideas challenged by 288–9
    implication(s) 326–7
    internal change programmes
    and 282–3, 284
    market research and 287–8
    questions for marketing 289
    in science 274–5
    in sport 293–5
    steam engines 274
    in television industry 286–7
    in theatrical productions
    279–80
    trust and 280
co-creator(s) 268, 279, 286–7
    learn to be 326–7
cognitive behavioural therapy 71
cognitive dissonance 65
Cold War 137–8
collaboration 45, 50, 287
    in economic activity 50–1
    factors affecting 304–6
    self-interest and 46
    see also co-creativity
collective madness of crowds 89,
    115
collective mind 88–90
collective planning (Soviet Russia)
    299
collective prediction, compared
    with opinion polls 94–5
Collin, Will 217
Collins, Michael 220, 221, 305

Comic Relief 2005, Peter Kay's
    video 264–5
communications
    as action 324–5
    as data transmission 178, 324
    funnelling effect 160
    implication(s) 324–5
    Milgram's research 160
    word of mouth 177
communism, jokes about 308–9
complexity
    meaning of term 108
    as way of seeing the world
    108–9
complicated, meaning of term 108
computer games, co-created
    272–3
computer industry, co-creativity in
    271–2
Conan Doyle, Sir Arthur 55
conformity
    application 141–2
    brainwashing and 138
    research 138–41, 151–4
connectedness 159–60
consciousness
    illusion of 67–70
    neural correlates 68
conspiracy theories 188, 258
consumer advocates 182
consumer concept 321
consumer tribal behaviour 85–6
consumers, customers as 150
continuous consciousness 11, 58–9
control
    illusion of 312–13
    surrendering 288–9, 313
Cooke, Viki 159
copying behaviour 37–8
Corner, I. 283
Cornish mines, engines 273–4
Cosmides, Leda 40, 259
Cova, Bernard 83, 84, 85, 86
CPM (critical path method) 300
Cranium, Inc. 223–4
creativity 268
    as joint effort 268
    see also co-creativity
credibility through repetition 187
Crick, Sir Francis 68
crime
    Campbell–Ormerod theory
    120–2
    causes 117
    punishment and 117, 121, *122*
    reduction in New York 117–19
    social deprivation and 117, 121,
    122
'crims'/'saints'/'floaters' model
    121–2, 306
crisis
    as impetus to change 307–8
    innovation and 308
CRM (customer relationship
    marketing) 7, 145
    implementation of 282–3
Crohn's disease, causes 185
cross-cultural studies 8–9, 79–80,
    91

crowd behaviour 88–90
  at gigs/theatres 136–7
  as collective madness 89, 115,
    123
crowd psychology 87
crowds, diffidence of British 136
cruelty, as norm 151, 154
cult brands 86
Curtis, Richard 171, 264
customer–customer word of mouth
  importance of 196
  measurement of 196–7, 198–200
customers
  as consumers 150
  most valuable 150
  as purpose of business 196
  usefulness to 150
'cutaneous rabbit' 69
cyborg 26
cynicism 256–7
  on BP's environmental agenda
    256
  origin of term 257–8
  reasons for 257

Dapretto, Mirella 44
data transmission, communications
  as 178, 324
database marketing 145
  use by charity sector 146
Davenport brothers [illusionists] 55
Davies, Russell, xii–xiv 178,
  239–40, 241
de Laliberte, Guy 278–9
de Waal, Frans 31, 41
decision making (before action)
  66, 73
decision markets 94–5
DecisionWatch 162
  examples of use 162–3
  learning from 164, 311, 324
depression 70
  causes 70–1, 96
  incidence 71, 72
  as social malfunction 72
  treatments 71–2
Descartes 11, 58
Diamond, Jared 30
Diana, Princess of Wales 4
Dichter, Ernst 11
difference between people 155–7
Diogenes 257
Dircks, Henry 56, 57
direct marketing, use by charity
  sector 146
distributed intelligence 110–11,
  327
distributed memory
  group 39
  individual 59–60
do-rethink-believe loop 66
dog
  behavioural characteristics 34
  as (original) Cynics' symbol 258
Domino Records 171
Dove product range (Unilever)
  'campaign for real beauty'
    246–8, 249
  mission for brand 243–4, 250

rebranding of 242–9
Dove Self-Esteem Fund 248
Doyle, Peter 155
Dunbar, Robin 36, 42, 69, 190
Durkheim, Emile 91
Dury, Ian 226, 251

early adopters 156
  in crowds 136
early development, effect of other
  people 37–8
early social interaction, effect on
  later behaviour 9, 38–9
eating disorders, in UK 248
ecological awareness, clothing
  company 211, 213–14
economic activity, collaboration
  and 50–1
Edelman's trust barometer 177, 178,
  192, 208
education, different from
  propaganda 89
EEG (electroencephalogram), mu
  wave pattern 44
egomania/egotism 135
  dismantling 150
Ehrenberg, Andrew 7, 66
Eichmann, Adolf 151
Electronic Arts Games 272, 273
Emerson, Ralph Waldo 87
emotion-driven thinking 63
empathy 41–2
emulation strategy 38
endogenous (naturally arising/
  system-generated) word-of-
  mouth 167, 184, 188, 194, 200,
  325
Enron 219
Enterprise Oil offices
  (Aberdeen) 114
Enterprise Rent-a-car, customer
  satisfaction data 198
environmental lobby, views about
  BP 255, 256
epidemiology metaphor 117, 119,
  159
equilibrium states (in physics) 119,
  120
  similarity in crime-effect
    relationships 121, 122
Erdos number 160
Eternal Sunshine of the Spotless
  Mind (movie) 59
European system of logic 80
Eveliegh, Polly 157
evidence-based thinking 275, 320
Exactitudes project 27
exogenous (marketing-stimulated)
  word-of-mouth 167, 184, 194,
  200, 325
expert opinion 93–5
Exxon Mobil 256
'eyes' picture, effect on honesty 27

factories, advert-making 217
false memories 60–1
Farr, Robert 91
fashion, influence of others on
  choice 143

Fehr, Ernst 49
feminization of Britain 4
Festinger, Leo 65
fickle consumers 157
film industry, use of word of mouth
  180
fire, as symbol 233–4
fire of belief 234–5
  lighting/relighting 14, 231–60
  questions for marketers
    259–60
firming cream, product launch of
  Dove range 244–5
floating voters 121, 307
  discouragement of 126
flocking behaviour, birds 110
Flood, Merrill 46
floral commemorations 1–4, 5,
  144
focus groups 10
  Chinese/Thai consumers 81
  consumer-to-consumer
    interaction in 129
  criticisms 177, 240, 287
Fogassi, Leonardo 39
football crowds
  'Mexican wave' 111–12
  singing 12, 40–1
force-for-good collectives/
  communities 21–4, 26
Fox, Kate 116
fractal mathematics 109
Frankl, Victor 208–9, 258
Fraser, Lorraine 187
Freud, Sigmund 9, 38, 89, 138, 276
Frost, Robert 263

Galbraith, J.K. 276–7
Gallup, George 92
game theory 46–7
Gandhi, Mahatma 21
Gantt charts 300
Gardner, Howard 275
Geachter, Simon 49
genetic similarities, chimpanzees
  and humans 29–30
Gilbreth, Frank 300
Gilbreth, Lillian 300
Giles, Alan 172
Girls Intelligence Agency 183
Giuliani, Rudy (Mayor of New York)
  119
Gladwell, Malcolm 117, 118, 119,
  159
global warming, BP's viewpoint
  254–5
Godes, David 197
Godin, Seth 149
Goebbels, Joseph 89
Golden, Hyman 236
Goodyear Tyre 137
Google, new products 304–5
'Gorillas in Our Midst' study 62
gossip 42, 95–6, 191, 308
government policy, reporting on 6
Graham, Alex 286
Graham, Martha (dancer) 275–6
Graham, Tessa 205
Grandin, Temple 61

Greek culture, compared with
    Chinese/Confucian culture
    80–1
Greenfield, Susan 68
Greenpeace 256
Griffiths, John 287–8
grooming
    human verbal communication as
        189–90
    language skills evolving through
        42, 190
    social relations and 31, 189, 190
group think 90
guerilla gardening movement 24
Gunn, David 118

Handy, Charles 229
happiness, factors affecting 38–9,
    96
Harlow, John 216–17
Hawthorne effect 283–4, 301
heart-transplant patients 68
Helbeing, Dirk 112
herd marketing principles 13–15,
    99–314
    belief 14, 203–30
    co-creativity 15, 261–89
    influence 14, 133–65
    interaction 14, 101–31
    letting go 15, 291–314
    (re)lighting the fire 14, 231–60
    us-talk/word-of-mouth
        communications 14,
        167–201
herd theory 7–8, 12
    evidence for 13, 17–98
Hieatt, David and Claire 210–14,
    229
Hillier, Bill 113
Hitler, Adolf 89
HMV (music retailer) 172
Hobbes, Thomas 46
Hoffman, Bob 83
Honda, Soichiro 240
Honda UK 239–41, 249, 250
honesty, factors affecting 27
how? questions 12, 322–3
howies (clothing company) 210–14
    ecological awareness 211, 213–14
    passion 211–12
    quality 210–11
HR departments 283, 301–2
Human Relations movement 301
Humphrey, Nick 79

'I'
    ideology 91
    illusion of 53–74
    and 'the Other' 9–10
    politics of 88
    research 92–3
    vs. 'Us' 75–98
'I saw this and I thought of you'
    (Royal Mail) campaign 281–2
ideology, definition 91
IKEA 221–2
illusion
    of consciousness 67–70
    of control 312–13

of 'I' 53–74
    of volition 67, 73
illusionists 55, 141–2
iMac 225
image 'change' 252–3
imitation strategy 38
inattentional blindness 62
Indian restaurants 22, 116
individualism
    growth in 24–5
    implication(s) 322
    Protestantism/Reformation
        rooted in 91
individualists
    Anglo-Saxon 78, 90
    interaction with others 9
individuals, unreliability as
    witnesses of mass behaviour
    322
infant mutation theory 34–6
infantile characteristics 33–4
    evolutionary advantages 34–6
influence 14, 133–65
    compared with persuasion 133,
        165
    implication(s) 324
    questions for marketing 165
influence diagram/map 163
influence of others, as basis for
    mass behaviour 5
influencers
    car purchase 162–3
    types 164
influentials (people) 157–8, 311,
    324
information-storage/-retrieval
    system, memory as 11, 59
'injection' experiment 140–1
innovation 284–5, 304
    crisis and 308
instinctive (belief-based) marketing
    205–6
    principles 207
Integration IMC 180
intellectual analysis, compared
    with belief 226–7
intelligence tests 79
interaction 14, 101–31
    in early life/developing years 9,
        38–9
    implications 130–1, 323
    mirror neurons and 39–40, 115
    numbers 115
    tacit 303–4
    in urinal use 105–7
'interaction' businesses 302
interactional jobs 302–3
interactive animals 110
interactive humans 110–11
interdependence of humans 8, 301
interesting businesses 195, 203,
    326
internal change programmes,
    co-creativity and 282–3, 284
international trade 50–1
Internet 149–50
    chatrooms 183, 197
    film reviews 180
    marketers' views 25–6, 149

medical information available
    271
music downloading from 170,
    172, 335n6/1
music industry's attitude 172,
    335n6/1
intuitive thinking 63, 74, 107
Iowa electronic markets 94
iPod 6, 225, 285
IT departments 283
IT support 303
Ives, Jonathon 225

Jackie Cooper PR 182
James, Carwyn 295–7
James, William 319–20
Japanese companies, management
    style 305
Jobs, Steve 224, 285
Johnson, Olivia 242
Join-me collective/movement 22–3
jokes 308–10
    epidemiological/political studies
        309–10
jumbo jet, complicated nature of
    108

Kahnemann, Daniel 62, 63, 64,
    107
Kamprad, Ingvar 221
Kane, Pat 276
Kanner, Leo 43
Karma-army 23
Katz, E. 176
Kaufman, Wendy ('the Snapple
    Lady') 236, 238
Kay, Peter 263–4, 267–8
    'Amarillo' song/video 264–5
    at Live 8 concert 266
Keller, Ed 157, 158, 174, 175, 179,
    180, 311
Kelling, George L. 117, 118
Kelly, Kevin 157, 313
Kim, W. Chan 251, 252
Kipling, Rudyard 87
Knight, Phil 222
Kotler, Philip 196
Kuhn, Thomas 274–5, 320

Lagnado, Silvia 244, 246
Laing, R.D. 72
language skills, origins 42, 190
Latin model of society 83–4
Lazarsfeld, P.F. 176
'lazy minds' view 62–4
Le Bon, Gustave 89, 115
lecture theatre, mass behaviour in
    107
letting go 15, 291–314, 327
    implication(s) 327
    questions for marketing 314
Lewis, Dennis 245
Libet, Benjamin 66
Libet test 66–7
lighting/relighting the fire of belief
    14–15, 231–60
    questions for marketers 259–60
line-of-sight considerations 113
Linux operating system 272

Littlewood, Joan 279–80
Live 8 charity concert 266
logo rebadging 252–3
loneliness 96
  managers 297–8
loyalty cards 147
loyalty metrics 195, 198

McCarthyite 'witch hunts' 138
machine, company as 298
McKenna, Regis 252
McKinsey
  on benchmarking 251
  on co-creative networks 285,
    287
  on tacit interactions 303–4
  on word of mouth 176
Macmillan theory of mass
    behaviour 4
McNaughton, John 253
majority view 140
mall-rat massacre 79
management, end of 313, 327
management style, purpose-driven
    businesses 305
managers, loneliness of 297–8
Mandela, Nelson 8, 82
Mandelbrot, Benoit 109
market research
  co-creativity and 287–8
  individualistic basis 10–11, 93
markets
  behavioural 128–9
  demand-side approach 128–9
  interaction and 127
Marky Mark and the Big Shorts
    135
  influence on audience 144–5
Marsden, Paul 199
Marsh, Arnold 236
Marsh, Leonard 236
mass behaviour
  as collective madness 89, 115
  complexity 108
  difficulty of changing 6–7
  F.H. Allport's model 92
  Macmillan model 4
  main factor affecting 5, 104,
    109, 115
  Schelling's model 104, 107
mass-customization 25
mass psychology 138
mathematical power law 147–8
Mauborgne, R. 251, 252
Mayo, Elton 301
mayonnaise 108, 334n4/2
Mayzlin, Dina 197
Mbeki, Thabo 8, 82
measles
  increase in infections 188
  see also MMR vaccine
media costs 174
MediaEdge, CIA data 176, 179, 180
medical information, availability
    271
Mediterranean culture 84
meetings 276–8
  co-creativity in 279
  combative nature of 277

lack of interaction in 137
social interaction in 193
'memetic' creativity 282
memory
  effect of act of remembering on
    60
  recovery techniques 60–1
  unreliability 11, 59, 73
Mercedes car(s), purchasing
    influences 162–3
mergers and acquisitions
  failures 236–8
  long-term effects 6
  reasons for 236
'metamessage' 244
metastable states (in physics)
    119–20
  similarity in crime-effect
    relationships 121, 122
metrics 195
'Mexican wave' 111–12
  applications
    public/urban space planning
      113–14
    traffic flow systems 112–13
micromanaging 300
micromotives, mass behaviour
    affected by 107
Microsoft, communication(s) from
    178
MICs (most influential customers)
    324
Milgram, Stanley 10, 151
  communications research 160
  obedience research 139
  punishment research 151–4
  military training, purpose 154
Mill, John Stuart 88, 169
Miller, Alice 9, 38, 71
mirror neurons 39–40, 115
  malfunctioning in autism 44
'mission, vision, values' statement
    235
mistrust in authority 177, 188, 271
MMR (measles/mumps/rubella)
    vaccination
  drop in uptake 188
  effects 185–6
  journalists' response 187
  scare stories about 185–7
  Wakefield study 185–6
mob rule/thinking 87, 123–7
mobile phones 149
  see also Motorola; Nokia; SMS
    text messaging
MOD (Ministry of Defence),
    computer system crash 265–6
Moore, Alan 86
Morgan, Adam 227
Morgan, Cliff 293
Morris, Desmond 31, 33, 189
Morrison, Blake 4
mother–child interaction 33
Motorola 280, 308
music industry 169–71
  attitude to Internet 172, 335n6/1
  reaction to Arctic Monkeys
    172–3
  way of operating 171–2

MVC (most valuable customer)
    150, 324
MySpace website 149, 150

Nagel, Thomas 69
naked apes
  humans as 32–3
  reasons for nakedness 32–6
Naked Chef TV series 214
Naked (media business) 216–18
Narnia tales (C.S. Lewis) 28
naturally influential people 157–8
negativity, in online environments
    309
neophilia (love of new things) 156
neotenic mutation 33–4
net recommendation score 198–9
neuromarketing 10
New York
  crime rate 117–19
  subway system 118–19
Newton, Sir Isaac 109, 275
Newtonian model 109
Nike 222
Nisbett, Richard 8–9, 79–80, 91
Nokia 305
normative view 140
novelty, susceptibility to 156
nucleation 120

objective setting, as conflict 306
Ocean's 11 (dream team) approach
    286–7
office design 114
Ogilvy, David 157
Ogilvy agency
  Dove rebranding campaign
    243–8
  IBM adverts 178, 179
  South African Breweries
    campaign 281
Oldridge, Mark 156
Oliver, Jamie 214–16
  restaurants 214–15
  school meals campaign 215
  TV shows 214, 215
One-Number theory 196, 198–200
  challenges 199
one-to-one marketing
  obsession with 131
  see also WoM (word of mouth)
one-to-one relationships 25
online bulletin boards, gossip and
    jokes on 310
open-air market, interaction of
    humans in 111
'open-source' research 159, 288
open-source software development
    272, 273, 285
Opinion Leader Research 158, 159,
    288
opinion polls
  compared with collective
    prediction 94–5
  individualism as basis 92–3
orang-utans 38
organic cotton jeans and t-shirts
    211, 214
organism, business as 304

organogram 310
oriental cultures, mass behaviour 8–9
Ormerod, Paul 120, 121
Osho/Rajneesh 276
'Others'/other people
  development influenced by 37–8
  interaction with 9
oversupply situation, how to get attention in 206, 241, 242

pair bonding 33
  reasons for 37
paradigm 275, 320
parallel lines experiment 139–40
Pareto's law 147, 148
paths in a square 111
Paulos, John Allen 63
paying people to talk about you 193
peace and reconciliation, in South Africa 8, 82–3
peer pressure 90, 143
peer review 175
peer-to-peer communications/ networking 149–50
  growth in 149, 191
peer-to-peer influence 137, 181
peer-to-peer value-exchange 269–70
Pepper, John Henry 56–7
Pepper's ghost 56–7
person-to-person influence 145, 148
personal belief 14, 227
  expression of 227
personal beliefs, businesses based on 207, 219
  Apple Computers 207, 224–5
  Cranium, Inc. 223–4
  Honda 239–41
  howies (clothing company) 210–11, 213–14
  IKEA 221–2
  Jamie Oliver 214, 216
  Naked media company 217
  Nike 222
  performance compared with other companies 220–1
  Snapple soft-drinks company 236
persuasion, compared with influence 133, 165
PERT 300
Pfeffer, Jeffrey 195
phantom limb syndrome 69
phase transitions 119–20
  similarity in crime-effect relationships 121, 122
Phillips, Melanie 187
Phillips, Stephen 162, 164
Phoenix Nights (TV series) 264–5
physical contact
  effects 41
  rules governing 116
Pictionary game 222
Pinker, Stephen 1, 8, 13, 58, 88, 190

placebo effect 142
  Asian viewpoint 142
'play ethic' 276
Pledgebank 26
Poland 309
politics of 'I' 88
Popbitch website 95–6
population growth of humans 29
Porras, Jerry 220, 221, 305
PortalPlayer 285
postmodern tribes, compared with traditional tribes 85–6
The Power of Dreams programme (Honda) 239, 240
'practice' networks 285, 286
The Pragmatics of Human Communication 253
Prahalad, C.K. 271
predictive research 93
prisoner's dilemma game 46–7
  co-operative approach 49
  collaborative strategies 49
  tit-for-tat strategy 48–9
pristinians 156
'process' networks 285, 286
promoters vs. detractors score 198–200
propaganda, different from education 89
prospect psychology 127
Protestantism, individualism and 91
Prozac, clinical trials 72
pub test 175
public opinion, F.H. Allport's model 92
public opinion polls/surveys 92–3
  on word of mouth 177
public relations 89
public sector, co-creative approach used by 288
public/urban space planning 113–14
punishment
  crime rate affected by 117, 121, 122
  research on 151–4
  separation from peers 32
purpose-driven businesses
  performance compared with other companies 220–1
  see also belief-led businesses
pygmy chimp (bonobo) 29, 32
pygmy thinking 227

Quaker 236–7
  acquisition of Snapple soft-drinks company by 237–8
quality, as company belief 210–11

'rainbow nation' (South Africa) 83
Ramachandran, Vilayanur 44
Rankin (fashion photographer) 246, 248
Rappaport, Anatol 48
real-world word of mouth 193–5
reassurer, as influencer 164
rebadging 252–3
rebranding

BP 254
Dove personal products (Unilever) 242–9
Honda UK 239–41
recommendation score, as the one number/metric 198–9, 325
reconciliation
  in South Africa 8, 82
  stages 82–3
recontextualization, of Honda UK 240–1
record industry, way of operating 171–2
Red Bee Media 286
Reeves, Rana 182
reflexive-apology rule 116
Reichheld, Frederick 198
  net recommendation score 198–9
'relation-canoes' 146–7
relationship building 147
relationship marketing 7, 178
relationships, business–customer 147–8
relighting the fire of belief 14–15, 231–60
  questions for marketers 259–60
researcher, as influencer 164
Reynolds, Craig 110
riots
  response to 126–7
  Sydney (Australia) 123–6
roadside floral memorials 1–2, 3, 12
Rogers, B. 283
Roman theology 233
Roper Organization, on word of mouth 176, 177
Ross, Jonathan 265
Rousseau, J.J. 233
Rowe, Dorothy 71
Royal College of Psychiatrists, on memory recovery 60–1
Royal Mail 179, 281–2
rugby 293–7
  Barbarians vs. All Blacks match 293–5
  coach 295–6
rules-of-thumb 62, 107, 115–16
rumour, human-to-human interaction 191

'say it with flowers' 1–4
Schachter, Stanley 140
Schelling, Thomas 104, 107, 108, 193
schizophrenia 72
school meals campaign 215
scientific breakthroughs 274–5
'scientific' management 299–300
  criticisms 300–1
Scrabble game 222–3
Sculley, John 224–5
Seabright, Paul 50–1
'séance box' 55
séance, simulated 141–2
seating choices 107, 108
self-interest, collaboration and 46
self-organization 112

sense of self, distorted, depression caused by 70–1
separation of Man from animals 28
separation from peers, as punishment 32
sexuality, as reason for nakedness 33
Shakespeare, William 87, 330
Shameless (TV series) 219
Sherif, Mustafer 138
shoes, factors influencing choice 143
'show, don't tell' 252–4
SIM City computer game 272
Simons, Daniel 61, 62
The Sims (computer game) 272–3
Singer, Jerome 140
'six degrees of separation' 160
Smith, Adam 45, 50
SMS text messaging 149, 191
    Motorola and 280
    response to in riot situations 126
    Sydney beach riots 123, 124, 125, 126
Snapple soft-drinks company 236–7, 249–50
    acquisition by Quaker 237–8
social apes 31–2
    brain size 36–7
social brain 39–40
social conformity *see* conformity
social deprivation, crime rate affected by 117, 121, *122*, 125
social influencers 158–9, 288, 311, 324
social intelligence theory 79
social interaction, learning through 38
social malfunctioning, depression caused by 72
social meaning 207
social psychology 9–10
    individualization of 91–2
    origins 91
social relations
    grooming and 31, 189, 190
    in human-to-human interactions 191
social species
    advantages 31
    humans as 19, 321
social status theory (depression) 72
society, Anglo-Saxon attitude to 90
software development, as co-operative activity 271
South Africa
    apartheid system 154
    transition to majority-rule government 8, 82–3
South African Breweries, Castle Lager '1894' campaign 281
Soviet Russia
    collective planning 299
    jokes 308–9
space planning 113–14
Spring Research 162, *163*

stardust, as measure of separation of humans from animals 27–8
steam engines 273–4
    co-creative improvements 274
Stephens, Anne 159
Stern, Howard 236, 238
'stickiness' concept 282
stock markets 127
'stooges' (in experiments) 140, 152
strategies, top-down, failure of 305
stream of consciousness 69, 73
stroking (physical contact) 42
    language skills evolving through 42, 190
successful apes 28–9
super-connectors 160–1, 311
super-social ape 19–52, 193, 201, 321
    implications 321–2
Sydney (Australia) riots 123–6
    analysis 125–6

tacit interactions 303–4
tactile human contact 41–2
Tait, Richard 222, 223, 224
talk
    compared with action 228, 311–12
    grooming and 42, 190
    jokes and 308–10
    social relations and 190–1
Tannen, Deborah 244
Taoism 313
target audience 155
Target (US retailer) 229
targeting 155, 161–2
Taylor, Frederick W. 298
    'scientific' approach to management 299–300
technology support 303
teenagers' behaviour 103
text messaging 12
Thatcher, Margaret 90
theatre, co-creativity in 279–80
time-and-motion study 298–9, 300
tone of voice 190
Tooby, John 40, 259
traffic control systems 112–13
trail-blazing consumers 156–7
travel, main function of 78
Trevithick, Richard 274
tribal life 42–5
trust, co-creativity and 280
Truth and Reconciliation Commission (South Africa) 8, 82
'turtles all the way down' 319–20
Tutu, Archbishop Desmond 8, 81, 82, 154
TV advertising
    B2B marketing and 178, 179
    compared with word of mouth 176
TV shows, prediction of future ratings 197
Twain, Mark 55

Ubuntu concept 81
    in South Africa 8, 82–3
Unilever personal products 242–9
urban planning and architecture 113–14
urinals, rules for use (by British men) 105–7
    one-metre rule 106–7
    one-space rule 105–6
us-talk 14, 167–201
    questions for marketing 201
    see also WoM (word of mouth)
USA
    Girl Scouts educational health programme 248–9
    presidential elections 94–5, 97
    terrorist attacks 95
    see also New York

value-chain analysis 269–70
    'Amarillo' song 269, *270*
    candy-bar manufacture 269, *270*
value-creation 268, 269
    see also creativity
van Schaik, Carel 38
Versluis, Arie 27
vestal virgins 233, 234
Victorian era 55–7
violence
    chimpanzees 32
    humans 29
viral marketing 181–2
visual information, processing by brain 61–2
'visual language of space' 113
volition, illusion of 67, 73
von Neumann, Johann 46

Waitrose 229
Wakefield, Dr Andrew 185, 186, 192
Wallace, Danny 21–3, 39
Walmart 229
Walworth boy scouts (drowning) 2
Warwick, Kevin 26
Watt, James 273–4
WCRS agency 282
'we-species'
    evidence for 19–52
    examples 26–7
Wegner, Daniel 67, 69
Weiden & Kennedy 178, 239
Weisberg, Lois 160–1
Welsh clothing company 210–14
Wertheimer, Max 139
'what we don't do' 235
'Where's Debbie?' 179, *180*
White, Roderick 25
Whiten, Andrew 38, 44
'who you are' 226
    putting into action 227
Wight, Robin 282
Wilde, Oscar 135, 195
Wilkins, Jon 217
Wilson, James Q. 117
wolves, role in human cultures 78
WoM (word of mouth) 14, 164, 167–201

Arctic Monkeys example
    169–71, 173–4, 184, 189
artificial/company-generated 182–3
in B2B and B2C
    marketing 178–9
endogenous (naturally arising/
    system-generated) 167, 184,
    188, 194, 200, 325
exogenous (marketing-
    stimulated) 167, 184, 194,
    200, 325
facts about 175–81
as global phenomenon 179–80

growth in importance 177–8
implication(s) 325–6
measurements 195–6, 325
MMR vaccine example 184–8
more important than other
    influences 176, 180, 325
not additive activity 184
questions for marketing 201
traditional marketing reaction
    to 181
WOMMA (Word of Mouth
    Marketing Association) 175
Woodruffe, Simon 205

Woolf, Arthur 274
word of mouth marketing 8,
    174–5
    relative unimportance of 194
    see also WoM
Worldcom 219

Yellowwood Consulting 159
YouTube website 149
Yttenbroek, Elly 27

zero budget game 253
Zimbardo, Phil 151